# The Guilded Pen

Seventh Edition — 2018

*The Guilded Pen, Seventh Edition* is a publication of the
San Diego Writers and Editors Guild
P. O. Box 881931
San Diego, CA 92168-1931
www.sdwritersguild.org

*The Guilded Pen, Seventh Edition* was published by Grey Castle Publishing
and printed by CreateSpace, an Amazon.com company. Copies are
available at www.greycastlepublishing.com , www.CreateSpace.com,
and from our website: www.sdwritersguild.org.

Marcia Buompensiero, Managing Editor
Ruth L. Wallace, Editor
Simone Arias, Editor (Poetry)

"Lady Ted and Beisbol" was previously published in *Irreverent
Forever* (2018). Reprinted by permission of the author and the
publisher, Grey Castle Publishing.

"Freeing the Genie" was previously published in *The Genie Who
Had Wishes of His Own* (2013). Reprinted by permission of the
author and the publisher, Plowshare Media.

Paperback price $15.00

**ISBN-13: 978-1726073813**

**ISBN-10: 1726073815**

# The Guilded Pen

Seventh Edition — 2018

An anthology of the
San Diego Writers and Editors Guild

# Table of Contents

| Contributors | Title/Page |
|---|---|

# Introduction

Since 2012, the SDWEG has published an anthology for its members. It is, simply put, a collection of poetry, essays, memoir, and imaginative short stories by our members.

The categories for submission are specific; but the opportunity for creativity is wide open. There is no standard to which a writer is expected to adhere. Of course, good grammar, correct sentence structure, a plot that moves forward in some logical way, and characters that are interesting are a good start.

Although writing is a singular effort, we need other people to give us their impressions of what we have written. So it is with the anthology. A single piece of work will have had many eyes and ears upon it before final publication.

What makes an anthology valuable to a writer is that it provides a platform to display a small sample of their talent for public viewing. The anthology is a showcase for an author's skill, imagination, and flair for storytelling. Here, authors can try something new, something outside their comfort zone, something beyond their usual genre — and get it out into the universe.

The SDWEG anthology is published for just those reasons. Not many authors have this opportunity. It is one of the many benefits of Guild membership.

— Mardie Schroeder, President
San Diego Writers and Editors Guild

— Marcia Buompensiero
Managing Editor

# Acknowledgments

*The Guilded Pen, Seventh Edition,* 2018 owes its existence to the SDWEG Board of Directors. Their dedication and foresight fostered the creation of a venue to showcase members' works and to carry on the mission to support the local writing arts.

**Board of Directors 2018**
Mardie Schroeder, President
Robert Doublebower, Vice President
Anne Janda, Immediate Past President
Laurie Asher, Secretary
Marcia Buompensiero, Treasurer
Richard Peterson, Membership Chair
Sandra Yeaman, Social Media Manager/Webmaster
Directors at Large:
Gered Beeby
Janet Hafner
Frank Newton, Newsletter Editor
Adolpho Sanchez
Ken Yaros

---

We are grateful to our editorial review panel who read, critiqued, and edited the submissions. Special thanks and appreciation goes to Vincent Adragna, Laurie Asher, Gered Beeby, Barbara Crothers, Robert Doublebower, Dave Feldman, Janet Hafner, Margaret Harmon, Frank Newton, Richard Peterson, Arthur Raybold, Ken Yaros, and Sandra Yeaman.

Marcia Buompensiero, Managing Editor
Ruth L. Wallace, Assistant Editor
Simone Arias, Assistant Editor (Poetry)

# San Diego Writers and Editors Guild

**Mission Statement**:   **To Promote, Support, and Encourage the Writing Art for Adults and Youth**

We are a nonprofit local group of writers and editors dedicated to improving our skills and helping others to do the same. Since 1979, the Guild has played an important role in furthering the goals of both novice and accomplished authors. No matter what your writing skill, we can help you get to the next level. Our members come from all over the region in search of support and to share their talents.

**Benefits of membership include:**
- Monthly meetings with informative speakers
- Marketing Support Group
- Monthly Newsletter (*The Writer's Life*)
- Membership Directory
- Manuscript Review Program
- Opportunity to publish your work in *The Guilded Pen*
- Opportunity to list yourself and your work in the SDWEG Speakers Bureau and Members' Works pages on our website
- Active Website and Social Media Presence
- Access to Online Resources for Writers
- Access to discounted space at the Annual Festival of Books
- Periodic presentation of awards: "The Rhoda Riddell Builders Award" — recognizing efforts to build/expand the Guild; "Special Achievements Awards" — for extraordinary service; and "The Odin Award" — to those who have been major stimulators of the writing arts in San Diego as evidenced by their body of published work.

Guild membership is open to all and guests are welcome to the meetings for a small donation. Visit: www.sdwritersguild.org.

Those who tell the stories
rule the world.

— *Hopi Native American Proverb*

# The Shepherd of Oruzgan

## *Michael Jude McMahon*

It had ceased to be a wonder to him, or even something he had a need to understand. Each year, at precisely the same time, the ewes gave birth to their lambs. The snows had barely melted, filling the stream, sending the water gushing down the mountain and into the welcoming valley. And the lambs were being born. They seemed to simply appear out of the dark of night.

He would hear a faint bleat a short distance away announcing their entrance into the world. He did not marvel at the sound. He was grateful for it, but he did not marvel. Nor did he rejoice and praise Allah. His expectation inhibited such enjoyment. He had learned to expect. Enjoyment was not gratification. He remembered the year of the drought when the stream did not give up its treasure in a sustained manner, and the sheep and the land suffered. Suffered terribly. The land was barren and dry, and the wool on the sheep was not fit to use for the carpets. The weavers had rejected it offhand at first but finally after much complaining had to make use of it on inferior products.

The merchants who came to purchase the carpets also complained. The prices they would get barely covered their transportation costs. Or so they said. But merchants are merchants and not to be trusted. They would always come out smiling. They would buy what they had a market for, and they knew their market well. It was the reason why they were merchants and Ahmad Zubair was a shepherd.

He was blessed with a sweet face when he was young. With long flowing hair he had a girlish appearance. The people down in the valley called him "*dokhtarak*." It did not please his father to hear him called so. He wanted a manly son and to hear his youngest boy referred to as "little girl" displeased him greatly. It did not please Ahmad Zubair either. He was left alone to play his

1

own war games, wielding his sword against invisible enemies on horses charging forth from invisible fortresses, firing invisible arrows and threatening death and destruction on the village townsfolk, who were saved from the wrath of the charging hordes by Ahmad Zubair and his invisible friend, Kadeen, both of whom would forever be hailed as heroes long after the name of "*dokhtarak*" was forgotten.

It was to his mother he turned in his darkest moments. She it was who taught him to read the language of the Qu'ran and the discord of religion with science and other endless truths. She taught him the old creeds along with the new, and encouraged him to perceive the "miracles of mythology" and nature. She taught him the value of the sheep he would one day be caring for in the hills. The fat rump breed of sheep. They were known as Afghan Arabi sheep, she had said with bursting pride, so that he too would be proud. If he felt resentful, she taught him to use it as a defense and to be resolute in molding himself to the world he lived in. "There are injustices," she told him, and quoted the holy book. "They who devour the possessions of orphans shall swallow fire into their bellies." He was not an orphan, nor would he ever devour the possessions of orphans. The thought of having fire in his belly would forever keep him from such insanity.

He was not sure when it was he resolved to remain forever in the hills. It was a great comfort to him to hear the sound of the running water and the bleating of the lambs. The birds too added their joy. Their chirping very often took over the pulse of the hills. He would look up to try to identify the direction from which the sound came. One here, one there, one everywhere. They flew low, and they flew high as all birds do. And their chirps and songs were in a language he felt he knew. Like the bleating of the lambs. In distress or in happiness. He felt he knew.

It was in that repose he felt the safest. High in the hills in the company of the natural world. He would not sweat; he was at one. Nor would he feel the cold icy winds coming down from the north penetrating his sheepskin coat and woolen hat. He would protect his beard from the rain showers. It was only a minor discomfort if it became sodden, but better to protect it. The animals seemed unperturbed by the changes that came to the hills.

2

Whether they were shorn or in their full winter coat, it mattered not to them. They were there. Unquestioning. Placing their faith in neither book nor snakestone but only in the finite presence of their being.

On a day when the rain and the winds were soft and easy, Ahmad Zubair saw the figure of a man approaching from the lower end of the valley. He appeared to be struggling, trying to cope with the steep slope of the hill. When he was no further than the distance of a long throw of a stone, the figure called out to him. The voice was not one he immediately recognized

"Ahmad Zubair, have you no welcome for me? I your compatriot from the village of your birth. Raise yourself up and show respect."

Reluctantly, Ahmad Zubair did as he was bid to do and rose from the rock upon which he was seated. The man's head was still bent to the short grass of the mountain, making his identification difficult to establish. As he approached, it became clear to Ahmad Zubair who it was he was soon to be in the company of.

Mohammed Nabi raised his head to expose his flowing beard and fierce eyes. He too lived a life of expectation. It showed in all he did. When Nabi came into the company of others he expected them to hold his truths and beliefs sacred. He considered himself a scholar of the Holy Scripture and all about him as pupils to be instructed in his scholarly wisdom. He was a man Ahmad Zubair knew well.

"It is not good for a man to live as you do, Zubair. Up here in these hills alone, away from the teachings of the Qu'ran and the blessings that go with it. What? Have you nothing to say for yourself? No greeting to a scholar of the holy book?"

"I am sorry, Taliban. I have grown unused to company. My manners sometimes fail me. Up here we, that is, myself and the animals, have grown to rely on our expectations. When we do not expect, we fall short. So, on behalf of myself and the animals, I apologize."

"Do I sense a derogatory tone in your voice, Ahmad Zubair? An apology from sheep? Whoever heard of such a thing? We are a civilized nation following in the footsteps of Mohammad. Civilized nations do not give a voice to sheep. Sheep are to be

3

served with rice or turned into carpets. They are good for nothing else."

"Of course, of course, Taliban. I alone apologize. You are right. Look at them, nibbling on the short grass, pulling it up by the roots. It takes a long time for it to grow strong and healthy again. If they were as scholarly as you they would eat only that which is on the surface and leave the roots to replenish themselves. That is why we move from pasture to pasture. Always in search of strong and healthy grass. But tell me, Taliban, what brings a man of your scholarly stature into the furthest reaches of the hills?"

"It is curious you should ask me that, Ahmad Zubair. Is it not obvious? Has it not occurred to you that I too am in search of 'strong and healthy grass,' just like your sheep?"

"Forgive me once more, Taliban Nabi. I am a simple shepherd who spends too much time alone with only the sheep for company. I do not follow your reasoning."

"Of course not. This time I beg your forgiveness. I have credited you with having more intelligence than you deserve. I will speak to you as plainly as I can so you will understand. But firstly, I have a need to quench my thirst. The journey has made my mouth as dry as the last drought. Hand me the water bottle."

Ahmad Zubair passed the scholar the leather pouch he himself had fashioned from the skin of a ram. He watched as his visitor raised the pouch filled from the cold mountain stream and satiated his parched mouth. As a boy, his mother had read a story to him about a Turkish Imam, Bayeldi, who had satiated himself on aubergines stewed in oil with tomatoes and spices. His overindulgence caused him to be ill for several days. He wished the same fate on Mohammad Nabi. He could only smile to himself at the thought. The precious liquid would only serve to quench Nabi's thirst and saturate his beard.

It would not be hard to understand why Ahmad Zubair wished harm to Mohammad Nabi. In the city of Tarin Kowt, where he and his mother had gone many years before to sell their wool and sheepskins, it was Nabi who wielded the stick and beat the women dressed in their burkhas for the slightest infraction of a code of conduct dictated by the Imams and the scholars. His mother had been feeling unwell in the scorching summer heat and

4

thrown up inside her veil. The retching caused her foot to be exposed and Nabi was not hesitant in showing his displeasure. The long cane swept across his mother's back. Ahmad Zubair felt as though he himself was the recipient of the blow.

He was barely out of puberty at the time. Still, it was sufficient for him to know the look on Mohammad Nabi's face. It was not of displeasure or anger. The fierce eyes displayed an emotion new to Ahmad Zubair. One he was only coming to know. It was not of the five senses, but located in his nether regions. He could see Nabi felt it in his loins. It was a violation of his mother. An act he had concealed from his young mind but was now resurging into a hardened thirst for revenge. His mother had told him that only the beasts suffer intemperate anger. Of what were the beasts she spoke of? Were they the newborn lambs bleating and prancing on the hills that he was sworn to protect from preying beasts? No. The beasts were the stick wielders with their querulous anger wounded by the display of a foot.

Ahmad Zubair continued to observe his visitor throughout his quenching. He watched as Nabi allowed the water to drain over his long beard and closed, seedy eyes.

"So, you wonder why I am here, Ahmad Zubair. Let me tell you. We need men such as yourself to help us in our time of need. To take up arms against the enemies of Islam. I have been assigned the task of recruiting men of worth. We consider you to be such a man. One who would obey an order without questioning from whom, or whence, it came. Do not underestimate this gift we are bestowing on you. Few are chosen. We have carefully evaluated you from information given to us by your fellows in the village who insist you are worthy to be drawn into our cause. We will find someone less worthy to tend to the sheep, and you will follow me down to the village to begin your training. So make preparations. Bid farewell to these creatures whose future lies in *birriani* and rugs."

"I am honored to be chosen, Taliban Nabi. It is something I have dreamed about. I did not expect to be seen as a shepherd until the end of my days. I wanted more. I wanted to be admired by those such as yourself. By the great scholars. Not by the little people with no aspirations, who see ambition as a vice. So tell me

5

what I must do."

"You have chosen well, Ahmad Zubair. You will go down in the annals of our history as one of the great martyrs. Songs of praise will be written about you and sung in the mosques throughout the world. There will be gatherings to shout your name from on high. You will be welcomed into the heavens in a triumphant cacophony of angels. I will leave now and send someone to care for your flock in a day or two. Then you may join us on our glorious journey in praise of Allah."

"May God be praised! May I accompany you down the hills for a while? I need to move the flock to another location, and I can show you a trail to make the journey less painful to your chest and legs."

It was delivered in a humorous way, but Mohammad Nabi was not the humorous kind. It was considered a sin. An affront to Allah.

It was known as the Goat Pass, though no goats were seen to take it. The old shepherds refused to herd their flock along it for fear of losing one or two on the narrow path. There were steep inclines the entire length of the rugged pass, and sure-footedness was for the goats but not the sheep. It was Kadir Khan who many years before had tried to take the path with his flock and paid the consequences. Four of his precious animals had tumbled over the side and broken up so badly on the coarse rocks that their meat and wool were rendered useless for consumption or otherwise. The entire shepherd kingdom heard of his misfortune and sympathized with him. They swore among themselves never to take the path; the loss was too great. The birds of prey were grateful. They did not expect such bounty. They fought and feasted over the carcasses.

Ahmad Zubair and Mohammad Nabi had little in common. The conversation on the journey from the depleted pastures and up to the pass was strained. Nabi felt a need to reassure Ahmad Zubair of the wisdom of his decision to leave the tender hills and bleating flock. His condescension towards his companion was evident the entire way. He made no effort to conceal it. Why should he? He was superior, after all. A scholar. He dwelled on it. And as his body floated down and struck the jagged rocks of the

6

cliff face like Kadir Khan's sheep, his wisdom dwindled, unlike the smile on the face of Ahmad Zubair.

# Freeing the Genie

## *Margaret Harmon*

A woman named Nina knew exactly what she wanted. In an antique shop to buy herself a birthday present—something exotic, she'd know it when she saw it—she found an ancient bronze oil lamp. It was covered with dust, but its elaborate handle and thick spout looked important, its ideal proportions the work of a master artist. So she scooped the lamp from the shelf and talked the shopkeeper into selling it for fifty dollars instead of seventy-five.

At home with a magnifying glass, she searched the lamp for hallmarks to see when and where it was made, and found one tiny cuneiform. The lamp's base was crafted with the same care as its spout, as though for the joy of creating, for the light it would give.

But it was grimy. So, though she respected patinas, she gentled it into warm water.

It trembled in her hands.

She stepped back.

It was silent.

She toweled it dry.

Fumes and vapor bubbled from the spout.

She shrieked and grabbed her fire extinguisher.

The fumes and vapor grew into an exquisite genie wearing little more than an emerald turban. He bathed her in a smile; dark eyelashes swept air when he blinked. He'd been sculpted by the Michelangelo of genies, and his gentle eyes emitted light instead of reflecting it. He bowed graciously from the spout. "For finding me in this curséd lamp, I grant you three wishes!"

He swelled and swayed above the lamp. "They must be personal—for *you alone*."

His lovely manners and kind voice softened her fears. And she had wishes! Silently, she prioritized. *This physically stunning*

9

*creature will understand.* "I wish to have perfect health. Please."

He looked at her. "But you seem—"

"Oh, I'm fine. I work out every day and eat organic food, but health is . . . "

The genie nodded. *Whooouuffff!* A great wind roared from the lamp and swirled around her body.

When it quieted, she felt racehorse-sleek, and energy filled her mind and muscles.

"Thank you!" she said.

He bowed beneficently. "And your second wish?"

"I want to be my boss's boss. Reorganizing our division at Battedyne could save the company and 500 jobs!"

The genie smiled. *Whooouuffff!* A great wind filled the room, rattling the windows.

The telephone rang.

"Shall I get that?"

He nodded.

It was the CEO of Battedyne. "Nina—Scott Hylund here. Good news! Jim Barnes is taking a job with the government, and I want you to replace him. Phil simply can't run your division, so I'm promoting you above him. Can you come in Monday prepared to be Division Chief?"

*I'll be my boss's boss! The genie* must *be magic.* "Of course," she said.

Scott paused. "Did Jim tell you he was planning to leave?"

"No. But I've been seeing ways to make us more effective. I'll bring my notes in Monday. I'm grateful for this chance."

She said goodbye to Scott and returned to the genie. "Thank you again! I'm my boss's boss!"

The genie straightened his turban. "Have you a third?"

Nina blushed. The genie's long-lashed eyes and rippling muscles awakened her third wish, but wariness stopped her tongue. "May I wait until tomorrow?"

He bowed. "Just rub the lamp." With a gentle hiss, he shrank back through the spout, and she set the lamp on the dining room table.

She exercised and cooked an organic dinner, trying to think of a different wish. But she knew exactly what she wanted: health,

10

fulfillment, and . . . It was too important to change.

The next day she bought four new suits, shoes, and a sleeker briefcase, and got a haircut.

After running on the beach and stretching, she ate dinner while organizing her notebook of ideas for refocusing her division.

The magic lamp hummed on the table.

She buffed it with a tea towel.

The lamp rocked and hissed as the genie swelled from its spout. "Yesssssssss?"

"Would you like to see—?"

"I would like very much to see the notes and suits. Your hair is beautiful."

She showed him the briefcase and modeled her suits, then explained how each idea would empower her company in a competitive market.

He listened intently.

~

Each day, Nina felt more at home in slender power suits and a corner office. Some of her ideas worked better than others, but coworkers at Battedyne found they could rely on her for honest, creative thinking.

Every evening after work and working out, Nina freed the genie to tell him her adventures. He floated above the lamp, smiling at her successes, wincing at disasters, asking questions until he understood.

She read him novels after dinner, twenty pages a night. He loved it. She played the piano and they sang duets.

One Tuesday night, Nina stopped reading *Moby Dick* mid-page and said, "You're magic, of course?"

He nodded. "The real thing, not sleight of hand. Genies work with talent, charisma, creativity, love." He leaned closer. "Genies search for people like you."

She lost her place in *Moby Dick*.

There was a long silence.

"Your third wish, Nina?"

She looked at the genie's glittering eyes, dear smile, powerful

11

torso, and smooth skin—and the genie blushed.

"But granting my third wish," she whispered, "will set you free."

The silence expanded.

She closed her book and looked at the genie. "I wish . . . to find my own true love."

The genie swelled taller, and there was a great cloud of steam in all colors known on earth plus some not yet encountered.

When the steam cleared, the lamp was empty.

She polished the lamp and put it in the center of her mantel.

~

A week later at Battedyne, the president of a new company, Tekktronixx International, arrived for an appointment with Nina. His tie was emerald silk and his dark eyelashes swept air when he blinked. He was so exquisitely sculpted that Nina's secretary overturned her coffee cup.

The secretary ushered him into the office, and Nina stood up but hung onto her desk.

When she reached forward to shake hands, he lifted her hand to his heart.

Her secretary backed out and closed the door.

# Old Kim

## *Al Converse*

Mr. Kimble occupied Room 123 in the old folks' home overlooking a small farming town in Ohio. Run by frugal and tidy Catholic nuns, the place displayed the same aged durability as Old Kim. Years of scrubbing left the number faded and the "one" completely gone from the room's sign. The hallway's wooden floor resembled planks in age and wear.

An afternoon beam of sunlight danced on suspended dust through the unfurnished hallway, landing on the spot where I scrubbed. Each day after school I earned a dollar an hour to clean the place's floors with soapy water. An hour and a half of work, a buck fifty, not bad for an eighth-grade kid in 1955.

A nun bustled into his room with some warm wet towels to make him comfortable. Everyone said he was dying.

When she left, I heard him calling me in a raspy voice.

"Hey kid," he said. "Come in. I gotta joke for you."

Old Kim, the jokester — he went around room to room, when he was well, telling shaggy dog jokes and other goofy witticisms. The old folks all looked forward to his daily rounds of mirth. His quips were never laugh-out-loud funny, but his good humor always carried the day and cheered up the place.

"Figured a way to communicate with ya after I die," he said.

I didn't know what to say. A thirteen-year-old kid, what could I say to the dying man?

"Huh," I said.

"Ya tell 'em this joke at my funeral. If they laugh, that means I got ta heaven. If they don't laugh, I'm in hell."

How me, a kid, could get up in church and say anything, much less tell a joke, didn't seem to bother him. He told me the corny anecdote and chuckled.

They held his funeral on a Saturday in the church near the old folks' home. I walked to the service a mile away from my home, wondering if I would chicken out.

The nuns and the few old residents who managed to amble over for the service sat scattered around in the pews — a respectable turnout.

The reverend gave a sermon, and invited people to get up and share their own thoughts about Old Kim. No one stood, but all looked around to see if someone would speak for the old guy. I got up.

Scared and shaky, I stumbled and fumbled my way up the steps to the altar podium. *I wanted to know.*

Then I started. "So this lawyer, this priest, and Mr. Kimble get to the pearly gate and Saint Peter sez, 'Stop, I heard this joke before.'"

A few chuckles began in the rear of the church; folks looked at each other saying "That's Old Kim all right." The chuckles rose to laughter. The laughter took a long time to die out.

# Thankful for Simple Things

## *Audrea Ireland Liszt*

Without a doubt, the Blitz on Liverpool, during World War II, was the time when our family was most thankful. We who escaped with our lives had much to be thankful for. With bombs exploding all around us, tomorrow was not a given. It was the small things in life which became important, like a hug, or even a smile from a stranger.

Prior to the war, people would be friendly, families would stand by each other, but they rarely expressed their affection. I can't ever remember my father telling us kids he loved us, yet we knew he did. The fears and uncertainty felt during the war years went unspoken but became evidenced in our kind and considerate actions toward each other.

Fears were never voiced, nor did they determine our decisions. When a warning air raid siren was heard during a meal, we quickly finished the food on our plates, or if eating a sandwich we would wrap it up and take it with us to the air raid shelter.

Mom had the essentials ever ready, right down to a spare battery for the torch. My little sister Peggy would grab her favorite Mom-made rag doll, a blanket, and her child's Donald Duck, government issue, gas mask. My brother and I carried blankets and pillows and something to drink. What mattered most was being together. Our togetherness in the air raid shelters never included my father. Dad was the team-leader of a rescue squad, extinguishing small fires and digging survivors and non-survivors out of the debris.

His job was hazardous, but also distressing. It was written on his face.

Although we were children, our hands were never idle. The older schoolchildren, if capable, helped where needed. Bombed-out sites were cleared away and planted with Victory Gardens.

15

Schooling in Liverpool went by the wayside during the Blitz. At school, we filled sandbags used to protect the walls of underground shelters, and they were also used on the beaches, tangled in barbed wire, to keep the enemy at bay.

Schoolchildren did what they could to help with the war effort. Les, my older brother, age 14, would help around the fire station, filling sandbags and keeping the fire buckets filled with water. He also spent time on roofs as a fire-watcher.

I unraveled knitted garments, salvaging what wool I could to be reused. As I could knit in the dark, while sitting in the air raid shelter, I knitted many a muffler for the boys on the front lines. All clothing in England was rationed during the war, and odds and ends of anything and everything that could be used was reused.

Women risked their lives cutting the silk parachutes off the German land mines when they landed and before they had exploded. The silky material was used for baby clothing and negligees. We also tore freshly laundered bed sheets into strips to provide bandages for the Red Cross.

The falling bombs were not only a threat to us, but they changed our lives and our way of life. Our street was cratered and pockmarked with bombed-out buildings. Sometimes all that was left of a row of row-houses were the iron fire grates. Les said our area looked like a mouthful of missing or broken teeth waiting to be pulled.

Many bombed-out homes looked like dollhouses with the insides exposed to the outside and stairs that once led to second floors standing above rubble.

Most bombed-out sites were cleared of debris and they became belly-filling Victory Gardens.

After an air raid, Les would look for shrapnel through the bombed-out streets, often wading through water from broken water mains. Boys in the neighborhood vied with each other to see who could collect the most. On one scary occasion, Dad took away from Les a live shell, which he had been proudly showing around.

Our English Sunday morning breakfast was codfish preserved in salt, which would last for donkey's years in its hardened form. It required 24 hours of soak time before being scrubbed clean and deboned. It was then cooked for an hour or more. If we had butter, it would be placed on the fish. Any leftover fish was mixed with mashed potatoes to become stinky fish cakes.

Salt fish was such a basic staple in Liverpool, especially among the poor, that it earned a lyrical line or two in many a Liverpool ditty. One was: "Now pork and beans may be a great American dish, but give me Sunday mornin' an' me owld salt fish, for Ma. . . I got the Liverpool Blues."

Another one was: "Sally Army sells fish, three ha´pence a dish, taste it and try it, if you can afford it, then buy it, Sally Army's salt fish — Sally Army's salt fish."

During the war, butter was rationed, and we ate whatever grease was available, especially beef drippings and hog fat. Mom always made sure that any animal we ate, whether bought from a butcher or accepted from a poacher, arrived wearing its own fur coat. Mom wanted to be absolutely, positively sure that we were not eating roof rabbit, the name given to a skinned and beheaded cat, often prepared and sold as a rabbit for stuffing and cooking.

This digesting of cats during the war affected my father. In 1941, he became a Desert Rat, serving with the British Eighth Army as an artillery gunner under Monty. He fought in Tobruk, El Alamein, and Tunisia, and after the Tunisian disaster for the Germans, my father found himself in Sicily as an army cook.

As I never saw my father cook a piece of toast or make himself a cup of tea, I can only believe that his cooking skills were nil. But I do recall two things my father said about the war. 1) That he was glad the Aussies were our allies, for he saw how brutally they treated their enemies. 2) As an army cook he always prepared far more than his soldiers could ever eat, for it broke his heart to see Italian mothers with hungry children scavenging food from the barrack's waste food bins.

Dad said he always cooked extra and also put out big vats of soup for the Italians. He also told us that the streets of Italy were bereft of "moggies" (Scouse for cats), for the starving Italians were killing and eating them. Dad seemed to be unaware that the same thing was happening in Liverpool when he was away.

There were plenty of wartime hustlers around, who as the saying goes would sell their mothers to make a few quid. They were called Spivs. They touted food and goods stolen from the docks, or off someone's lorry. As food was also rationed, some grocery stores would not display certain scarce items, but kept them under the counter for those special customers who could and would pay the exorbitant asking price. But, overall the people I met were overly kind to us children; we sang in the air raid shelters, and the adults entertained us children.

And, not all people were dishonest. Mr. Strofsky, our generous greengrocer, treated everyone fairly. Whenever he received a bag of onions, he would place one on a purple pillow in the center of his greengrocer's window.

Once the onion was espied, a queue would form, and those pungent pearls were given by him, one to a customer. When down to the last few, and with too many eager housewives waiting and wanting, Mr. Strofsky would resort to raffling them off — no charge.

His customers would then pick numbers out of the hat, hoping they would be lucky enough to take one home. Nothing, but nothing, smells as good as the aroma of frying onion, the basic ingredient for onion gravy to be poured over bangers (sausage) and mash. And what pray tell is an Irish stew without a Spanish onion? Now I ask you? And that's how it was during wartime, when the simplest thing could bring one pleasure. Or the need to eat meant that we ate things we would never have dreamed of consuming prior to the war.

One other simple pleasure available to all at little cost was storytelling. I can recall many a memorable evening, whether in the shelter or at home hogging the warmth from a dying coal fire, it having done its cooking for the day. If we were without imagination, Gran would tell us to close our eyes and think. My brother could always come up with something scary. We also played gramophone records and sang along.

We learned to be thankful, along with patience and perseverance. And while I can't ever recall being told, "It's better to give than to receive," we knew who made the sacrifices. It was our parents.

Nor did we have to be told not to be selfish, for we knew that we'd get our fair share. I also learned that there was no shame in being poor, that life is not always the way it's supposed to be. It's just the way it is. The way we cope with it is what makes the difference.

# A Mexican Mother's Day Reflection

## *Francisco Cota-Robles Newton*
## *(Frank Newton)*

What goes into the selection or formulation of a name? Sometimes it's pure impulse. A Hawaiian woman once explained to me how she named the second of her seven sons. "The doctor walked into the maternity ward and asked me what I was going to name my baby. At that moment I happened to be reading a magazine article about President Eisenhower, and so it popped into my head to name him Eisen."

More commonly, it's a matter of family tradition—as in, "There's always been a David in our family." Or sometimes it's holiday happenstance. I have a relative who is named "Noel" due expressly to his December-25 birthday. And then, I've known countless couples who spent weeks on end scouring naming books and websites, agonizing the entire time over their final choice.

But once in a while, a name results from a key life experience, and the name pays a heartfelt tribute to that profoundly meaningful incident. Such is the case for the maternal branch of my family tree—the Cota-Robles clan of Sonora, Mexico.

*Cota-Robles* is not just an uncommon family name in Mexico, it is a unique surname. There is only one Cota-Robles family. This is because my mother's father, Amado Cota-Robles, formulated the name intentionally. Instead of simply taking his father's last name "Cota," which would have been the customary thing to do, Amado deliberately attached his mother's family name, "Robles." And in this willful act, there lies a tale worth telling.

Imagine the dusty pueblo of Hermosillo in Sonora, Mexico, in the early -1890s. There is a bright-eyed, vivacious child, aged 13 or 14—long black hair, a sweet smile and a mischievous sparkle in

21

her ebony eyes. She is bubbling with joy this one Friday afternoon because she is sporting a colorful new dress, frilled and ribboned. It's doubly cherished because it is not only pretty, it was hand-made just for her by her doting mother and grandmother.

Then her father — my great-grandfather — comes home and plops down at the kitchen table. A baker, he's been working since the wee hours of the morning, and now he's bushed. The girl rushes excitedly to his side, greeting him with a hug.

"Daddy, look at my beautiful new dress!" she exclaims with delight.

Tired and grumpy, he glances at it. "And what is this?"

"Grandma made it for me for the dance this Saturday at the church hall. My first dance! I can't wait!" She's so excited she seems about to burst.

"What dance? Nobody told me about this." He gets grumpier.

"Mommy said I could go," she pleads.

"No... you're too young. I don't think you should go," he abruptly decides. "No... you didn't ask me for permission... so no!"

"Whaattt?!" she wails in disbelief. The harsh declaration, so unjust, so utterly unexpected, stuns her. She steps back, dismayed, tears of hurt and anger well up instantly. "Daddy, no!" she half screams, half cries.

"No, you should have asked me first," he concludes firmly.

She runs to Mama, sobbing. But father has decided and the matter is settled. Inconsolable, she runs to her room and slams the door.

Later she is called to supper and arrives in a bitter mood, obstinate. Her father barks, "I told you to take off that dress." When she refuses, he angrily sends her to bed.

Now her mood is darker and more defiant. She refuses to take off her cherished dress or to go to bed, as these are her father's two explicit demands. Instead, she decides to lie down in her pretty party dress on the concrete floor of her bedroom, without any bed covers.

Unfortunately beyond her reckoning, on arid desert nights concrete tends to chill, becoming bitterly cold; so when her mother comes in later to check, she finds her child lying on the bare floor,

22

shivering and sneezing. She puts her to bed, but already the child is aching and coughing. In the morning she has a fever and the cough is worse.

During the day, her fever rises and the cough turns hoarse and wracking. Alarmed, the doctor is called and his face is grim after his diagnosis. The child has pneumonia... this at a time long before the discovery of penicillin.

Desperate, they ply her with every conceivable remedy – soups, teas, honey salves, and even the arcane ministrations of a *curandera* (native healer). Sadly, all to no avail.

There, high and dry, tucked into her warm bed, many miles from any lake or sea, the little girl drowns... her lungs filled with the toxic fluids produced by her own frail body.

The family is devastated by the tragedy. Not only are my great-grandmother and her mother utterly disconsolate, but my great-grandfather is crushed and never forgives himself. Still off to the side, below the adults' attention, perhaps the most deeply touched is my grandfather — the girl's little brother, Amado. He dearly loved his older sister; and as he grew older, he never forgot her and he never forgave his father's culpability in her death.

Thus, when Amado became an adult and set off from home, he decided not to honor his father by using only his father's surname, Cota. No. He added the maiden name of his beloved mother, Robles.

What's more, when Amado married and held his first child in his arms, he named the little girl in memory of his long-lost sister, Isabel. This is how Isabel Cota-Robles came to be named... and in due time, she became my own dearly loved mother.

# Analog

## *Jenna Benson*

What a surprise that one set of hands
controls every human being on earth.
The new version of sands
Passing through a small hole in glass
Makes our days here so precious.

What makes us tick is what holds us together.
But it's that subtle tock that drives us to the edge.
On the toughest days we must weather,
We are never alone; time is always our partner
Ready to tell us where we went wrong.

How human it is to lose interest in our passion
The one thing that truly drives us;
Pushes us and in time allows us to grow in fashion,
Even through the pain of it all.
We have to start creating memories for ourselves.

The years passed by are not wasted,

Surely, we have made a difference.

The luxury of life has only been tasted,

Wandering in the dark alleys and cursing at the sky,

Lost in yourself.


The hands move across the clock at the same speed
every day.

No matter what changes,

And no matter what you say,

The seconds in each day never falter.


If we do not destroy ourselves we will,

One day,

Venture to the stars.

# The Lifeguard

## *Charles H. Currier*

**It was a da k and s ormy night.**

"Great," Richard grumbled to himself, "The ribbon's shot and I still haven't come up with a decent opening line. I can't even write crappy clichés, much less something worth reading."

He yanked the page out of the antique Corona typewriter sitting on a desk in the living room of his deceased uncle's Lake Michigan beach house. The age-hardened rubber roller, with its internal gearing, too gummed up with dried grease to rotate easily, didn't budge as the paper slid out from under it. Richard thought a typewriter should make that dramatic ratchet noise he loved hearing in an old movie when the star reporter, about to miss his deadline, pulls out a finished piece with flair. He then hands it off to a waiting copy boy who rushes it to the editor's desk.

~

The previous evening at his Chicago apartment, Richard, forty-seven and an award-winning mystery writer, had mentioned this peculiar fetish to his twenty-four-year-old girlfriend, Cindy, while they reclined on the couch. He was watching a youthful Jimmy Cagney on TCM in one of the actor's 1930s newsman roles. Cindy was texting someone, as usual.

"Are you paying any attention to me?" Richard asked.

"Uh huh," Cindy said with no real enthusiasm before brightening. "Oh, see what I got today. Like 'em?" She waved her new nails, with gold unicorn stickers, inches from his face. He swatted them away, eliciting an "Ow!" from her. She pouted while holding the slighted fingers. "That's not nice, and besides, I'll bet you haven't used a typewriter in years."

27

"I know I know, but when I did, that sound indicated accomplishment, of completing something important. It used to give me a euphoric feeling, something like a satisfying morning constitutional."

"Huh?"

"You know a dump." Laughing, he gave her a sideways glance.

She frowned. "What, are you? Constipated? You're gross."

He turned back to the movie, "Yeah, that's me, constipated."

~

Richard had driven to the beach house on Michigan's western shore to escape both the Windy City and Windy Cindy. Silence to her was a void to be filled. Silence to him was something needed to overcome the worst writer's block he had ever suffered.

Traffic had been light for a Friday afternoon. When he turned onto the county road leading to his uncle's lakefront property, he came upon a flagman controlling traffic. Several Michigan Gas and Electric boom trucks were repairing downed lines. Richard lowered his window and asked the worker, "What's up?"

"A windstorm came through yesterday. Electricity and cell service will be out until Monday if you're going to be at the shore."

"No well water, huh?" Richard asked. The man shrugged his shoulders.

It was four when Richard arrived at the house. He unlocked the back door and entered the kitchen. A check of the faucet confirmed his expectations: no water. The same for the light switches: no power. He opened the cabinet drawer in the hallway usually stocked with flashlights and candles. It was empty. That seemed strange until he remembered a crew had been hired to clean and winterize the place after Uncle Dick died in September. *No doubt they helped themselves to a few items in the process.*

He entered the dining room and set his Apple laptop on the table. He opened it and groaned. In his haste to leave the city, he had nabbed Cindy's by mistake. *Crap, I don't know her access code and the battery's almost dead. Oh well, I'll charge it in the car and call her for the code from the gas station pay phone in the morning. Wait, did*

*I see the charger in the glove box? Damn her. She nagged me never to leave anything in the car that might get stolen.* Cindy had pointed out the charger specifically. To avoid an argument, Richard had taken it inside. He remembered thinking at the time, *who the hell would break into a car to steal a three dollar phone charger?*

Their most recent fight began as he was leaving for the beach house and had continued on his cell phone while he drove north. They bickered for over an hour. As he crossed the Indiana-Michigan state line, she was crying. Richard had had enough and turned off his phone. He switched on the car's radio and found a classic rock channel out of Kalamazoo. He smiled; it was playing Paul Simon's, "Fifty Ways to Leave Your Lover."

~

He glared at the useless typewriter in front of him, then ran his fingers through his thinning hair. Three years ago, he could walk through any airport newsstand in the country and see his name on book covers alongside Patterson, Grisham, and Cussler. Not anymore. His publisher had called him saying he needed to see progress on his next story or their book deal would be history.

Richard crumpled the nearly blank sheet of typing paper into a tight ball and tossed it, free throw style, toward the fireplace. It had been a struggle to get the fire lit. Being November, the logs and kindling stacked outside under a canvas tarp were damp. It took all the matches and newspaper he could find to get the flames going. Now, with a good bed of coals glowing, wood he added dried and caught with only a slight delay. Outside, the temperature was in the mid-thirties; inside, even with the fire going, it didn't feel much warmer. The recalcitrant typewriter notwithstanding, he hadn't yet mastered typing with gloves on.

Richard stood, stretched, turned up the collar of his winter jacket, and added another chunk of wood. Crossing the room, he looked out a window that faced west. It was late, and there was nothing to be seen except occasional lightning strikes stinging the lake's surface miles out. A storm was approaching.

Returning to the chair behind the desk, he leaned back and looked at the ceiling. Some of the tongue and groove boards overhead had water stains and were bowed. He knew the bathroom had a cast-iron bathtub and was directly above him. Unnerved, he stood on his tiptoes and tested the slats by pushing upwards. Satisfied there was no immediate danger, he resumed his seat and laced his fingers behind his head. He chuckled. The warped boards brought back memories of his summer vacations here as a kid.

Every day, he and his cousin John had been plunked into that upstairs tub by Aunt Millie to wash off any beach sand still clinging to their legs and feet, or hiding in the folds of their bathing suits. Their splash wars, beginning at the lake, continued in the tub with each boy attempting to sink the other's toy-boat armada. The recurring puddles left on the floor from these naval engagements drove Aunt Millie crazy.

"You're going to ruin the linoleum. Now stop it," she'd say.

Richard guessed these daily floods, although mopped with towels, probably had contributed to the possible wood rot issue. He made a mental note to mention it to John, now the house's owner.

Swiveling in the chair, he surveyed the living room's outdated furniture. It reminded him of a South Chicago thrift store. Two armchairs and a sofa still wore the same purple and orange paisley-patterned coverings from bygone years. Very little in the house had been modernized since its construction—indeed, not since Richard was a child. Closing his eyes, he breathed in. The smoke from eight decades of summer evening fires in the old fireplace had left its mark, penetrating the knotted throw rugs, draperies, and upholstery. He found the woodsy aroma comforting.

Rising from the chair, Richard lay on the old couch before the fire and listened to the wind-driven rain beating against the windows and siding. Waves crashed on the shore. His eyes wandered to rows of faded hardbacks on shelves wedged between the walls' exposed studs. He knew the extensive collection existed because his uncle had been a Professor of English Literature at Northwestern.

One book caught Richard's attention as it protruded from the others. It looked ready to fall. No family members had been to the house since his uncle's death. *I wonder if Uncle Dick left it like that.*

30

Richard removed the volume from the shelf. It was Melville's, *Moby Dick*.

As he opened the cover to check the edition, a scalloped-edged snapshot fell to the floor. Picking up the black-and-white photo, he turned the image toward the fire. It showed a couple standing on a dock beside a wooden speedboat. The young man was his Uncle Dick wearing trunks and a sleeveless tee-shirt with LIFEGUARD printed on the front. Richard thought this cool, having worked as a lifeguard in college.

The woman wore a headscarf, tight sweater, and a skirt hemmed at the knees, a style popular in the 1950s. A pair of bobby sox and saddle shoes completed her ensemble. She was leaning into Dick with one hand on his right shoulder, the other squeezing his bicep.

Something about the photo narrowed Richard's eyes. He fumbled for the magnifying glass he'd noticed in the desk's drawer. When her face came into focus, he experienced an involuntary shudder brought on by an obscure memory. Had he seen her before? He thought so, but how, where? Looking lower on the photo, he thought he saw a baby bump. Writing on the back of the picture seemed to confirm this, "September, '59, Dick, sweetheart, we three will be forever happy."

One thing Richard knew for sure, this wasn't Aunt Millie. *So, who was she? A summer fling? Do I have a cousin somewhere I don't know?*

He remembered hearing that Millie and Dick married in December 1960, right after the Kennedy election. Still perplexed, he laid the photo on the desk and returned Moby to its original slot. He took a deep breath. *Okay, quit stalling. It's time to get back to my opus.*

Richard sat back at the ancient typing machine. He remembered seeing a leather case with "Corona" embossed on the cover in the corner of the house's attic years earlier. *It's a long shot, but maybe there's a spool of useable ribbon in there.*

He stood, turned, took a step, and froze. Something about going into that attic in the dark spooked him. *What can I use for light? My iPhone.* He pulled it out of his pocket and turned it on. A warning appeared saying its power level was down to less than ten percent. Now he wished he had hung up on Cindy earlier. He would have to conserve the battery as best he could.

Leaving the living room to go into the unlit areas of the house, he flashed the phone's camera strobe to burn an image in his mind's eye of what was ahead of him. Before the scene on his retina faded, he moved forward avoiding anything he might trip over. He flashed it again and again, each time creating a new still photo in his brain. Climbing the stairs to the second floor, he made his way along the hall. The floorboards creaked with every step. He flashed the bathroom and its claw-foot tub. He flashed the bedroom in which he and John had slept on sagging twin beds then toward the end of the hall where a narrow stairway rose to the attic. Nothing happened. The battery was spent.

The hair on the back of his neck bristled at the thought of climbing those steps even without a light. He and his cousin had camped in that very attic. When Uncle Dick had come to tuck them in, he was drunk, stinking drunk. A memory of a scary story his uncle had told them came rushing back to Richard. It was about a young man and a young woman who were returning home in a speedboat from a dinner-dance at a nearby waterfront resort. On a moonless night, a sudden storm came up. The woman fell overboard. The young man swept the beam of his flashlight across the wind-whipped water until he saw her scarf floating on the surface. He jumped in after her, but she sank away from him into the vast expanse of deep water. By the end of the story, Uncle Dick was fighting back tears and mumbling to himself. He tromped down the stairs and turned off the attic's single light, leaving the two boys in near darkness within the cavernous room.

Cousin John had nodded right off. Eight-year-old Richard hadn't. He lay terrified, hiding in his sleeping bag, afraid to move or speak, transfixed on an apparition floating inside the window at the far end of the attic. *What if it's the dead woman?* For hours he lay there silent, even peeing in his bag rather than reveal his presence to the wraith.

In the morning, his tormentor had turned out to be nothing more than a sail his uncle had been airing out in the breeze from the open window. Richard, embarrassed, never told anyone about that night. Nonetheless, it was the last time he would sleep in that

32

room.

~

Suddenly it dawned on him. *That must have been her in the photo, the woman in his uncle's story who drowned. But how would her face seem familiar to me? She died before I was born, and why couldn't Dick save her? He was a trained lifeguard. It should have been easy. Oh Christ, maybe he didn't want to.*

Richard's mind raced. In the darkness of the second floor, he leaned against the wall and laughed, quietly at first, then louder. *Screw the attic.* He now knew the story he would write, and he needed to get it on paper pronto. By the time he had made it down the stairs, his mind was already into the third chapter.

While feeling his way back to the living room, he entered the hallway where he had searched the cabinet drawer earlier for candles and a flashlight. Then it struck him. *She's in there.* He opened that same drawer and removed a newspaper lining its bottom. Returning to the light of the fire, he sat on the sofa gazing at what he held in his hands. Yellowed, torn, and stained from decades of age and waxy residue, yet still discernible, was page three of a local newspaper dated September 27, 1959. The caption under her photo said she was Nancy O'Connor, dead at age nineteen.

~

The typewriter was heavy as Richard placed it on the floor. Inside the desk, he located a pencil, a legal pad, and a pocketknife. Opening the blade, he carved a fresh point on the Dixon Ticonderoga number two, and, by the light of the fire, wrote, *'Twas a dark and stormy night above Lake Michigan, while, on its surface, the chop was dangerous as they struggled to drag her bloated, blue body from the wintry water...*

# Out with the Old and in with the New

## *Barbara Crothers*

Not long ago one of my friends sent a notice stating that the downtown portion of Wausau, Wisconsin, would again undergo change, with new and updated shopping and entertainment facilities on Third Street.

I was immediately thrown back into the late '70s when I worked on the original project that "under the threat of condemnation, HUD would provide for, along with other governmental agencies, the demolition of and building of a new Downtown Shopping Center Project covering eight blocks of privately-held buildings dating from the early 1800s." These old brick buildings, some three or four stories tall, were empty, could not be heated properly, and could not easily be brought up to code. Several of them housed elderly, disabled seniors, living on meager incomes.

Three agencies provided funding for that project. Therefore, the law firm I was employed by won the contract to establish an office in the designated area; keep three sets of files open for viewing at any time by one or more of those participating agencies; provide space for the Relocation Experts; provide expert appraisers to establish fair values of the buildings and certain ornamental antique fixtures in those buildings; and pay current owners for their property. We would provide enough staff to handle the daily operations of that on-site office. Not only would I remain the Office Manager at the firm but also serve as the newly established office-Manager-Coordinator in one of the "better" buildings on Third Street. I would work with the City Attorney, judges, owners, The Redevelopment Authority, attend all meetings and report same to the attorneys at the firm. I would also travel to HUD in Washington, DC, and an affiliated law firm in Chicago. (They provided transportation for me in their firm's official Lear Jet!) The timeframe projected for the whole was stated from start to finish of all work at approximately five years.

I assisted in streamlining all elements of the tasks necessary, created a work binder with letters, etc., and gave seminars upon completion of the project in other communities wishing to do a like-manner project to upgrade their aging centers. Our project was completed in two and one-half years! When it was finished, the City Attorney and I flew all over the state discussing and distributing our methods, standardized correspondence, and file system to those wishing to accomplish like projects around the state. We charged for those seminars, with proceeds going into the firm's coffers.

Above all, I remember many of those elderly folks being forced to move out of the area and being relocated in affordable, warm housing within a general neighborhood close-by; they are still clear in my mind.

~

The old man walked slowly against the wind on the other side of the street in front of the empty furniture store. His progress was slow. The wind tore at his long coat; he wore no hat. For every step he took forward, the wind pushed him back two. I guessed he came from the Farmer's Tavern just around the corner. During the first part of the month he was drunk every day walking home, bent over with his head facing the sidewalk. Toward the last part of the month, he did not stagger, but walked up and down the sidewalk, finally meeting some of his neighbors for a chat; he was almost handsome, clean-shaven, and still wearing that long dark brown coat.

A couple of weeks before Christmas that year, the old man poked his head in the front door of the office and shouted, "Leave us alone!" He closed the door carefully, like a polite child, and stepped back into the swirl of snow.

I walked to the front of the office and saw a group of elderly men and one woman envelop him and scuttle away like newspapers caught by the wind, out of my sight.

Early, the last week in November, Marge, my secretary, mailed the next batch of letters, giving notice that the time had come for the residents of this area to begin looking for new places to live; they had ninety days within which to comply.

The letter further stated:

> "If you desire help, please contact this office. You will be paid a relocation benefit and all moving expenses. You will be provided with similar or better facilities at similar rents by our Relocation Experts, who will assist you in finding newer homes and the assistance you require to make that move."

Marge adjusted the thermostat again and squared the corner of the stack of files on her desk. "My God, I don't believe it! Look! Here comes that old man again."

The office Marge and I occupied was on the ground floor of one of the ancient brick buildings situated along Third Street. It was difficult to heat. Some days I worked all day with my coat on. One morning it was just a bit above zero degrees. We did jumping jacks to warm up enough to do the necessary work. It, too, would be one of those buildings razed once all were empty and inventoried prior to destruction.

All the ornate, lovely, reusable fixtures, any remaining furniture still usable was listed to be sold at auction or catalogued by qualified appraisers. The underground network of tunnel-hallways that once carried heat from the monster coal furnace in the basement to the rooms and offices located in each building was cleared, and any open spaces were located, cleared, and listed prior to demolition.

I personally travelled through those underground tunnels one cold evening with a bunch of skeleton keys and a flashlight in my hand. The dark hall was a labyrinth of cobwebs, old signs, boxes, doors that opened onto grassy squares open to the sky, and a speakeasy or rathskeller-type place from the 1920s. High ceilings of imprinted tin squares covered some of the ceilings--a time capsule locked away for years! Outside access at street level was filled in with bricks, with dirt packed in between them. From the inside, just past the door, was a flight of stairs leading up to the outside sidewalk. I could almost hear the ragtime piano playing as

I backed out of that room and back into the darker hallway.

He walked in, sort of side-stepping, through the front door, over to Marge's desk, placed both hands on the edge, swayed a little and said, "You the Mall Lady?"

"No, she is," and pointed with her shoulder in my direction. He turned toward me. He had one brown eye, bulging, staring straight ahead and a soft hazel one that looked at me. Even from this distance I could smell he had been drinking for a long time. He pulled a letter from the inside pocket of his overcoat and threw it on my desk.

"You tellin' me I gotta move. Well, I won't, and neither will Edward or Art or Regina or any of the others. We got no place else to go; so if you tear the hotel down, you gotta do it with us in it." He left without another word.

I put a small Christmas tree in the front window, requisitioned some comfortable chairs from the City Hall warehouse, and bought a coffee pot. Every day as we worked on the files for the project that HUD required, the smell of fresh coffee filled the air in the office and escaped out onto the street where the residents dared each other to pass from time to time.

As Christmas neared, Marge and I took turns bringing fresh baked cookies to go with the coffee. We brought small gifts to place under the tree in the window.

He came in again on Wednesday, just before Christmas. His hair was combed, and he didn't stink!

"Sorry about the other day, but the Judge said that he would buy me a bottle if I could scare you. My name is Herman, Herman Adams. I live in room 407 in the Washington House Hotel...well, upstairs in this building. Been there for thirty-five years now, but I suppose you know that. You folks seem to know just about everything there is to know about us and this area."

"Herman, would you like some coffee and a cookie or two? Come, let's sit over here and get acquainted."

He wrapped his large, work-worn hands around the cup and started talking. "We really don't want to move, you know? We've lived here for so long and we all know each other. Regina borrows cigarettes from everybody and never pays them back. She stinks and doesn't comb her hair, but we don't let nobody bother her

38

either. She wears that coat all the time, but she has about three dresses. She gets a hundred and forty-five dollars a month in a check that comes on the first, but she's broke long before she gets another check. Her rent is seventeen dollars because she just has a bed. Doesn't need a closet and the bathroom is down the hall."

He poured coffee in my cup and helped himself to a chocolate-chip cookie. I could tell that Marge was trying to hear what he was saying over the sound of her typing the endless reports and letters that filled each file.

"She has been here only about eleven years and she never told anybody where she came from or if she has any people around." Herman shook a crumb from the front of his coat.

"Edward has lived in his room for longer than I have. He is the cripple who has the walker. Lord, he sure is mean sometimes. Goes down the steps to get out on the street because he don't have a window in his room, but he can't hardly get back up the stairs. It's forty-three steps, you know? When he's down on the street and has to go to the bathroom, sometimes he don't make it. I scrub the steps sometimes because Rose...she works for the Judge, you know...it is really part of her job, but she has arthritis and it's pretty hard for her to scrub them. So I do it. Besides, it gives me something to do. Sometimes she pays me but most of the time she don't." He paused in his story, smoothed his hair and looked out the window for a long time.

We chatted for a little while longer. Herman saw Edward waving at him through the window. "I guess I gotta go and help Edward up the stairs now. Oh, did you know that top floor is where the pigeons live? Must've been like that for years 'cuz of all the pigeon poop piled up there. It has skylights, broken ones where they get in. No one goes up there 'cuz it stinks, but they don't bother us, so I guess it's not hurtin' anyone though. Just thought I'd let you know."

"Thanks, Herman, but we do know about that, too. It really isn't healthy for you all either. That's just one more reason for this project to get done. I do appreciate you letting me know though."

I handed Herman several cookies wrapped in a large paper napkin. "Maybe you can share these with the others out there."

Herman nodded his head, took the small bundle and put it in

his pocket and walked out the door.

The next day Margie and I both brought cookies and made more pots of coffee. I added a tablet, some stamps, a few pencils and envelopes to the other small wrapped gifts under the tree. The red and green ribbons and shiny wrapping paper covered several packs of cigarettes, some packages of gum, small amounts of hard Christmas candy, nuts, a few handkerchiefs, and a paper of bobby-pins. Others held razors, combs, aftershave, and a small bottle of cologne. We were bridging the gaps in ways that eventually brought these people into the office.

One more day until the Christmas holiday brought Herman inside again. "Edward sure can be mean sometimes. Now, he don't want anyone else coming in here; says you're his girlfriends . . . both of you. Says he's the only one who can come in."

"Herman, do you think that is true? Or maybe Edward just wants to think he has been here the longest and, well, that this was his home first."

"I guess he can talk better than me; I didn't do much talking all the time I worked on the San Francisco Bay Bridge. Worked on that bridge for thirty-two years. Painted it from one end to the other and when it was all painted, had to go back and paint it all over again . . . the salt water was hard on the metal; rusted in places, so had it all to do again. I hated that job, loved it, too. Yeah, after a while, I felt that it belonged to me, and I had to take care of it. Yeah, I can see that about Edward. I'll not let it get to me — we been friends too long, you know?"

"Maybe just say something to him like that. He just needs a little attention now that all of you are in the same boat, so to speak."

Herman smiled a bit, stuck his hands in his pockets and started to walk out the door. "Say, Herman, won't you invite the others in? I'll bring in a few more chairs from the back and maybe we can share some coffee, a bite or two of those cookies, and everyone can get a little something for Christmas. What do you think? Think that is a good idea?"

He nodded as his smile grew bigger, turning up the edges of his mouth. I saw him through the window talking with the others.

The following week, Herman let us know, "When we move,

40

could you have those guys find a place where we can still live close to each other? Maybe have it somewhere about half-way between The Farmer's Tav and St. Mary's Catholic Church…yes, we all think that would be real fine."

# San Diego County Jail

## *Chloe Kerns Edge*

My first-grade teacher took care of my cat when I went to jail. I had just turned twenty-one. Mama Kitty had four babies while I was down. I thought it was great when telling my teacher, Esther Young, what I had done and why I had to go to jail and that my biggest worry was what I would do with my kitty for who-knows-how-long, and she offered, "Well, I'd be glad to take care of her. That way I'll see you when you come back, find out if you learned anything." I never thought about providing or paying for food. I was locked into fear. I just took my cat over and thanked her and said goodbye.

I had been arrested with my boyfriend in November of 1964, for sales of narcotics. It was his sale. He sold a lid of pot to a guy in an old Mercury who had been introduced to us by Patrick Fiddler. Patrick was our friend, or so we thought. We were a bunch of college kids living in Mission Beach and Patrick had been popped at the Arizona border with some kilos. He turned state's evidence and rolled over on forty-four of us. It turned out that not all of us were college kids. We were on TV getting busted. They said it was the biggest bust in San Diego ever. I had two co-defendants — my boyfriend, Roy, and our roommate, Frank.

I had endured a jury trial, during which I wore conservative clothes and kept my mouth shut, like the attorney told me. I still believed in "truth, justice and the American way." It was 1964 and few people knew about drugs back then. Drugs hadn't become mainstream knowledge. I was charged with Sales of Narcotics, Conspiracy to Sell Narcotics, Possession of Narcotics and Cohabitation. It was illegal to live with someone with whom you were not married back then. The trial lasted days. I studied my jurors.

After I was convicted, my charges were dropped from Sales of Narcotics to Possession of Narcotics. It was possession of marijuana. The codes were H&S 11530 and H&S 11531. It was a Health and Safety Code issue in the early sixties. What I had actually done was respond to my boyfriend's request, "Baby, hand me that lid on the bookcase." There had been a man in the old Mercury outside. I handed him the lid. He gave it to the man in the car. That was conspiracy. I was out on bail, waiting for the sentencing.

My bail had been $55,000, which used to be a lot of money. My Dad was so mad that he went to his friend who owned the liquor store and got it in small bills, took it down to the County Jail in a big bag and made them count it.

A lady cop came to tell me that my bail had arrived and she brought me a bundle of my possessions. I got my few things together — letters mostly — and changed into my street clothes. We had no idea that it would take so long to count the money. It took most of the day. I waited and waited. My Dad still had a smirk on his face when I saw him. For once, he wasn't mad at me, he was mad at the cops in the jail.

I had been twenty-one for a month. I had to wait until after Christmas to be sentenced and this was the most unpleasant time. It is better to know the worst than not to know. I could have gotten five years or one. Between the time I was convicted and the day I was sentenced, when I was out on bail, Roy and I got married to get rid of the co-habitation charge. We had a quickly assembled wedding at the Christ Lutheran Church on Cass Street, where I had spent my Sunday mornings and Wednesday nights in my childhood. Pastor Quentin P. Garman officiated. In attendance were most of the forty-four recently arrested felons and my family. Roy's family was in Boston.

When it was time to walk me down the aisle, my Dad said, "I can't do this. I can't give you to him. Look at him." He was pointing toward the front of the church where Roy was standing.

"Dad! Look what I'm wearing! I'm getting married!"

"I can't do it" he said. I looked around the church to find someone bigger than my Dad, and sped down the outside aisle to my best friend, Richard.

"Hey, man! C'mere!" I whispered. He followed me into the narthex at the back of the church. "I need help. My Dad won't walk me down the aisle. Will you?"

He gently touched my elbow and motioned me toward the door. Leaning toward my ear, he said, "I love you way more than he does. I understand how your Dad feels. If you really want me to do this, I love you so much, I will." Richard walked me down the aisle. Soon after, I got pregnant, but I wouldn't know this for a couple of months.

I was sentenced to five-to-life, dropped to a year in County Jail, followed by five years probation. They took me right from the sentencing through the back door in handcuffs. I could hear my Dad sobbing deeply as the door slammed shut.

They booked me, which means a mug shot, an interview during which they inquire about any identifying marks or scars, a full body and cavity search followed by an issue of jail clothes. At that time, females wore an ugly brown dress with stripes woven into the fabric.

Stunned, I was escorted by two sets of cops into elevators, through catwalks and into the "B" Tank. The old County Jail — walls, bars, ceilings — was painted in a dull shade of pale, flat green. The color was depressing. The area they enclose, "B" Tank, on the second floor, was divided into three sections. On the right were sixteen sets of bunk beds in two rows of eight in the dorm room, which was a long, wide room open on one side except for the bars. Eight bunk beds were in a row against the inside wall, and the other eight bunks were along the bars. At the opposite end were four steel tables and round steel stools, all attached to the floor so they couldn't be thrown. Thirty-two women lived in this cage, when it was full. Even the TV had bars around it, attaching it to the wall. Most people didn't watch it. The cops controlled what was on it and when it was on.

The dayroom was where we ate, played dominoes, and had AA meetings with the women who came in and sat on the catwalk on the other side of the bars and talked to us about being sober and how wonderful it was. We could buy coffee and use hot water from the tap to make tepid instant coffee. If we had money on the books we could buy candy, but no gum. Gum messes up locks.

I had a friend named Katie whom I met when I got there, and we played a lot of dominoes together. She was from southeast San Diego, and she had five kids. She had stolen a strainer from the Safeway on Imperial, and she was sentenced to six months in jail. Soon after she told me that I stopped believing in God.

In between the bunk beds and the tables were showers and toilets. Minimal and sparse. Out in the open, we peed and pooped without privacy. Someone would rig up sheets in an effort to get a minimum of privacy, but it didn't last long because the cops who came by regularly to count us had to be able to see everyone. The toilet seats were steel and cold. The shower smelled like mold and urine.

The repeated counting of the inmates was absurd. The first thing I learned was that to get out, there were fourteen locked doors and no cop had more than seven keys. It was a police team effort to get from any floor to the street.

Before I'd been there for thirty days, I was the tank captain, and my bed was next to the big metal doors, first bunk, bottom bed. You didn't just go in and out of the tank. The big steel doors to the catwalk would open, the prisoner goes into a holding area. Then the doors to the catwalk would slam shut and the door to the tank would open. The prisoner walks in. Never were the two doors open at once. This was very loud. The metal doors slammed and locked every time someone went in or out. My job was to keep control in the tank, to talk to women who were all older than I, to help people if I could, to quell disagreements, and, in general, keep order.

By March, I knew I was pregnant but I didn't tell anyone. When I started to show, they shackled my ankles and handcuffed my wrists behind me and took me through the fourteen doors to a cop car. The cop drove me to County Hospital Maternity Clinic, where there were always at least fifty women waiting in the huge waiting room. Walking in leg irons is noisy, and I shuffled in small steps along the right aisle, down the hall to the doctor, attracting a lot of attention. They put me in the stirrups wearing the ankle chains. This happened every month. One time the lady doctor stared down the cop. I was on my back with my heels in the metal stirrups looking at the doctor lady, who was staring at

46

the cop standing behind my right shoulder. Nothing happened. It was a long couple of minutes, and I couldn't see the cop. Suddenly the doctor exploded, "Get these god-damned chains off her! What is *wrong* with you?" He moved fast to unlock the leg irons and then she told him to wait outside. Cool doctor. It wasn't always that good.

What I often wondered was, how come the cops didn't know you can't take your panties off wearing ankle chains?

There is no sound like the finality of an electric door slamming in a locked facility. I worried about that noise. As my baby grew, I became concerned that she would have hearing problems because of the slamming of the doors. My bed, as tank captain, was right next to the entry, so when anyone came in or left the tank, the doors slammed four times. I would grab my pillow and hold it over my belly through the tedious in-and-out business.

From time to time an angry woman would join us, spreading venom in the tank. When I was five months pregnant a tall girl came in with a big attitude, wanting to fight. Soon it was obvious she wanted to fight with me. I remember the second I realized that if I did not take her down, I would lose control of the tank. When she came at me I reciprocated, threw a good one into her face, then caught her shoulders and kicked her foot out from under her. She went down. Not only were the cops not mad, they were proud of me, smiled at me as they removed her. I was confused.

The months went by. My mom, who was fighting cancer, would drive out to Camp Morena, where my new husband was serving his time, to pick up a letter on Saturday. Then she'd drive down to the County Jail to visit me on Sunday and hold the letter up to the double glass between us so I could read it. She thought my baby should have a mom and a dad, and she wanted us to stay together. She was being helpful, doing what she could.

She was also as afraid as I was that my baby would be born into captivity. As the months went by, she hired a friend of ours, Paul Peterson, then head of the Democratic Central Committee, and a fine attorney, to have a judge modify my sentence so the baby could be born free. I had gone into jail as a disillusioned twenty-one-year-old and I became a cynical felon while I was there. My only hope was the baby growing inside me.

47

In September, I got out, had my baby girl and took care of my new baby and my dying mom, lying on twin beds staring at each other for a month. She died on October 15, 1965. I have never been so sad.

Soon after, we moved to Vista because the probation office in San Diego never went north of Del Mar to bust into a probationer's home a 4:30 in the morning and shake it down. There was no substation in Vista yet.

On the way, we went to Esther Young's house to pick up Mama Kitty and the four babies. She hugged me with tears in her eyes. My mom was also her friend. She looked at me long and close. She asked me if I'd learned anything.

"Yes," I said, "I did. Compared to the general female population in County Jail, I am a very good domino player and my cardinal rule for the rest of my life is: Do not get caught!"

What I didn't tell her was that I no longer believed in Justice in America, I thought the cops were crooked, and that Truth was relative to what side you were on.

I also knew that I would miss my mom forever.

# QH 101

## *Janet Hafner*

"I'm sorry, sir, there's been a delay . . . quarters for you and your family won't be available for three weeks." The young lieutenant at the 29 Palms housing office stands like a Marine — back straight, uniform creased to perfection. His eyes shift from my husband's frown to the floor.

I think, *I wouldn't want to be the guy who tells a senior officer he doesn't have housing.*

My husband grows taller. He inhales enough air to cover the entire nine hundred and ninety-eight square miles of this Marine Corps base.

"I won't ask why I wasn't notified," my husband says. I recognize the tone — official, commanding, severe — his "in charge" voice. His jaws flex around clenched teeth. "I could've kept my family in comfortable quarters in San Diego. Now, where's my family going to be housed?"

The air molecules buzz. The junior officer leans over the desk, fumbles with a file folder, stalls for a second and says, "Sir, we've made . . ."

Arnie interrupts, "My wife and my two-year-old son are with me. Our living quarters MUST be appropriate." His green eyes hide a smoldering fire. Glitches like this are unacceptable. He holds back.

"Sir . . ." the snap in the 'sir' tells me the lieutenant is about to add more disappointing news. He draws air. "Sir, you and your family are scheduled for QH 101 behind the Officers Club. I'm sure . . ."

"What kind of accommodations is it?"

"Sir . . . it's one of our newest temporary housing units — private bath and kitchen."

Arnie's inner volcano rumbles. No motion yet, but his cheeks

49

look like rosy apples.

"Let's check it out," I say. *I know better than to interfere but . . .* Arnie's glare scorches. *That's a warning about what may follow.*

The lieutenant says, "Sir, I'll take you over there now."

We pile into the jeep. The Officers Club is up ahead. The jeep pulls in behind the club.

"What? No, no, NO . . ." my husband bellows. "This . . . this is a Quonset hut—not housing. Absolutely not." My husband bolts out of the jeep with the lieutenant two paces behind. They're gone.

My body stiffens against the jeep's seat. Four letter words crash into each other inside my mouth. Nothing spills out.

I blink at the semi-cylindrical metal shelter with one of its ends staring at me. I've seen these buildings in war movies—barracks, storage sheds and agricultural hot houses.

"Where are your windows?" I ask the Quonset hut. "It's time for us to be friends. You're going to be our new . . . temporary . . . home."

The sun is overhead. The steel corrugated structure repels the sun's beams. They ricochet into my eyes. "Be nice," I say, "I'm going to live inside you."

My feet hit the ground. Sand oozes into my shoes. I take them off and pour every grain back where it belongs. My eyes scan the neighborhood—no grass, no trees, just sand. My hand reaches out. I stroke the sizzling metal. "Hot . . . so . . . you're QH 101. Not sure how I feel about you yet. You know . . . you're a freakin' metal dome. Well, whatever they call you, I'll call you Sid. Don't ask me why. It's Sid for now. Maybe when I look inside, I'll change my mind and give you another name. For now, I hope you're okay with Sid." My heart's tempo tells me I'm anxious about what I'll find inside.

As I walk around to the other end, I ask, "Why don't you have any eyes, Sid? You know—two openings so I can peek inside?" I squint at the gleaming glaring Sid. As I approach the door, my feet sink into the soft sand.

"Oh, you do have eyes." Two three-foot square windows flank an oversize metal door. *Of course, they installed your peeps where only six-foot-tall Marines can look into the building. I'll have to stand on a chair if I want to see in or out.* "Okay, Sid, it's time to take a look."

The mega-door lumbers out of my way like a desert tortoise revealing . . . "Oh my God, Sid, you're almost naked," I mumble. "You're sparse, inadequate, bare . . . ah . . . but well lit." Four floodlights sheltered by half-dome metallic shades dangle from the twenty-foot ceiling. *It should be easy to find anyone or anything that gets lost in here.* I chuckle out loud. My husband and the Lieutenant whose job it is to make us comfortable turn and stare in my direction.

"Are you talking to me?" My husband's booming voice plows toward me from what looks like half a football field away.

"It's nothing," I raise my voice enough so it carries down to where they're standing.

The men return to their conversation. *Well, let me see what you've got. Hmm, wood paneling — ceiling . . . floor . . . walls - a nice homey touch.*

"What did you say, Sid?" I listen. "Oh, I see — there's insulation behind the paneling. That's good."

"Janet, are you talking to me? Come over here and tell me what's so important."

"He always sounds like that, Sid. I'm used to it," I whisper. I turn to face my husband.

"It's nothing," I call. I really want to tell him I'm having a conversation with Sid our sturdy structure, but he wouldn't understand.

I whisper, "Everything's good, Sid. We've got metal beds, a couple of chairs, the Marine Corps version of an uncomfortable couch, and a table." I think that might be a refrigerator in the corner. It stands like a lone sentry.

Giant steps get me face-to-face with Arnie and the Lieutenant. My husband asks, "Well?"

The Lieutenant, whose cheeks have gotten redder, asks, "What do you think, Ma'am?"

*Does he really want me to answer that?* I choose my words carefully. "It definitely has possibilities. I'll feel more at home when our shipment gets here."

Arnie's jaw moves in and out. Hands roll into fists.

"At least the boy will have lots of room to play," my husband says.

I've never understood why my husband calls our son, "the boy." Maybe it's because they share the same name.

"Yes, it's true. Outside a giant sandbox and inside . . . well, who wouldn't love a football field."

The corners of the Lieutenant's lips pull back into a weak smile. Arnie's lips don't move.

~

Sid's door creaks. Before I can reach it, it opens.

"Hello, anybody in here?" a cheery voice calls. I recognize the voice.

"Come in," I say.

Margie is a Marine wife whose husband, Garland, has been stationed with Arnie before. "Where's Gar?"

Gar steps into the doorway. "Look who we brought with us."

"Mommy, Mommy." Arms reach out for me and then my arms wrap around our son. He tightens his hold around my neck. Tension vanishes.

"Oh, Margie, I can't tell you how much I appreciate you babysitting Arnold while we check-out our new accommodations."

"You're not going to tell me this is your housing assignment, are you? Please tell me I'm wrong!"

Margie talks like a racing locomotive so in the space of a breath I jump in, "It's just temporary, Margie, a couple of weeks, that's all."

Gar's base voice sounds off, "We'll have time to talk about this later. Right now, it's cocktail time at the Officers' Club."

A squirming two-year-old struggles to the floor. And then he takes off yelling, "Yippee, yippee, yippeeeeeee."

"Are we ready for this, Sid?" I ask.

Margie spins around. Her eyes search for Sid. "Who's Sid?"

I grin.

# Belief

## *Barbara Huntington*

When I was a child, the butterfly of belief
brushed a filmy wing across my forehead
"Chase me, chase me."
Through churchyards and headstones
I reached out and grasped, soft wings against my palm
I held, released her, slept

In my youth, she hid behind napalm clouds of war,
fluttered above a guitar in songs of peace and equality,
forgotten in the headiness of first love
lit briefly in the comfort of second
Not knowing if I really held her, pretended her presence
for my children

In middle age, children gone to chase their own butterflies,
no infinite sky, no fluttering form, a shadowed memory
in the dark cramped rooms of death, parents, friends,
my dying love, his mind and body gone before the breath stopped
Mocking, mutant memories, no place for butterflies
Too fearful to sleep

My hand numb with grasping what wasn't there

I felt a tiny foot light on my forehead

"Chase me, chase me."

Fields of possibilities mimicked a thousand butterflies

without revealing the one who called,

I envied those who knew

the objects of the chase lived forever in their hands,

I slept

Is she still there just beyond my cushion?

"Chase me, chase me."

The chase is slower now

beyond mountain, ashram, Bodhi Tree

always beyond, beyond, a soft brush, a light touch

hovers, gentle beyond my reach,

I sleep

Life can only be understood
backwards, but it must be lived
forwards.

— *Søren Kierkegaard*

# "C"

## *Jenna Benson*

Was it too much for you? Did you have to leave?

I know you'd think I'm stupid for writing this.
I know you'd think I'm stupid for still crying.

But I'll always be wishing you were still here-
Missing the stupid jokes,
The nights that turned into days.
The things you would say that would make us laugh so hard
We would write them down and hang them on the fridge.

To me you were:
New adventures
Unique people
Better experiences
A better life –
A more cherished, happy existence.
I wish we still had you.
 I can't listen to your music
Can't look at your pictures.

You haunt me

But in the best way.

I still hear you,

See you in my head, every day.

If only you could have stayed longer,

And shown the whole world what you were made of.

# Manta Ray Dive

## *Janice Coy*

Our small dive boat is moored near Kona International Airport at Keahole. Spinner dolphins led us here, bodies leaping in paroxysms of joy. The sun is low; rays of fading gold and pink splash the ocean's surface. Airplanes roar overhead, lights blinking. But we're here searching for ocean fliers — giant manta rays.

About 100 giant manta rays, creatures with a fourteen-to-fifteen-foot wing span and open mouths like the front grill of a Chevy Impala, inhabit the waters off the Kona Coast of Hawaii. Mantas feed here, so a rock circle where divers can kneel and watch was built at a depth of thirty feet on the sandy ocean floor. Mantas return because the divers' flashlight beams attract plankton, the manta's food source.

We jump into the twilight ocean and descend in a trail of bubbles. Gray shadows disappear into inky blackness when the sun slides below the horizon. I feel as if I'm entering a vast cave with no boundaries of walls or ceiling. Our flashlights are mere firefly pricks in the midst of such total darkness.

The water temperature is in the mid-70s, and we wear full black wetsuits with hoods. It's hard to distinguish individuals with dive masks obscuring eyes and nose and breathing regulators distending mouths. We follow our dive master — acolytes traveling to the sacred place.

At the rock circle, we kneel and aim our flashlights up. Snorkelers float at the water's surface and shine their flashlights down. Plankton is thick in the light, swarming on the backs of my hands. I resist the urge to wipe away the squirmy mess.

Suddenly, a manta ray soars by, its open mouth welcoming the plankton sacrifice we're offering. My heart thuds and I duck as the ray skims overhead. Others do the same as if we're paying homage to this strange being. Another manta ray glides towards the snorkelers and executes graceful flips inches away from their reaching hands. A third flies over us, knocking a diver on his heels. I want to touch the manta's silvery skin; I'm sure it feels smooth and rubbery soft like a snake's belly. But awe holds my hands back.

I think about the stygian darkness of an ancient Mayan cave I visited once. The Mayans believed a cave was the opening to the underworld, and that the stalactites were mythical beings. What if the manta rays have come loose from the frozen formations to flap above us — giant bats from hell?

Leaving the rock circle is difficult. The mantas are still flying, but our air supply is running low and we must return to the surface to breathe. We climb aboard the boat in silence, ridding ourselves of oxygen tanks and wetsuits.

The night above smells of seawater and airplane exhaust. I wrap myself in a warm towel; run my fingers through wet, tangled hair. An airplane lifts off the nearby runway soaring into the sky on fixed wings. I lick the salt on my lips, and I think of the manta rays swooping below in mystical flight.

# Thesis

## *Gered Beeby*

It boasted of being one of the most beautiful university campuses anywhere. Perched on high ground above the Pacific Ocean, the University of California at San Diego (UCSD) also purported to be the best assemblage of bio-research facilities anywhere. This was a place where knowledge was created. Miracles could be discovered. Scientific history could be written and careers could be launched — or never published and never begun.

The natural drama played out before Kevin. Turbulent wisps of cloud swept past and through the bent, yet resilient trees that fortified the school's western edge. Only slightly chilled, his Midwestern origins lent credence to a saying he had heard more than once: "Tell yourself this is February." The dreamlike setting offered soothing support for events, perhaps less dreamlike, to come.

With the process of science inevitably came the process of review. And more to the point for a doctoral candidate was the prospect of justification. Even more unsettling from the painstaking process of advancing science was a persistent and underlying fear. New ideas always faced this threat — the specter of rejection.

Kevin faced that unwelcome possibility.

His thesis advisor was tasked with the initial overture in this age-old ritual of academia. Selection, he reflected, in many ways could not be better — or worse. Known throughout UCSD as a stickler for exactness, his advisor often possessed a charm that kindled more than academic respect.

With no classes scheduled, her Office Hours could potentially last all day. Kevin considered himself lucky when he found no other students outside her door. The sign read simply "Professor

Chu, Genetics." Cultural assimilation was nothing new for a world famous institution such as UCSD.

Kevin mentally sorted through several ideas surrounding his soon-to-come thesis review date. He knocked briefly at the door and entered.

Professor Chu looked up from her desk, "Good morning, Kevin." She pushed back from the desk and stood. Fairly tall, she wore the traditional high-collared dress of patterned Chinese silk. Magenta highlights harmonized with her fair skin, black hair and ruby lips. Also, no one could miss the slit along one side of her skirt. Today's rumor was there was a social get-together for faculty after classes. Perhaps Madam was ready now.

She graciously extended her hand toward one of the guest chairs and they both took their seats.

Those in authority often gain labels irrespective of their actual names. College students were no exception. Some names came and were rejected early. "China Doll" would never do. "Madam Chu" also materialized, although no one verified whether she was ever married. Then there was the question of her age. Most guessed her late thirties.

For Kevin, the generations-old contrast of Occident versus Orient remained alive and well. The West, no matter how sophisticated it wanted to be, often harbored a sense of mystery for the culture of the East. Another not so secret name eventually evolved for this young, full professor of genetics. Quaint in a theatrical sense and a decided holdover from earlier times, this name finally stuck—The Dragon Lady.

The brief formalities now over, Professor Chu produced a folder from her side credenza. Placed flat on the desk, she perused the several sheets within for nearly a minute. Kevin believed that somehow even this rapid sweep of the contents was unnecessary. Elbows propped on the desk with her hands gently folded she addressed him with what many knew to call The Stare.

After an interminable duration, she spoke.

"Kevin, as scientific advisor on your project I find your conclusions forward-looking, cutting-edge in the extreme, and at numerous levels, downright astounding. But as your guide through this miasma of highest-level academia, I have obligations to the institutional demands of this university."

She paused then moved her high-backed chair to one side and closer to her doctoral candidate student. Her hands rested easily on the chair arms and her fingers rhythmically caressed the ends. Kevin also could not miss the oversized jade ring on her right hand.

"Outline for me again the attributes that you insist exist only for this one-of-a-kind human subject. By the way, you may need to do something about that name — Joseph Little-Guy. Don't you think we have evolved past this kind of thing?"

Kevin cleared his throat, "Sorry, but no can do, Madam ... uh, Professor Chu. That is his legal name. His mother is like a reborn, flower child. Her family is also wealthy and more than a bit eccentric. The child is totally in the family care. I've only been able to visit once since he was born."

"Hold right there," Professor Chu raised a restraining finger. "Review once again this birth. You say the presumed father is deceased?"

"Yes, Ma'am."

"And yet this father was killed in some kind of barroom brawl nearly two years prior to the birth?"

"I realize that sounds more than a little fantastic, Professor." Kevin could feel his own agitation on the rise.

"This smacks of science fiction." Professor Chu rested her elbows on the chair arms and placed her fingertips together. "But for the sake of resolution, go ahead with your story."

Kevin nodded and continued. "It is more than a story, Professor. These findings are what the facts show. Please don't forget that it was you who handed me this case a while back. And that nobody else had any clue about what was going on."

Professor Chu eased back into her chair. Her open palm gesture bade him continue.

"As of now, Joseph ... that is, the child is presumably healthy. Even though he is over a year old, he still looks like a premature newborn. Compounding this reality, the mother is estimated to have been over two years in gestation with him.

"Instead of reality as you put it, Kevin, this young person appears more of a genetic mystery. Your notes say you performed

63

a full genome analysis?

"That's true. But again, that was only accomplished through a kind of subterfuge. A small tissue sample was obtained with the cover story that our hospital needed it to detect allergic effects, if any. Anyway, that xenophobic collection of rich egocentrics that call themselves a family actually bought it."

"Summarize again what your analysis showed."

Kevin swallowed. "At risk of sounding repetitive, what we found, simply put, was... nothing."

Professor Chu resumed her grand inquisitor mode. "Mister Kevin, this requires a great deal more elaboration."

"I realize that, but this is all that can be found. Whatever gene-factor that may be causing these results remains somehow hidden. With all the Junk DNA in humans and all other creatures for that matter, this anomaly could be lurking anywhere."

"And it may not exist al all. Yet you manage to label your postulated, highly hypothetical gene with a name: The Slow Factor. Is this what you want your formal thesis statement to say? Come now, sir, we are both scientists. And further, you are not willing to state or even speculate whether the end result of this proposed genetic collaboration is from some extraordinarily rare recessive gene in humans, or equally speculative, a one-time, one-of-a-kind mutation."

Kevin caught himself drumming fingers on his chair arms. For all her brilliance, he did not need a lecture on scientific discipline from Madam Chu. "I may only be a rough-hewn farm boy from the wilds of Wisconsin, but I am trying to make sense of an event that seems to have no precedent in medical history. You have read the extent of my research. You must realize ..."

"And I, Kevin, am only a refugee girl from Grant Avenue, San Francisco, who is also striving for a consistent rationale from all that has been found. Please trust and believe that I am on your side. We are both orphans in this storm that is certain to be coming."

Professor Chu took a moment and visibly relaxed in her chair. "Yes, I will do my best to secure grant funding. This will require a multi-disciplinary approach with you as lead investigator, of course. Ironically, one of our biggest obstacles may be publicity.

Normally that's not a problem for research programs, but this is so frankly sensational. Further irony lies in the fact the infant child's family is so monumentally reclusive. This could actually help."

"Thank you, Professor." Kevin relished his welling of relaxation. "And I know the secrecy surrounding everything could rival the Manhattan Project. If this gets revealed too soon, there are sure to be crazies out there. Some would claim little Joseph is the product of some outer space, alien implant."

"That's a new one," Professor Chu suppressed a laugh, "but in some respects is no less sensational than one of your own postulations. You project one possible development timetable for Mister Joseph Little Guy. And this could be a real hard sell."

"My thesis lays it out fairly clear," Kevin was already defending himself. "Also, by all indications he has a very strong immune system."

"And he may well need that robust system," The Dragon Lady returned. The Stare bore into him. "The scientific community will need to take a deep breath on this one. Barring accident, or some other incident, when armed with his Slow Factor you project young Mister Joseph's lifespan would extend on the order of five hundred years."

# The Other Side of History

## *Joe Naiman*

In my spare time I research and write sports history books, so I'm used to documenting history. I'm not used to being the history, but that's what happened March 14 on Crawford High School's new baseball diamond.

Crawford High School, whose graduations include mine in 1982, opened in 1957 and the first baseball games were played in 1958. The original baseball diamond south of Trojan Avenue was modified in 1959 when classroom bungalows resulted in the field being moved slightly north and in 1977 when the removal of the bungalows relocated the field south and allowed for tennis courts to be added between the baseball field and Trojan Avenue.

In 2015 the San Diego Unified School District undertook a renovation of Crawford which moved the baseball field to the site of the original football stadium (which also hosted soccer games and track and field meets) while relocating the stadium to the site of the former baseball diamond, tennis courts, administration building, and northern classroom buildings. The new football stadium opened in October 2017 and the baseball diamond was ready for this spring's games.

March 14 was Opening Day for Crawford's baseball season, but since Crawford would be playing in the new stadium it was a special Opening Day. Although rain fell earlier that day, the weather allowed the historical game to be played that afternoon.

The game had a scheduled 3:30 p.m. start. I positioned myself at the Woodstock's Pizza lunch buffet, which allowed me to arrive at the ballpark about 1:50. Some of the players were already on the field.

Ronell Jones, who is Crawford's coach, arrived shortly afterwards. Ronell had actually arrived earlier, but the bucket he brought contained the chalk to mark the baselines had other

67

items. So he had to visit a store to purchase white paint. He explained the situation to me. That put us on the subject of supplies, and I asked how much baseballs cost. Ronell responded that a case of 12 baseballs typically cost between $50 and $60.

Because the game would be the first on Crawford's new field, I wanted to preserve some significant balls such as the first hit regardless of which team reached base on that and the first Crawford hit. I mentioned that desire to Ronell and offered to pay for the balls which were preserved.

Ronell had a similar idea. He asked me to throw out the ceremonial first pitch.

The thought of a ceremonial first pitch had occurred to me, but I hadn't envisioned throwing it. Ash Hayes, who was Crawford's original coach, is now 94 and would have been my first choice. Ash's wife responded to my e-mail notice about the first game being March 14 if weather permitted, and asked about the scheduled starting time. But Ash did not attend the game nor did any of the other former Crawford baseball coaches. None of the former Crawford players, who later played professional baseball, were able to attend either.

I accepted the honor of throwing out the first ball. I began hoping that I could throw the pitch the 60-foot, 6-inch distance from the pitcher's mound to the plate. I realized that I hadn't thrown a baseball since I was watching a practice on the former field and returned a foul ball that went over the fence. I also couldn't recall having thrown a pitch from a regulation-distance mound to the plate.

I did remember some information about throwing baseballs more accurately. In the 1970s, I played for College Park Little League and was a student at San Diego State University's Summer Youth Fitness Program, where I later spent three years as an assistant baseball coach. I remembered that positioning my fingers on the seams would result in a straighter throw.

Shortly before the start of the game Ronell called for me to throw the first pitch and gave me the ball. I walked to the mound. I did not remove my Crawford letter jacket. (Which still fits if I don't button it!)

I put my fingers on the seams and threw. The ball went past

home plate and into the glove of Crawford catcher Pollo Sanchez. It was close to the right side of the plate; but, from 60 feet 6 inches away I really couldn't tell if I put the ball over the plate. I thought I might have hit a right-handed batter, had one been there. After I returned to the stands, I was told that the pitch went over the right corner of the plate, and I knew the throw was close enough to Pollo that he was able to catch the ball in the air.

Ronell gave me the ball from that pitch. I put it in my briefcase, and later obtained the balls from the first hit and from the first Crawford hit. I'm hoping those historic balls will eventually be preserved in a trophy case at Crawford.

In the future it will be noted that High Tech High senior Aaron Schumacher tripled in the top of the first inning for the first hit on Crawford's new field. The first Crawford hit was a third-inning single by junior Malik Vongsouthi, who eventually scored when freshman Rudy Mendoza singled for the first Crawford run batted in on the new field. That part of Crawford baseball history is now documented.

And shortly before the actual first pitch on Crawford's diamond, I was on the other side of history.

# Transubstantiation

## *Arthur Raybold*

As a twelve-year-old member of the Episcopal Boys' Choir at Grace Church, New Bedford, Massachusetts, I was subjected to a very long service of hymns, prayers, announcements, a sermon, and communion. After having served in the choir for two years, I knew the entire communion service by heart. If the priest collapsed, I could easily have taken over.

Early on, I was curious about the wine and wafer the priest gave out and the solemn words, "This is my body which is given for you."

One day, I asked Dick Adshead, another choir boy, "What does this mean?"

"You don't know that?"

"No. Do you?"

"It means the wafer becomes Jesus's body and the wine becomes his blood and by taking it in, your sins are forgiven."

"How can that be possible?" I asked with a screwed-up face.

"That's what those kneeling people believe."

"Do you?"

"I don't know. I've not been confirmed so I haven't tried it."

"So the wine turns into Jesus's blood. It sounds terrible. We don't drink people's blood."

"We drink animal blood so this is the same thing except spiritual."

"Who told you this?"

"My Mom and Dad. They teach Sunday school."

~

The next trip to choir practice, we walked over the bridge from Fairhaven to New Bedford, and I said, "Rich, do you believe taking the bread and wine takes away sin?"

"Sure do. God gave his son, Jesus, as a sacrifice so we could go to heaven."

"You really believe that?" My voice was getting louder. "Gods are gods. They don't have to sacrifice their children for us. They should just tell us," I shouted. 'Do the commandments or else.'"

"We are not strong enough. We need help. So God helps us overcome our sins with Jesus's magic blood. That's all there is to it."

"Phew!" I spewed.

"Don't you listen to the sermons? Reverend Loring talks about it every Sunday."

"I go into a trance. Communion keeps me awake because I want to know if he makes a mistake."

"He can't make a mistake," said Dick. "He's reading out of the Book of Common Prayer."

"What about all those people who never go to church? My Mom. My Dad out there reading the Sunday paper and smoking in his car?"

"They don't go to heaven. They die and go to some other not so nice place."

This sounded pretty good and Rich was a friend. Soon after we were confirmed, my parents showed up for this momentous event. My Mom came forward for communion, and I noticed she took the wafer, waited for the wine, and dipped the body of Jesus into the wine and consumed both at once.

I had never tasted wine before, and it was somewhat bitter. I had trouble consciously chewing on Jesus's body before swallowing. Nothing magical happened, so being an optimist, I thought something good would happen later. My dad did not take communion. He was brought up a Baptist, and maybe they don't have communion.

~

After church one Sunday when Rich and I both served as acolytes for the same service, we discussed our first communion. "Nothing special happened, Rich, and I was disturbed by having to chew the body part."

"Well, nothing special for me either. These things take time.

Maybe we were not prepared to receive Jesus, so no magic could take place. We're young. We have to be patient."

I marveled at his maturity—not being upset or having felt cheated but instead concentrating on a positive future.

About this time, the choir girls began to interest me most of all. They seemed like pretty little angels. I think one or two had their eyes on me. I was glad not to worry about them changing into something quite different.

# Tavern Tales

## *Fred Crothers*

I knew I was in trouble the first day I opened Freddie's Bungalow Tavern. A bunch of loggers walked in, and one of them said, "Wow, look at this cute little guy; let's bend him right over the bar!" What is the obvious retort to this kind of message? I didn't know, so I chose to ignore the comment and simply asked, "What'll you have to drink?"

This was one of many incidents that led me to reinvent myself. Obviously, this crowd required more than a nice guy to serve them drinks. A bartender is always the butt of jokes and should possess a quick wit and a good sense of humor. I worked with the public most of my life, and thought I knew and understood most people from all walks of life, but this was a totally different environment for me. Every day was a learning experience.

One afternoon I had a visit with a local sheriff's deputy, Todd, who stopped in for a short beer. He asked me if he could work as a part-time bartender. I was always glad to have part-time workers and readily agreed. He said he was interested and would stop by a couple of times to let me show him the ropes.

I met with him a couple of afternoons and arranged for him to work my night shift so Dawn and I could drive into Portland for a movie. We got home in time to ask Todd how it went. He told me he stayed busy most of the time and the difficult part was preparing and serving chicken dinners and keeping everyone supplied with drinks. He had some weirdo order a can of Bud and throw it down before he could even walk into the kitchen. As soon as he left the room, the guy was banging his can on the counter yelling for another beer.

Todd came back several times and served him another can, but finally it got to him. He walked back in behind the bar and said to the guy, "If you want to drown yourself go jump in the effing river, but if you want another beer don't bang on the bar." I thought his comment was classic and wished I'd said it. Todd never came back but I wasn't too surprised; sometimes bartending is not as easy as it looks.

When I worked the third shift (12 a.m. to 7 a.m.) at Douglas Aircraft in Long Beach, California, I had a novel experience. Like most people who work hard for a living, the shift ending usually called for drinks, so a bunch of us guys would hit Curley's Bar on top of Signal Hill for an eye opener. We drank a lot of beer, ate pickled pig's feet and lots of those spicy pickled eggs.

Curley was a huge guy, stout, heavily muscled like a former wrestler, with wild grey curly hair and a full bushy beard. He was a no-nonsense guy and sported a big, nickel-plated revolver shoved in his wide leather belt. Curley cashed company checks for the riggers who tended the oil wells nearby, requiring a need for him to keep a lot of cash on hand and a tight rein on the place.

His bar was one of the roughest places I've ever seen, like something out of a wild-west show, but I hardly ever saw anyone get out of line. Most of his clientele were covered with oil and dirt from head to toe, and the floor was covered with ankle-deep, filthy sawdust that hadn't been changed in years. The ocean view would have been outstanding, but the windows were so grimy and smudged most people never even noticed. I didn't get much sleep working third shift, but it certainly was an interesting time in my life.

I never dreamed I'd someday be the owner-manager of a tavern like those I frequented as a curly-haired paperboy of nine. I grew up in Coos Bay, a small logging town in northwest Oregon. Most of my early school years, I delivered a morning newspaper, the Portland *Oregonian*. This required getting up early in the cold, dark, rainy mornings, saddling up my trusty steed (a Schwinn bike), proceeding to a pick-up point to find my bundle of papers. I'd spend a half hour folding the papers, usually in a triangle shape that I threw long and hard like a tomahawk. Later, I graduated to rolling the papers and securing them with rubber bands. My wide canvas paper-bag was draped across the handle bars and rested on the front fender. I think there were about 120 papers stuffed into the bag. I remember skunky old apartment buildings where I quietly entered and stepped softly along a mile-long corridor, dropping the papers at each apartment door. Sometimes I would lie down on the filthy old red carpet, flat out, to rest and get warm.

I enjoyed the delivery process especially on the few level streets where I could whiz along the sidewalk and make some fancy throws to a high porch. Other neighborhoods required parking my bike and hiking up the vertical hillsides to pitch the papers up on sky-high landings. Fortunately, a few of these obscure sites had metal tubes on posts that I could stuff the paper in at the bottom of the driveway. Sunday deliveries were always a nightmare, with heavy, overstuffed papers. Many times, my good ol' Dad would take pity on me and drive me around the route so I wouldn't have to make so many trips.

Oddly enough, I liked the delivery process but hated to collect from the customers at the end of the month. Some people were kind and paid their bill on my first collection try, but others were very reluctant to pay and would avoid me for days; some were crabby about the high-cost of subscribing, threatening to quit, and some were just never home. The first collection attempt was usually good, but then it got harder to go back. I did receive tips from many of my customers and nice gifts at Christmas, which offset the ill treatment I received from a few. I remember ironing the scroungy old dollar bills so I'd have a neat stack for the paper route manager when he came to collect from me.

I carried the *Oregonian* papers for many of my school years, and it paid for many of life's little pleasures — like trips to the monster movies, (Frankenstein, Dracula, and the Wolf Man), and triple-layered soft Dairy Queen ice-cream cones for after.

When I was about ten, I heard about a part-time job offering with our local paper, *The Coos Bay Times*. I went to the office and signed up for one of these jobs for after school. I was quickly hired, given basic instructions about selling on the street, and shoved out the door with my allotted twenty papers. There weren't any hard and fast rules about when or where a person might sell papers, just sell them and come back for more.

I soon established my territory in the taverns, which included: The Anchor Inn, The Pastime, The Town, and The Blue Moon. It

77

was a little scary at first to walk into these noisy, dark, smoke-filled rooms, filled with lots of rough looking men; but I soon found out that most of them liked me and considered me quite a novelty. They would often ask me, "how many papers you got?" I hurriedly counted them and gave them a number. The paper sold for a dime and many times they'd say, "Okay kid, I'll take em all!" One guy bought all my papers and handed them back to me saying, "Hell kid, I can't even read, take em back and sell em again!" Even if they only bought one paper, they would often give me a dollar and say, "Keep the change."

One time a guy grabbed me up, stood me on the bar and said, "Come on you cheapskates, this kid's working his way through college, pass the damn hat!" They quickly passed the hat, gave me all the money and shoved me out the door.

Another time a guy at the Blue Moon Tavern called me over and said, "I'll give you twenty dollars if you tear up all those papers and throw them all around the bar." He handed me the twenty and I did just what he said. The bartender yelled, "Pick up those papers and get your ass out of here!"

I made a lot of money in those days and learned a lot about life. I can still recall the songs emanating from blaring juke boxes, such as "Good Night Irene," "Red Sails in the Sunset," and "I'll Sail My Ship Alone." I'll always remember walking up the aisle behind the bar stools, looking up at those huge, gallon jars of pickled pig's feet, pickled eggs, and ugly sausages floating in some vile liquid, all in a row on the highly polished bars. I couldn't imagine why anyone would eat such things. Many years later I found out these gross looking snacks were regular fare in taverns and taste great with beer. I remember, too, some grizzled, snaggle-toothed old guy with a fat, juicy pickled pigs foot in his dirty old mitt saying to me, "The closer to the bone, the sweeter the meat!"

# A Few Pearls About Balboa Park

## *Laurie Asher*

We've all been to the now famous Balboa Park. Originally named City Park, most of us know the origin of its buildings – the celebration of the opening of the Panama Canal in 1915, which connected the Atlantic and Pacific Oceans. San Diego's hope was to be the first port of call in the United States for ships travelling north after going through the canal.

Balboa Park was built to sponsor the Panama California Exposition in 1915 and 1916.

But we have to go back to 1868 when Alonzo Horton, newly arrived in San Diego, had the foresight to see far ahead into San Diego's future; and convinced the City to set aside 1,400 acres as open space – City Park.

Regarding the expo, there are many stories about the buildings and the event itself.

After three-and-a-half years of preparation, a groundbreaking ceremony was held, and pigeons were brought in and released for the occasion – I guess we couldn't afford doves at the time. And yes, they are still there, generationally speaking – the pigeons, that is. At the time, the entire population of San Diego was 40,000.

Even now, it seems there may still be more pigeons than people in San Diego.

A little known fact about the expo was that we had a competitor for bragging rights: San Francisco also built a *village* for their international exposition as a means of recovery from their recent devastating fire.

Balboa Park sits on 1,200 acres and is considered the largest cultural park in the nation. This was the perfect foundation for the expo, and although both the exhibits and structures in the park were meant to be temporary, San Francisco tore down its structures shortly after the expo ended, while San Diego fortuitously kept theirs intact. And this decision had lasting repercussions for our city.

Most of the buildings were meant to last for two to three years, many made from wood, plaster of paris, and chicken wire. Over the years, these existing buildings have been reinforced from their foundations up. All existing building have been required to meet modern day earthquake standards. A few buildings, such as the Spreckels Theatre/Organ Pavilion, were always meant to be a permanent venue, and over the years and there have been many famous performers gracing the stage. The Beatles and the Rolling Stones played there during the early part of their careers. Many other performances from the Marx Brothers, John Phillip Sousa, Charley Chaplin, to David Bowie and the Doobie Brothers have graced the stage over the decades, since the Spreckels brothers, of sugar fame and fortune, donated the funds to build this grand outdoor theatre. *(Wasn't that SWEET of them)?*

In 1915, San Diego opened its two-year exposition to much fanfare featuring the unique architectural buildings borrowing from Spanish Colonial, European, and Mexican architecture. In the second year, the expo was renamed The *International* Expo to reflect the steady flow of hundreds of thousands of international visitors.

Many dignitaries visited such as Thomas Edison, William Jennings Bryan, famous singers and actors of the time, Secretary of the Navy Franklin Roosevelt and his wife, Eleanor, William Howard Taft, and Theodore Roosevelt, who quipped, "These rare and phenomenal buildings ought to be preserved forever." Sage advice which our city fathers have taken to heart over the decades.

You might be wondering how millions of people arrived at the expo over its first two-year run?

Some came by horse and carriage. Some even came in those newfangled motor vehicles. But by far, most arrived via the electric trolley. While many out-of-towners and other visitors came to San Diego by train, they quickly jumped on the trolley at Broadway and were delivered directly to the expo, took the underground walkway and entered the park.

What trolley? What underground walkway, you ask? These

structures were built along Park Boulevard, the eastern entrance near the Prado arches. But all evidence of the trolley service and tunnel has since been covered over with earth, grass, trees and shrubs. Imagine if the trolley still existed today. You wouldn't have to shoot someone's tires out to beat them to the last parking space in the Reuben S. Fleet Science Center's parking lot. And one other interesting feature of the park during the expo—at a specific time daily down at the reflecting pool, near the famous botanical gardens, a gong was struck under the water to call the fish to feeding time, and they all came, every time, gaping mouths awaiting. It is believed that many of the koi carp we see today are thought to be direct descendants of the original "troupe of fish."

Did you know that the San Diego Chargers played at the Balboa Stadium until 1966? (Do we even care anymore?)

And when the Liberty Bell was on tour in 1915, Philadelphia selected the San Diego Expo in Balboa Park as one of its stops. At that time, it was possible for tourists to touch the bell and its famous crack. However, it remained under guard twenty-four hours a day.

The expo caused the "red tile roof" craze in San Diego because so many of the expo's buildings featured them. No one had ever seen one on a home before then.

And there was a nudist colony as part of the exposition when it reopened for the 1935-36 season. Originally created for the 1915 opening as an attraction, it was called Zorro Garden Nudist Colony. Actors played the parts of the nudies. Weird, huh?

Many San Diego residents are surprised to learn that during WWI, Balboa Park became an important wartime metropolis, providing training grounds, administrative offices, and hospital space. And, again, during WWII, Balboa Park was conscripted for military use. The History Museum and the Museum of Man were closed to the public for wartime purposes, and their contents were sent to private residents for safekeeping during this time. The federal government paid San Diego $790,000 for the use of this land.

It was incidents such as these that influenced military agencies to permanently anchor in San Diego.

Our current San Diego Zoo was also a direct result of Balboa

Park's expo. A few lions in box cages were a feature attraction at the expo. However, the creation of our zoo started with the following animals according to the census of the day: one elk, nine deer, twenty-one goats, one alligator, three buffalo, five monkeys, and two porcupines. Now, of course, its influence is worldwide.

The city prepared for the expo by building hotels, upgrading roads and even renaming D Street to Broadway, which they thought had more appeal.

Today, there is still a very large open-air architectural "boneyard" pit where pieces that have fallen off buildings, or were deemed too dangerous to remain, are stored. Very few visitors even know where this is.

As a direct result of the expo, Balboa Park has become an oasis in the middle of the City of San Diego.

The park, with its 15,000 trees and 2 million plants, includes its showcase Moreton Bay Fig tree. Planted in 1915 as a small sapling, the huge Moreton Bay Fig has grown to more than 78 feet tall and 123 feet wide (according to 1996 statistics). This magnificent tree has thrived in its park setting, just as has San Diego has done over the years.

So here is a novel idea: Keep a copy of this story about Balboa Park in your glove box. Then, when you take those fifth cousins, thrice removed, who show up on your doorstep, uninvited, shouting, "Surprise," to Balboa Park, you'll have more to share with them besides, "Uh, do you want to go see those roses again, Cousin Elmer?"

# Golf and English are Tricky Games

## *Tom Leech*

At our lodge over by the gulf,
We love to play that fun game of golf,
The course is right there by the beach,
Past that tall tree we know as a beech.

Before our game we sip some tea,
It helps us focus at that first tee.
Tactic one is to stop and pray --
Dear Lord help us whip that other prey.

Golf often comes with a "whether,"
It's hard to tell with nature's weather,
One thing for sure we're never bored,
Can't say that when we meet with the Board.

On the course the question is "would,"
Hit with an iron or better with wood?
Smack it wrong and you've bought your bier,
Sink it just right and slurp up their beer.

Lunch is when we gather to meet,
And gobble down fish & chips or meat,
A treat is when our chums we bruise –
They have to pay for mugs of fresh brews.

Now pay the bill, a standard rite,
First make sure the numbers add up right,
Same guy always gives us our check,
His name is Jose, he's not a Czech.

Next round up as a golf cart passed,
Ready to play with some lessons past,
With golf some are against or for,
But all love to shout that neat word "Fore!"

# My Precious!

## *Terri Trainor*

**Editorial Suggestions, Reaction 1:**

"But no! That's my precious!"

The slashes on the page look like wounds. The question marks point to missing parts. The dialogue suggestions insult each character's sense of self. My poor little precious looks wounded and deflated—in need of both amputations and enhancements. My characters are screaming in horror—some angry, some heartbroken, some sassy sarcastic. They turn on each other rather than merging in cooperative harmony.

My poor little precious!

Wisely, I recognize that I'm in "momma mode" and step away from the computer. Let's give this a few nights to dance with my subconscious.

**Editorial Suggestions, Reaction 2:**

OK, let's try this again. All the characters and paragraphs sit quietly in a circle, prepared to negotiate some compromises. They've decided to trust me, their creator, as I revisit the suggested changes.

I re-read my precious. This time, it's easier to notice the flaws—the places where my fingers didn't keep pace with my imagination. Places that, without the cacophony of the characters' voices in my head, no longer feel cohesive.

Now, my editor's suggestions feel like the wise warm words of an NFL coach urging my creation towards unimagined magnificence. As the characters try on the suggestions, they nod appreciatively—feeling more authentically expressive. The characters learn their team roles and start to cooperate. To express appropriately.

And my little precious learns to play well with the imaginations of other readers.

# The Synthetic or Amy's Evolution

## *Alia Berkeley*

The flashing lights blinded Dr. Steiml through his thick-lensed glasses, his smile slight and reserved. After the flashing stopped, he stepped over to the podium and slightly stooped to the microphone. The room quieted to a hush.

"I am Dr. Bryan Steiml. When Amy came to us with her first injury, little did we know we would embark on a study of human evolution and tap into the possibilities of extending lives." Loud, low-toned murmurs erupted through the crowd.

"When you say "evolution" what do you mean by that?" A voice broke through in the audience. "Are we all to become synthetics? What about reproduction? When I think of evolution, I think of a species slowly changing over time—eras—biologically, where DNA is morphed through the generations. Without the capability of reproduction, where is the evolution?"

The question didn't daunt Dr. Steiml. His face remained neutral. He had grown accustomed to criticism.

"Well, I can't speak for our subject on her attempts at reproduction…"

Slight laughter ensued.

"…but there have been some attempts in the lab at reproduction. So far, in vitro reproduction has looked promising."

He stopped there as the murmurs grew louder. Dr. Steiml had no interest in further testing the synthetic capabilities of reproduction written into his contract at his employers' insistence. He knew he had already surpassed the abilities of mankind and was just waiting for everyone else to catch up. Thus, he hired second rate scientists to do the tasks he considered menial to please the administrators auditing the study.

Another hand shot up quickly in the front.

"How do you even go about transferring consciousness. Is she even the same person she was or is she just a robotic version of who she once was?"

"No, no. She is very much organic. *Synthetic* organic, that is. We've used organic nanotechnology to help regenerate and reproduce cells, skin cells, soft tissue and such, on the outside, whereas her structure — bones — are made of a special, newly developed, organic alloy that is compatible with the organic nanotechnology. Unlike bones, with this organic alloy…" Organic alloy, he knew, was an oxymoron, but the general public seemed to think "organic" was the most significant part of the experiment. "…there is no need for constant breakdown and re-structure. In fact, Amy, you can throw away those calcium supplements." He directed his comment off-stage. His tone was flat and dry, yet, there were gentle chuckles in the audience.

"Imagine never feeling pain or catching a cold — or any sickness — being able to heal rapidly if injured.

"But to get back to your question: transferring consciousness. We mapped out the synapses in her brain, including the grey matter etc., where her memories were coded and identified those areas lacking memories yet to be written. We used that nanotechnology to transfer data. Memories, thoughts, opinions, feelings…

"Rather than me ramble on about the technical details, why don't we hear Amy's story? Ladies and gentleman, I introduce Amy Yakamoto."

Amy stepped out onto the stage and stopped on cue. Her ameliorated body was able to maintain a cool temperature of 77°F under the hot lights. She stood blankly as the lights flashed until she remembered to smile. It wasn't a true smile, but a memory of a smile that she recalled one should do in front of a camera, one that mimicked pleasantry. Her pupils adjusted rapidly to the changes in light.

The faces in the crowd were not the stone-cold analytical ones of the doctors and scientists, before whom she stood naked as they assessed her, but faces of astonishment, disbelief, shock.

Dr. Steiml stepped aside allowing Amy to approach the podium.

"Demon!" A voice yelled from the back of the auditorium.

Amy frowned slightly as Dr. Steiml whispered in her ear. In that moment, the history of how she started on this journey until now flashed through her mind. It all started with a knee...

~

Amy was running as she usually did at dusk in the nearby park to decompress from the day's stresses. Something startled her. As she turned her attention towards it, she slipped and fell hard on her right knee shattering her knee cap on a rock. She screamed loudly. Another runner who heard her cries found her sobbing and whimpering. As he tried to help her up, she collapsed, again, with searing pain as bones shifted and ligaments stretched. Someone called an ambulance for her. She was taken to the ER where she was advised that she'll forever walk with a limp. They fitted her with a knee brace before she was sent home, and wrote her a prescription for strong pain killers.

In the months following, she went on short term disability and relied heavily on her husband, Steve, to help her out — a humiliating process. Having that independence snatched away from her was devastating, leading her to cry uncontrollably at times. Adjusting to his new role in the household was also difficult for her husband, which he emoted through endless griping.

After almost a year, Amy still walked with a limp. She pleaded with doctors, sought second, third, fourth, fifth opinions until, one day, she found, by chance, a study, for experimental joint replacement. Steve was aghast when she told him she applied, thought it was unproven medicine. They fought heatedly until their 4-year-old, Benji, cried. Amy would usually throw on her running shoes before it ever reached that point.

However, Amy was accepted into the study which was explained to her as "cutting edge" technology that permanently repaired joints without further need for future revisions. Amy homed in on the phrase "permanently repair." After further tests and examinations, Amy had surgery. Recovery was swift followed by an adjustment period of strengthening atrophied muscles. Once it all healed, her knee felt fantastic. She squatted without the kneecap shifting or cartilage snagging. She could pick up Benji who was now 5 ½ years-old. However, soon the right leg was far stronger than the left, causing issues.

During check-up, she addressed it with the doctors. Lack of coordination between the two knees, and frequently having to correct her gait, exhausted her mentally and physically. Running was a complete disaster; she was not able to reach that elation, that release, which used to rush over her after every run.

The treatment wasn't approved for healthy joints and tissue. But it had been months, she argued, that coordination should be equal in both legs, that she shouldn't have to concentrate this hard.

Rules were rules, unless she wanted to pay for it, which would drain their savings and some of Benji's college fund. Amy suggested this to her husband who scoffed and called her vile things. She disappeared into the garage after taking left over narcotics. Grabbing Steve's hammer hanging on the peg board over his tidy workspace, she smashed her left knee cap without hesitation, crying out in pain.

Steve rushed into the garage. When he spied the hammer on the ground and Amy gripping her left knee, he muttered: "You selfish bitch."

"Is Mommy ok?" Benji asked as the automatic door closed, shutting him out.

Steve opened the garage door by hitting the garage door opener on the wall with his fist so the ambulance would find her. He stomped back into the house as Benji repeated his question.

"Mommy's—" But the rest of Steve's response was cut off when the door shut again automatically. Sirens rose to a crescendo before abruptly cutting off in front of the house.

Two days later, Amy was accepted back into the study after the hospital sent over her x-ray and MRI results.

The surgery on her left knee was also successful; everything was back to "normal." She could run longer and faster than before. Over time, however, her muscles around her knee were tiring, as if they couldn't keep up with her enhancements.

Amy addressed this at her six-month check-up. The "genius" head of the study, introduced as Dr. Steiml, was there. While the doctors examined and questioned her, he sat quietly in the corner with his arms crossed. Then, they put her on a treadmill and observed while she walked, ran, then sprinted. Finally, they left her, still gowned, back in the cold exam room. She shivered a bit as she flipped through the same magazine several times. Amy began to wonder if they forgot her until Dr. Steiml returned.

"You've taken well to the therapy, Amy," he stated as he reached down for her leg and extended it while placing his other hand on top of her knee. "You bring up an interesting question." He let her leg go and reached for the other one. His hands were freezing. "I'd like to work with you further on this. You have some time to think about my proposition."

That's when he went into detail about how they would replace bits of her, starting with muscles in her legs and seeing where it went from there. She would sign consent forms for each procedure. She took this proposal home to Steve. They argued, she ran, and then they made love for the first time in months. After that, he told her that he was sold on the therapy since it was at a minimal monetary cost to them.

Gradually, they replaced the lower half of her body—bones, connective tissue, muscle, nerves and peripheral vascular system. It took a whole team of doctors working long hours and multiple surgeries. After the nerves were replaced, Amy started to feel…different. She had been warned, though, that there would be changes—some subtle, some obvious. Her skin felt electric, as if there was a constant static charge. It also looked smoother, near pore-less. When they tested for sensation up and down her legs with various objects, the textures all felt similar, but the pressure differed. For instance, a cotton ball had far lighter pressure than the pin they poked her with, which had a tiny firm pressure. Also, pain was no issue. The doctors told her they manipulated sensations of pain so that she no longer recognized if something hurt but could still sense the difference in objects. Learning to walk again was difficult at first…training the muscles to respond, getting balance and posture right. It took several more surgeries to replace her organs, vascular system, skin, and nervous system on her torso saving her head, face and brain for last. That was the hardest to get used to, the idea that they were going to replace her face and brain.

91

No, not replace, enhance.

Prior to her final surgery, she admitted to herself, at last, that maybe she had taken things too far. What if she wasn't the same person? What if they severely disfigured her? Everything up until now had worked flawlessly. Still, it didn't stop her the day before from picking up the phone and nearly calling off the last surgery...it was, after all, her choice. But, she had come so far — six years. So Amy went on a long run, enjoying the strength and enrichments she had acclimatized to, feeling the release of those endorphins. The run took her longer than normal, but her mind eventually cleared.

~

The story Amy told the auditorium was vastly abridged and mostly written for her. She began it once the room was cleared of the protestors. As she spoke, her voice was smooth velvet, unfaltering. She captured their attention as their eyes grew bigger and their skeptical faces slowly softened.

Then, her husband and son stepped out. Steve told his story about the astonishment of her transformation. He was charming, like when they first met, and talked about what little differences there were in terms of personality. His lines were mostly written for him, too, except a joke or two that were pre-approved. Her son didn't speak at all but stood stiffly in front of Amy as she held his shoulders. Later, they drove home in silence. Benji slept peacefully in the back with his mouth slightly gaping.

Before the conference, she didn't feel anxiety or excitement. She felt the same as she did after she woke up from surgery with her renewed cognition — an insouciance. If she did display emotion, it was mimicked from memory, or she based her emotion on the reaction of others around her. Amy also had a wealth, a data bank, of memories available to her leading all the way back to her birth.

"I suppose you won't sleep," Steve stated as he yawned wearily.

"I suppose not," she replied flatly.

"I don't get it."

When they pulled into the driveway, he left her to bring in

Benji who stumbled groggily towards the door. Amy pressed the button to close the garage door which still had a crack in it from when Steve hit it.

The next day was like any other summer day. Steve had gone out on some errand. Benji asked Amy if he could have ice cream. They walked to the ice cream parlor, about a 15-minute walk. She easily matched her speed to her son's. When they entered the ice cream parlor, the tone quieted as one woman quickly shuffled her unaware daughter out the door while she messily licked her dripping ice cream.

"May I help you?" The young server asked.

"Benji?" Amy looked down at her son.

"Ummm...vanilla and chocolate swirl."

"One scoop or two."

"Two please."

"And for you, uh, ma'am," the server asked while scooping up the ice cream.

"I'm fine thanks."

"Don't you eat?" A man asked behind her.

"Excuse me?" She replied when she turned to face him.

A woman approached her and pinched a large chunk of her cheek. Her smooth skin slid slowly out of the woman's slightly sticky fingers.

"She feels funny," the woman scoffed.

"Mommy?!" Benji panicked.

More people poured into the ice cream parlor, their faces a mix of anger and disgust. She guided Benji to the door abandoning the ice cream the server had propped in a cone holder. A peculiar new sensation rippled through her as a tidal wave of memories of disgust poured through her: the look Steve gave her when she smashed her knee, or the lecture her father gave her when she got a B+ rather than an A on her homework. She hurried Benji out the door too fast for his shorter stride, nearly pushing him over. As they rushed along the sidewalk, she thought about what she used to do when she was upset. She picked up the pace without hesitation and sprinted down the street in her sandals. Benji ran behind her as fast as his legs could carry him.

"Mommmmmeeeeee! Waaaaiiiittt!"

She continued on at a sprint past their modest house to the park nearby. The memories of why she would run were archived within her, and she wondered if she would get that same elated response.

But, there was nothing.

# The Nursing Home

## *Barbara Huntington*

In mid-October, the El Cajon Valley blows dry with the Santa Ana winds, but dark comes early and with it the first chill nights. As I descend into the hazy dusk, my headlights join a sinuous river disappearing past a giant granite outcropping, still reflecting the last red of the sunset. Other drivers speed by, eager to get home to warm dinners, but though I poke in the slow lane from my job at the university, eventually I must turn off, past the strip malls, the liquor store, the fifties tract houses, to turn into the parking lot of Melrose Manor.

My vision of a stately southern mansion contrasts starkly with this mishmash of stucco and glass. A pine and a shaggy palm rise above the cracked pavement and dead grass. The Liquidambar trees have already felt the evening cold, their leaves in last red scream before the dry wind sucks their life and color and abandons them brown and crumpled on the asphalt.

By the door an early jack-'o-lantern that won't see Halloween succumbs to mold, lid long gone, its bouquet of chrysanthemums adding to the slime. My steps slow as I stare at the glass panes in the door and reflect on the weary grey-haired woman backlit by the lights from the industrial complex across the lot. Taking a breath, I yank the door open and imagine an audible sigh from the moist air that has been waiting to escape. As I pull the door closed behind me, more damp heat tries to smother me with the heaviness of overcooked vegetables and pasta, adult diapers yet to be changed, the rancid odor of old people that cannot be covered by the overpowering scent of the lilies in the vase where I sign in.

I try not to stare at the desiccated bodies lined up in wheelchairs before me, but their eyes are on me. Accusing eyes, prisoners' eyes, eyes that no one lives behind. They hate this place, but they are part of it and their eyes brand me as an intruder. Fred is not among them.

I sign in and walk through the halls, past the cage of scruffy luckless finches and a woman with swollen ankles who sorts medications at her stainless steel cart. I glance in the common room, the battered grand piano in the corner. Four days ago when they brought Fred here from the hospital, he made a beeline for that piano. For a moment he forgot his shaky Parkinson's hands to pound out a Beatles tune. When the manor matrons, intent on Mahjong at a distant table, yelled that he was disturbing their game, I realized that at sixty-seven, he was too young for that crowd. The bossy women are in the piano room now. He isn't.

It has been a hard transition. The second day he gamely went to bingo and gallantly stood up for a confused old lady clutching a teddy bear they barred from playing. The old biddies hated Fred, and he knew it. He threatened their final domain. Fred, the elementary school principal everyone loved. I had tried to get him into a better nursing home. I visited some beauties, and they all had openings until I applied officially. After they checked our finances, they figured out my strategy of paying full price up front and then going on MediCal.

After twelve years holding a job during the day and caring for Fred and his cadre of little children hallucinations at night, I was tired. When one morning I found him unresponsive, his oxygen off, and melted ice cream all over the house, I sighed, reattached the oxygen cannula to his nose, and called a neighbor and the nursing hotline. No, I didn't just call 911 because I had called them so many times in the past only to have him sent home again, that I felt I needed support in my decision. By the time the paramedics arrived, Fred was awake, his oxygen levels were almost normal, and it took a little convincing to have them take him, once again, to emergency. To their credit, he had called 911 more than once when his hallucinations told him I needed help and was caught in the chair he had turned over. At the hospital, I overheard one doc tell another that the only reason Fred was there was because I wanted to have him committed to a nursing home. Fred was responsive, talkative, lucid, and I had to get our kids on my cell phone to convince him to remain for observation. The staff continued to blame me as a conniving woman until the sun went down and Fred told them he was holding hostages in his room to keep the cops from taking him for some unnamed crime.

The next day I had visited nursing homes and carefully analyzed each one until I whittled it down to the only one that would take him. By the end of the week, Fred and his hallucinations were on their way to Melrose Manor by ambulance while I followed behind, attempting to find positives, like the grand piano, to point out to him.

Now I entered his room where he sat in his lounging chair, the oxygen tube around his neck, not in his nose. I assumed it had not touched the floor so I gently replaced it and asked if the nurse had brought his meds. He didn't think so, but wasn't sure.

When his food tray came in, he was shaking so hard I had to feed him while he told me how the children in the corner were laughing at him. He coughed up a large green glob, which I caught with a tissue and lobbed into his overflowing wastebasket. Now I knew why the air was so moist. There was probably a basket like this in every room. Each inhabitant was filling tissues with snot, tears, and large masses of coughed up phlegm. Having lived with Fred's denizens for years, it was easy for me to visualize every resident of the ambitiously named manor, filling tissues and wastebaskets as they, themselves, dried and shriveled, eventually disappeared. As I shoveled food into his mouth, Fred suddenly looked at me with his Parkinson's startled-deer-in-the-headlights look, closed his eyes, and snored.

I wish I could remember if I kissed him goodnight before I tiptoed out to the nurses' station to find out about his meds and to remind them to check his oxygen. I entered the pass code and let myself out the door. Stepping carefully to avoid the now totally collapsed pumpkin, I pulled the cool delicious dry air into my lungs and kept the car windows down on the half-hour drive home.

As I entered the dark house, our old dog whined softly. I fed her, stroked her silky head, downed a bowl of cereal for dinner, and went to bed. About 10:30 pm, I surfaced to my ringing phone.

"We called 911, he is in E.R. Unresponsive."

Driving back on the empty dark freeway, windows closed against the cold, I wondered if he had removed his oxygen cannula and if it had fallen on the dirty floor. I fantasized the manor matrons as witches sneaking into his darkened room and gleefully removing it, perhaps aided by the evil little children in the corner. At the hospital, I saw x-rays of his filling lungs. They had been clear when he left the hospital.

Family gathered, but Fred never regained consciousness. Would he have lived if I had found the strength to keep him home just a little longer? Death by nursing home. How many others have been killed by Melrose Manor? Like the pumpkin, he didn't make it to Halloween.

# Roses & Thorns

## *Gary Winters*

It started out as just another family discussion at the dinner table. Mom and Dad and four girls in a typical American family shouting match. It ended when they laughed at the eldest sister for her transgender views. Jessica picked up the crockery salad bowl and flung it down on the table. The tempered glass exploded causing dinner and discussion to be over. All over.

Jessica had learned to get her own way by temperamental outbursts. If that didn't work she could always fall back on her body. She went to the Miss New Mexico beauty contest as a sure thing, but came away as the runner-up.

When the dust from the beauty-pageant whirlwind cleared, Jessica found herself out of the picture. An also ran. A nobody. She stewed in her own juice.

"Even after I went to all the trouble to tint my hair with Miss Clairol Champagne," she whined to her butch girlfriend. "Just look at Miss New Mexico's ass," she said after they made love on the waterbed. "Can you imagine how many beans and tacos she had to cram down her throat to get her butt to jiggle like that?" They giggled and went back to what they were doing.

Jessica was right. Miss New Mexico did like frijoles and tacos. She craved chili peppers. She was a hot-blooded Latina and proud of it.

Jessica called Miss New Mexico on the telephone. "Let's get together for a drink." Her shoulders hunched. "Don't invite anyone else. Just the two of us," she cooed.

"Sure, come on over. Bring a bottle of tequila. Make it Cuervo Gold. I'm out. Been partying, you know."

Jessica showed up at Miss New Mexico's apartment with a bag of limes and a liter of Jose Cuervo. And a Mexicali switchblade in her purse. The place looked like a flower shop. Roses, red and white and yellow, everywhere—even on the floor.

They got to drinking and talking, Jessica slicing limes with her switchblade. When the tequila was sloshing in the bottom of the bottle Miss Jiggle-Butt said, "I was born in Albuquerque, but I spent my teenage years in Guadalajara. It's the second largest city in Mexico. Oh man, those years.

"My boyfriend was a taxi driver. He taught me how to take care of myself in the big city. Guadalajara's a tough town. Beautiful but tough." She chuckled. "In those days my friends and I made fun of beauty queens. Funny how things change." She had to laugh out loud.

Right in the middle of Miss New Mexico's stupid laugh Jessica clutched the switchblade and lunged at her.

~

A light drizzle gently misted the living-room windows. The dark wavy-haired Albuquerque homicide detective lifted the tousled hair with a ballpoint pen and looked at the face on the floor. His gaze moved to the knife stuck in the victim's neck with GUADALAJARA emblazoned on the handle. He pried the switchblade from the dead woman's cold hand and bagged it. Then he put his arm around Miss New Mexico's shoulders and let her cry it out.

# Cindy and Frank

## *Robert Doublebower*

Her dad said don't go yet. Wait a bit. But the Datsun had been loaded. All her stuff, hauled to college, then hauled back, was now carefully sorted into needed and not needed and stowed in the car.

"They got a storm. Down around Antigua, or somewhere."

Cindy didn't care about any storm. She had gotten her acceptance letter for training school two long weeks ago, and that mattered way more than any tropical disturbance. *Antigua's far away, right?*

Her dad remembered Cindy growing up, as far back as seventh grade, with a fascination for airlines and big planes. She'd had her first plane ride back around then, and the whole experience had resonated with her. She wanted, more than anything, to be a stewardess.

The pictures in her room back then had still run heavily to The Beatles and Bobby Rydell, but 707s and, of course, his Majesty, the Concorde, had their corner. Yeah, she knew early-on there'd be the months of Newark-Detroit-Rochester-Newark, but, still, what could be more glamorous than flying? Eventually... L.A., Seattle ... Las Vegas. And all those people.

Cindy prided herself on her people skills. She'd been on cheer squad, of course, and every high school and college service committee knew her name.

"Don't worry, Dad, I'll be fine. It's only a four-or five-hour drive down to Jacksonville. Six at the most. Sun's out, look. I'll be back after the first three weeks. There's a break. I wrote the number of the hotel where we're all staying on the phone pad. I'll try to call whenever I can. I don't know if all the rooms have phones."

They hugged each other and he looked down at his little girl.

The college farewell had been tougher.

"Love you."

"Love you, too," and with that, the Datsun, with one squealing brake shoe, set off for the Interstate. And Cindy had a secret.

~

Frank Grafton was already on the Interstate. His old Malibu groaned and swayed as he wheeled north, blue sky ahead, an ominous gray off to the east. The hurricane out there had gotten a little stronger since sun-up, but all the weather-guessers on the radio had it drifting north, then northeast. Tough luck, Bermuda, but life here in the Sunshine State is as advertised.

A little rest. He knew what they meant. He'd been a deacon at that damned church in Clearwater for going on 18 years. He'd been through five pastors and six assistant ministers, but had he gotten his shot at the top job? Not so's you'd notice.

The only really cheap flight to Charlotte was out of Jacksonville, so the church board had "suggested" he drive there, rather than Miami. Cheap bastards. It wasn't like they weren't making money, for chris'sake. Florida is so automatic. Before platooning off to the Waffle House every Sunday morning, the oldsters that continually drifted south had to have a place to go to drink in the goodness of the Lord.

Speaking of which, Frank decided the time had come to stop for a little pick-me-up, a nooner or two, to relieve the flat monotony of the central Florida grasslands. The church's corporate board up in Hot'lanta maintained a sort of R&R retreat in Charlotte for clergy members who had become, say, too vulnerable to the temptations they fought in their zeal to save souls. A week or two of dry-out... I mean, prayer and Bible study... and the weakened fabric of their overtaxed souls would be made whole again.

*A little rest, my ass.* Frank had a secret, too.

~

Cindy had been driving and thinking of Ramon. She wanted to reach out and touch his wild hair and his skin the color of chestnut. They'd met the middle of senior year. He was not at all like the boys back home. Their run-up from dating to sleepovers had been meteoric. He'd gotten a job in Jacksonville and planned to move into his own place down here next week. Well, sorta' their place. Cindy and Ramon were going to see how it went. For her, this presented a new moral landscape. She hoped, somehow, it wouldn't make her a bad stewardess.

An hour outside the city, big raindrops began to splatter the Datsun's windshield. The tropical disturbance had taken a hard left. Twenty minutes later the wipers were hard-pressed to keep up. Palms along the highway started to wind-whip. Official check-in at the hotel went 'til 8 p.m. Cindy hoped she wouldn't be the last one.

~

An hour after he had pulled off, Frank paid his tab and strolled out to his car. Overhead, the Sunshine State postcard had been replaced by a scudding cloud layer, and a brisk breeze had kicked up. By the time he eased into the Interstate flow, Frank had settled into a decidedly vindictive mood, powered, in no small measure, by 12-year-old Scotch. *A little rest, my ass.*

He may not be top dog back in Clearwater, but he'd been there long enough to know a thing or two about their record-keeping. The proceeds from their "Swing into Spring with the Lord" bash back in April were proving hard to track back into the General Fund. Didn't seem to make it into the Mission Fund, or the Building Fund, either. Probably just a bookkeeping screw-up. But he had a friend back at the *Clearwater Sentinel* who would find this "interesting." Questions in the press, maybe an outside audit, guilt by innuendo… Who knows? Maybe even a resignation and a job opening. He chuckled and flipped on the wipers.

~

Cindy and Frank were coming from inland, but the hurricane, as usual, arrived by sea. The ebb tide of the river had met the storm surge from offshore, and the downtown was flooding. Cindy made it to the Hammond Blvd. exit, just outside the Beltway, before state troopers, in slickers and rain hats, began escorting them off the highway. They told locals heading

103

downtown to go back home. Darkness loomed within the hour. Out-of-towners were advised to follow the red and blue lights to the shelter.

Frank arrived at the Hammond Blvd. exit a few minutes later.

Cindy fretted. What would all this do to training school? They'd be late getting started. Late finishing. Ramon still planned to move into his place next week, right? She also had to call home.

The line in which she stood shuffled forward a few spaces. "REGISTRATION" read the well-worn sign-with-arrow. Outside, the wind howled, and inside the humidity slowly crept up. And the guy behind her in line smelled like whiskey.

Frank shook his head and looked at the floor. *Sure! Of course. Why not throw in a couple of nights in a hurricane shelter?* He had planned to call his friend at the *Sentinel* from the airport, but obviously not now. The bank of pay-phones he saw on the way in had a three minute limit posted, and "personnel" were there to remind you.

Damn the luck. His future hung in the balance. The registration line formed a giant "L" along two walls of a junior college event center. The cavernous hall had cots arranged over the entire floor in neat rows. They'd done this before. When the line jumped ahead another space, Frank leaned in to the girl in front of him, and said, "'Scuse me. Know what we're in line for?"

Cindy stiffened a little and closed her eyes. She'd rather get back to thinking about Ramon.

"Registration," she said with a half turn. "They also give you a little bag with soap and stuff. Looks like we're staying the night."

"Yeah, I figgered."

Frank went back to mulling his future. Three minutes wouldn't be near long enough to spin his tale with any credibility. How to make it all sound credible?

The line moved again. People walked from the registration desk, through the maze of cots, to the one assigned to them, as more people got in line. A food line began to take shape against the back wall. Home, sweet, home.

Fifteen minutes went by and then Frank leaned in again. "Y'all got family here?"

Cindy had just been thinking very much about family, as a

matter of fact, but wasn't sure how to answer that one. Maybe the question would pass. It did.

Another 10 minutes, and Frank, again, "Y'all from here?"

Cindy had had enough. She turned to face Frank, stuck out her hand and said, "Hi, my name's Cindy. No, how about you? From here?" People person.

That he didn't expect. Frank returned a short handshake. "Frank Grafton. No, me neither. From down south. Clearwater." They both looked around some more, now a shared vision.

"Amazing how they do all this, isn't it." Cindy said.

"I guess so," Frank said back, looking around. "Somebody's making some bucks on it, I'll bet."

Had Cindy been listening, that would have sounded cynical, but she had lapsed back into thinking of Ramon. How long would this storm hold him up?

"My boyfriend's moving down here next week," Cindy blurted out.

Frank had been looking over at the food line, but turned back. "Oh yeah? Serious type."

Cindy smiled.

Frank felt chatty. "*I* married *my* junior college sweetheart… back in the day. But that was a-ways back. Didn't last, though."

Then with a grunting laugh, "Just like the next two. I got business up in Charlotte, but sure wanted to use the phone at the airport."

"My boyfriend's moving down here next week to start a job with the county government. I hope the storm doesn't mess that up. I hope. We can't wait to see each other. We've been writing each other ever since school got out."

"County job, huh? I hope he has it in writing. Sometimes counties think they have more money than they actually have, then something like this hits…."

"Actually, I came down here to start stewardess school. For Braniff. They're the best. But who knows when that'll start now. What do you do, Mr. Grafton?"

"Oh, I am a minister, deacon actually, at the First Gospel, down in Clearwater."

"A preacher! I didn't take you for one. My family had a friend that did that, back in Georgia. Do you find it rewarding?"

"Heh, I think our pastor might."

"Pardon," said Cindy. Frank jumped at the chance to try out his story. He gave Cindy the abridged version of the 'Swing into Spring' event. How the money seemed hard to trace. How an audit might be necessary. He even alluded to the possibility of heads rolling at the church, and the opportunities that might open for him.

Cindy had never heard anything like this up close. She said, "That sounds kind'a serious. Are you sure about all this?"

"No, not particularly. But I figger if people start shakin' trees, who knows what'll fall out."

For the first time all day, a frown darkened Cindy's face.

"But, hey, enough about me." Frank suddenly brightened.

"So, y'all thinking about getting married?"

"Right now we just want to be together." Cindy settled on that as the best way to put it. "But, you know, maybe...."

Frank sighed, low and barely audible, but Cindy noticed.

"Sounds great," said Frank. "I hope all these variables work out."

"Variables?" asked Cindy.

"Yeah, you know, the job, this storm, your training school. Lots of moving parts, here, right?

Yesterday it all seemed so linear and solid.

"So, Mr. Grafton, what do you think your newspaper friend will do?"

"Don't know, really. Make some calls. Ask some questions. Do you think they have a bar in these places?"

Cindy didn't know about that, but she recalled a story from home. "I remember we had a girl back in high school, got accused of some stuff between her and a coach. We all had heard about it, but nobody knew for sure. She said this, the coach said that, parents got involved, the district investigated, and you know what happened? The home-ec teacher and an assistant principal got fired. The home-ec teacher! She wasn't even involved! Go figure."

Frank took his turn to frown. Had he not thought of this? House-of-cards?

Cindy's thoughts turned back to Ramon. *The county would certainly need more people now, not less, to recover from the storm, right? His apartment hadn't been damaged, had it? How long would they be in this shelter? What if... ?* Their place in line had long since turned the "L", and they were in the home stretch.

Frank stood uncharacteristically quiet for a few minutes. Then, "Did you hear any more about the storm on your way in?"

"No," said Cindy. "Just that it turned left and here we are. I wonder if they'll call off training school?"

Frank thought back to the slights he'd endured over the years, and then to some of the recent head-butting with higher-ups. A phrase kept occurring to him. Collateral damage.

Cindy tried to think back to the acceptance letter. Did they mention an alternative date? How long from now?

They were now only six people away from the registration table. Cindy had suddenly become slightly anxious. She had to get to a phone and call Ramon. And home.

Frank was slowly losing his interest in calling the *Sentinel*. He'd see how he felt after Charlotte.

# Wasted

## *Peggy Hinaekian*

She was sitting at the edge of the pool gazing at the turquoise water, listening to the birds and the swooshing trees and thinking about her youth. The most elusive and intangible escape artist she had ever come across. It had come and gone without her ever realizing it. One day it had been there, and the next day it was gone.

She was wealthy, she could buy anything she wanted, but unfortunately time was not for sale.

*God, why did you let me waste my days? Why did you let me pursue dead-end dreams? Why did you not make me realize the importance of time? I should have cherished every minute of it, doing the meaningful things. But no, you let me go astray thinking my youth was there forever, never realizing that old age would creep up sooner than I thought. I am in the phase of debilitating old age, full of wisdom that does not serve me anymore.*

She had lots of plans before passing to the other side. But did she have time to accomplish all that she wanted to do?

This phase in her life shall also pass, and she would go six feet under bemoaning the passing of precious time. Had it been worthwhile to fuss over meaningless things? Certainly not.

She should have been wise from the beginning and realized that life lasted but a second and it should not have been wasted. She always came back to that same word.

WASTED.

# Flight Risk

## *Jenna Benson*

I am endangered and I am in danger.

My tears turn to fireworks
And my fear to joy
My nature has been nurtured
My heart finally understands your ploy

I am begging to learn new things.
If passing trees are my lessons,
Each one that strikes my wings
Shall leave a lasting impression

Every moon brings new strength
A new thought, realization, mistake
The sun shines brightly, but it does not make
The changes until I do

Leaving all I knew
Flight risk
Finally finding happiness
In the abyss

# Warrior

## *Gary Winters*

One night at La Cabra Cantina in Baja California, I noticed a man with something a little bit different about him. In the dim light his right hand looked strange.

I strolled over to him and in a quiet way invited him to a glass of beer. "I have one," he said, "but I'd be glad to have a drink with you."

He was a Yaqui, the only unconquered tribe in Mexico. After a few swallows of beer I asked about his hand. He held it up.

Strangest thing I ever saw.

An eagle's upper beak attached to two inches of bone was lashed onto his middle finger with fishing line. I marveled at the primitive weapon perfected by nature.

He had caught my amazement and smiled, just a little. After some thought he said, "I will trade you my eagle's beak for a caguama" — a quart of beer.

I didn't hesitate and was now the owner of a weapon that could rip a man's carotid artery or take out an eye fast as he could blink.

I slipped it on, gave it a few wraps, and my mind wandered out into the vast desert regions of Sonora, Chihuahua, New Mexico, Arizona, Texas, California.

And then there I was drinking beer with a man who spoke Cáhita, pulled back into the present as the proud owner of an eagle's beak.

# Transporting Issues

## *Lawrence Carleton*

I took my place on the launch platform in Transporter B in preparation for going to Substation Draco, where an ensign had caught his hand in a blender. They needed a medical specialist in limb regeneration, so there I was. Ensign Arthur Dennis, the on-duty controller of the transporter, verified that the beam path was sufficiently clear, told me to be still, and energized the device.

Transporters are cutting edge technology, and space station Waterloo and its substation satellites are the first to deploy them for regular use.

This was my first time in a transporter, but I'd asked questions and read up on what to expect. There was the initial whir and things momentarily went blank. When I opened my eyes again I looked around expecting to find myself on Draco. It didn't take me long to realize I was still there in Transporter B.

Arthur Dennis rechecked all the controls and monitors. "Well, I've heard that this happens sometimes. Maybe some impurity in the beam path has caused an auto-abort. I'll check with Uncle Ben to see whether I should just try again."

"Uncle Ben" is Dr. Benjamin Forager, the supervisor of transportation for our station. He was one of the chief engineers in the team which developed the technology.

After Ensign Dennis left the bay I decided I should go in search of a bathroom. It took me longer than expected to locate one. I hurried back, worried that I was causing a delay. I paused just as I approached the doorway to think of how I'd explain myself. I saw Arthur and Uncle Ben standing at the control panel and discussing the incident. "It's the oddest thing," Dennis said. "Nothing happened while I was here for several minutes, but now Substation Draco reports that Lizzie Ryan got there and is attending to the ensign. False alarm, sir. Sorry to bother you."

115

Uncle Ben commented, "These things happen, Arthur, it's always wise to be careful, no harm done." I slid away from the doorway as Uncle Ben left to return to his office.

What to do? The transporter is supposed to disassemble your body into a code which is beamed to a distant spot separated from your current location mostly by space, then at the distant spot render the code back into the original you. People who have been transported report that they have full function of memory and the same awareness of body parts, etc. They have every reason to believe that they are the same person who stood in the transporter a few seconds or, at most, minutes earlier.

I sensed that it would be unwise just to go back to my quarters. In fact, it would be hard not to be seen going there. I decided I didn't want to be seen. Medics' quarters were in a different part of the space station some distance from the transporter bays, but engineers were scattered throughout. Prince Sauvage's place wasn't far. He'd invited me there on previous occasions, though not for discussions of technology. I decided it was time to pay him a visit.

Actually, I hoped he wouldn't be there, but he was. He was in pajamas at his desk. I entered quietly and looked around. I spied the little bookshelf he once described so fondly to me, with its three books: 1) *Fahrenheit* 451 — Prince liked to remark that we don't burn books any more, we don't even publish them in paper — it's all electronic, accessed by reader devices. He's the only person I know who still chooses paper over electronic when he can; 2) *Things Fall Apart* by Chinua Achebe, his distant relative; and 3) *No Easy Walk to Freedom,* by Nelson Mandela, a copy so beaten up that it would fall apart if anyone tried to read it. Prince just felt good knowing it was there. This was totally unexpected for me when he told me about it, given the way we first met — the Halloween costume party. He was there in his Wakanda outfit, which for him wasn't much more than a loincloth, gloves, and a scary necklace. He was totally into the role, his enthusiasm growing into danger of getting out of hand. (I, by the way, went as Wonder Woman, and wasn't wearing much more than he.) That was the occasion of my first declining his invitation to visit his quarters.

Now, after more no-thank-yous, here I was for the first time. He didn't seem to notice me as I approached. He muttered to himself "what am I missing? What, what am I missing?" as he looked back and forth between two piles of documents which on my closer peek turned out to be about our space station's transporters. He suddenly looked up as I leaned in to get a better view.

He said softly, almost whispering, "Am I dreaming, or have you at last taken up my offer?" I looked into his brown eyes and said, "I need you awake so you can help me." His smile nearly melted me. I continued. "I had an incident with one of our transporters."

"So you're the one. Troublemaker," he chided, but I could see he was smiling. "Now I see what happened. It made a copy of you at Substation Draco but didn't erase you from the launch pad. Somehow they lost track of you and thought it was just a delayed delivery. They don't know you're still here on our Battlestar Galactica."

"How did you know?" I said. I told him in detail what had happened.

"Well, you're right not to want to be seen. They can't afford this kind of thing to be known. Stay here. Please stay here." I wasn't sure whether this was simply for my protection or there were ulterior motives in play.

Prince continued. "Do you remember Todd Friendly? It might have been before you got here. The same thing happened to him and he reported it to Uncle Ben, who made him keep it a secret. He didn't mention to Dr. Forager that he'd already told his fellow engineers, including Vince, Kwame, and me, but he didn't let the secret out to any others. Within 24 hours Todd was gone. 'Reassigned,' Dr. Benjamin Forager replied when we asked him, but he never said where, and there's no record other than the entry which says only that.

"You're here for now, kiddo, at least for the night. I've got spare jammies. Here!" He grabbed a pair from a drawer and tossed them at me. After I stood there assessing the situation for a few seconds he smiled and assured me his motives were pure — this time.

When I came out of the bathroom he was standing by his bed. The sheets were drawn to one side, and a bedroll had been spread on the floor. "Your choice," he indicated.

I didn't have to think. I knew what I wanted. I strode up to him, pulled off this pajama top, ran my fingertips over his perfectly muscled chest, looked deeply into his eyes, and kissed him softly. "I've made my choice," I murmured. He kissed me hard.

I was helpless in his hands. Soon I was naked on my back in his bed, panties gone, thighs parted, as he leaned in for the kill. He transported me in a way I'd never experienced, safe and free in my own land of dreams.

Early next morning, in the fashion we have mornings in a space station, I heard voices outside the door. Vince and Kwame were there with Prince. "You banged Lizzie Ryan? The Queen of Tease bites the dust! We all thought no one could have her — especially you. You're the champ, Prince — oh that's right you're the Prince! You must continue to bear in mind, though, that she is too good for you. What's she like?"

"I have been favored by a goddess," Prince replied, "but we've got a situation, and how we handle it is crucial both for Elizabeth's safety and that of anyone who leaves this home away from home of ours. Come in. We've got to think."

I pulled the sheet around me as they entered and said their hellos. I could feel myself blush.

At first in the days to come our main thinking gravitated to getting me back to earth and away from the authorities who'd disappeared Todd. It would have to be by shuttle, given our experience with transporters. We'd probably have to invent or steal an identity to get me on some shuttle, and we'd have to line up someone we could trust on the other end to handle my case.

Soon I realized I could be helpful to the guys' project. I wanted to stay and fight. After all, it's my project too. And what I know of biology should be helpful in understanding what various parts of the system are meant to address.

Meanwhile after some weeks delay "Lizzie Ryan" returned by shuttle from her visit to the substation and, upon going back to her/my quarters, reported some of her things missing. Witnesses

118

had caught glimpses of someone who looked like Lizzie lurking near the quarters, and soon Commander Valjean issued a bulletin warning of a possible stowaway.

The three amigos were pretty clever moving me around and providing me with necessities. This added instability made it harder for me to contribute to the cause, but with my specialized help we did get the feeling we were getting close. But about six weeks after my transporter mishap the authorities caught me in Prince's bathroom. I'd spent a lot of time there that day, suffering from nausea – what was that we drank to celebrate Vince's birthday the night before? I had assumed it wasn't alcoholic – now I wished I had some of my mother's menudo. I didn't move fast enough when I heard people coming.

Joan Valjean, as Commander of Space Station Waterloo, took charge of the investigation. It began focusing on me as a security breach, but after they added Prince as my main accomplice his statements turned it into a transporter issue.

Commander Valjean called a formal hearing and held it in her boardroom. Advocates called witnesses to testify to the identity of both Lizzies. We each were grilled on our verifiable personal memories, on the customary assumption that continuous memory establishes identity - even though we all know that everyone has noticeable gaps in her remembrance of personal history. Still, our memories matched except for the understandable differences covering the most recent several weeks. We each also had been subjected to a complete physical exam and DNA analysis. The Commander was satisfied that the "transported" Lizzie was a duplicate of the original Lizzie. Since obviously the two existed at the same time, it was clear that the transported one was made by copying, not by decomposing, beaming, and recomposing the original.

That raised the question of what happened to the originals after they were copied in the normal cases, given the two known cases in which they remained after the "transporting."

The examination also produced an unexpected bonus: Prince and I were pregnant. Genealogically speaking, we were going to have a healthy Irish-Mexican-Igbo-Zulu girl. The first American to be conceived in space was on the way!

This piece of luck afforded Commander Valjean an opening for a face-saving solution. We are now officially conducting a study of human reproduction in space, with my Lizzie counterpart as a control and me as the variable. (She hated being called "Twin Lizzie" so now we all address her as "Betsy.") This is getting all the publicity. Quietly in the background, thanks to documentation and testimony from Prince, Vince, Kwame, and me, Uncle Ben, and a few co-conspirators, have gone back to earth to serve time.

We also have a standing committee to weigh the elements of personal identity in the light of true duplication via transporter. A transporter makes such a thorough duplicate that all memories held by the original are reconstructed in the transported copy. In what way, if any, is the transported person different in these two cases: 1) the transporter decomposed the original person (me) and recomposed (me) on Substation Draco; 2) the transporter analyzed the original person (me) and composed the copy (Betsy) on Substation Draco.

The person on Draco on her own cannot tell the difference. Subjecting the person on Draco to physical and mental examination cannot determine a difference. On what basis can we say the person on Draco is me (Lizzie) in one case and a duplicate (Betsy) in the other? The obvious difference, that in one case and not the other, there is a me (Lizzie) back on the Waterloo, does not seem to have any bearing on the nature of the person on Draco.

I want to say the transported copy has the same personal history as the original up to the point in time when the copy is made. (Has, or acquires?) It certainly feels the same to the copy as it does to the original. You could say that Betsy was created at age 23, but I think it makes more sense to say we shared the same personal history until we diverged at that age.

This has become an issue now that we've taken out the "cleanup" step — i.e., disposal of the body – from the transporters. This is thanks to Prince, Vince, and Kwame's further research. The break came from examining old paper documentation of the devices. The electronic documentation had been altered to hide the fact that there was a cleanup step, but it hadn't occurred to

Uncle Ben et al that someone might have been making a paper trail.

These days our associates know that when we send someone via transporter they come to stay.

~

Well, that's our story. I'll write it down for general consumption. I think I'll dedicate it to our baby-girl-in-progress. Will you like that, incipient child? I have to go on shift pretty soon. Several severed limb patients, my specialty. Maybe next time I'll tell you about Aunt Betsy and her two boyfriends.

"Your mommy had three."

"Prince! How long have you been there?"

"I think I heard most of the narrative."

"In truth, I think I kind of knew all along you'd be the one."

"You had me fooled."

"Well, you had a reputation. I didn't want to make it too easy for you."

"You succeeded in that. Anyway, I came to walk with you to your shift."

"Ouch! That was a nasty kick, little girl-to-be. Show your mother some mercy."

"Darling, help me up."

"I always do."

Humor is just another defense
against the universe.

—*Mel Brooks*

# Self-Reliance ... REALLY

## *Amy E. Zajac*

An interesting fact for most of us is that our perception of ourselves is one of youth, strength, and total self-reliance for our own accomplishments. I look in the mirror and see an aging person who doesn't fit with my personal innate feeling that I'm still young. I am close to seventy years old and still do everything for myself, except move heavy items.

Since I moved recently, I am learning how to adjust to a much smaller apartment, and part of that adjustment is with my bathroom. I know it sounds like that should be simple, but we create an idea of what our facility should be like, making it comfortable for all our needs.

One important piece of information is that I share my bathroom with my two cats, Monty and KC. They are my dear friends and their litter box has a permanent space wherever I live. They are good about using it correctly and regularly. Happily, they keep my home clean, despite cats' reputations that odor follows them wherever they live. Fortunately, I don't have that issue, with the exception that their presence makes my space smaller, especially my bathroom.

My new bathroom has a stand-up shower only, no bathtub. It's nice. It's as long as a tub. The litter box fits nicely next to the end of the shower. There is a shelf above half of the litter box. I use this shelf for supplies to clean the litter.

One convenience I'm used to, and this apartment does not offer, is a hand shower. I've always used one to aid with not only rinsing myself, but also rinsing the whole shower as I finish. I proceeded to place old accessories that I brought from my last apartment. I moved the stepladder into the small space and easily made the change, because I knew the product from the past. After I placed the hand-held shower piece into the older cradle, I

125

worried that it was too high for me to reach later. I hoped it would be okay. You probably guessed; it was too high. I couldn't reach it without the stepladder.

I proceeded to go online to make a purchase of a simple part to accommodate the change I wanted, a new cradle-type holder. I found a suction type, which would be a simple fix. It arrived after a few days and I planned out in my mind how I would modify the simple plumbing accessory.

I determined how high it needed to be, so I could reach it this time, and then placed the suction holder on the tile. It was a strong suction, so I knew it would hold. I then tried to set the hand-held piece in the new holder. It didn't fit...REALLY...the advertisement said it would fit all standard plumbing fixtures!

Okay...like I said earlier...I'm self-reliant; it was my fault I didn't measure...I just took their word for it. Hence a reorder came next. I changed the idea a little. I ordered a new base for the hand-held piece that would fit the suction-type holder, measuring this time...a lesson learned.

It arrived a couple of days later, and I once again proceeded to install the pieces, checking first that the hand-held base fit the suction holder for the wall. It did. Installation was swift, adding the two pieces.

Just as I placed the suction holder on the tile, I heard a slight tap on the floor of the shower right at the base of ladder. I looked down to see the tiny screw cover, which would keep it from rusting, roll through the drain slat and down the drain! REALLY...

Now most people would have let it go there, but darn...my perfectionism was inching its way to the surface of my mood. Yes...you guessed it again. After learning that I couldn't replace the fancy plug, I ordered another suction holder for the wall. I now have spare parts in my utility closet which can help the plumber I'll hire the next time I feel my self-reliance starting to show through again!

# School Days and Miss Moore

## *Kenneth Yaros*

Every five years, the postman brings another high school reunion invitation. I'll set it down, and then walk over to the bookcase to verify that my school yearbooks are still there. They contain many photos of friends and events I'd almost forgotten. Nearly all those years were chaotic, even dangerous, yet today I look back on them with nostalgia. Over two hundred of us showed up for our fifty-fifth high school reunion in 2016. Some of us had scarcely changed, others were unrecognizable. But nothing could stop us from reconnecting.

In June 1961, I stood in line for high school graduation. We waited to be called upon that gloomy morning at the band shell in the park, in Reading, Pennsylvania. I shuffled impatiently in the drizzle, anxious to receive my diploma and to shake the principal's hand. Sadly, all my friends didn't graduate. If it wasn't for a unique experience in ninth grade involving Ms. Moore, I could have easily been among them.

I consider myself fortunate. Unlike most of my friends who were undecided about their futures, I felt confident in my plans. It hadn't always been that way. But by the middle of eleventh grade I had already chosen a career path. In a few months I would be attending Albright College, then hopefully go to dental school.

It didn't concern me that day that I'd never again see many of my classmates, or a ninth grade teacher who unknowingly helped me mature in so many ways. A firm handshake and a smile assured me public school was in my past. My diploma was the first tangible key to pursuing my future.

~

When I look back at my elementary school experience, it is a wonder anything turned out right. We moved often. I attended at

127

least one different school every year. Just showing up for class could be awkward and sometimes dangerous for me, being the only Jewish child in many schools.

Fifth and sixth grades were particularly unpleasant. Bullies harassed a number of us before and after school. Any day could result in another fight. A swollen eye, bloody nose or a torn shirt was not an unusual sight as we pledged allegiance. On the school bus my tormentors sang rude songs and left a mess for the driver. In class, I found it useful to keep a low profile, which was pretty easy since my surname began with a Y. I usually sat in the back of the room.

In the fall of 1955, I entered seventh grade at Northeast Junior High School, in Reading, my ninth school since kindergarten. It would take me forty-five minutes to walk from our apartment, miles away from the bullies the year before. Attending junior high remained an amorphous thought the summer of 1955. I had no grand expectations. After all, what could be so interesting about another school?

My parents bought me a sturdy brown leatherette schoolbag with silver buckles, and packed it with a cheese sandwich and a candy apple for my first day of class. They sent me off with hugs, expressing hopes that I would finally have a good school experience.

I walked alone to class, passing a myriad of one-hundred-year-old faded two-story brick row homes and unfamiliar faces. Pervasive odors of fried bacon and cars coughing to start filled the hilly, narrow streets of my route.

That first morning I came upon a small bakery specializing in cream-filled doughnuts. The aroma stopped me. A lady in the shop wearing a frilly white apron and matching hat saw me standing in front of her display window. She came out and gave me a chocolate doughnut. Nothing like that ever happened before. I thought maybe it was a good omen. I savored every creamy bite.

A half an hour later, we freshmen congregated at the front of a building which looked like a medieval fortress, a substantial brick-and-stone three-story structure framed by thickly leafed poplar trees.

Moments after I arrived, a loud bell rang. The heavy doors

were swung open to let us into an enormous gothic-style foyer. North East Junior High School would be my school for the next three years. The cool, spacious corridors with glossy floors smelling of fresh wax were the widest and cleanest I had ever seen. Bright, airy classrooms rimmed a central auditorium, which soon became one of my favorite places.

Most students didn't know one another in seventh grade since we came from six different primary schools. It was a good opportunity to make new friends. We were assigned homerooms and introduced to departmentalism. A long piercing bell sounded at the beginning and end of each class, giving us three minutes to advance to our next classroom.

Each morning at 8:55, three short buzzes over the PA system signaled announcements from the principal's office. The broadcasts reminded us of the activities that day, upcoming events, safety drills, and the location of the floating detention room.

Sometimes the head office would allow an honor student to do the announcements. That would set up snickers and giggles that could be heard in the hallways. None of my friends would have ever qualified for announcement duty.

Students mocked teachers for their idiosyncrasies. But it didn't end there. Almost no pupil would escape our wrath either. A quiet girl with long, dark, scraggly hair was soon labeled the cootie girl. Others had equally undesirable names. My nickname was Owl. I never found out why, but it stuck. There was always plenty to gossip about.

One of my favorite activities was going to assembly. Friday mornings, over 700 twelve-to fourteen-year-olds, plus our teachers, would file into the handsome wood-paneled auditorium. I seldom knew what the program would be; likely because I didn't pay much attention to the morning announcements, but it was always fun.

After we found our seats and quieted down, the program would start with the Pledge of Allegiance and a short non-denominational prayer lead by the principal.

We heard motivational speakers talking about what made our country great, or what it took to succeed. We got to see highlights of the final game of the World Series, a film of center fielder Willie Mays making that incredible catch in 1954, and many projections of world news. We watched seasonal plays and musical productions, but most of all we looked forward to singing. It was the first time ever I sensed the camaraderie and pride of belonging to something bigger than my Scout troop or our small family.

Most teachers were World War II veterans. They treated us like Army recruits. Mr. Potts was typical. He was the boys' physical education teacher. We called it gym then. He tried to run our classes like an Army drill sergeant. Students had to line up. He'd usually pick on the tallest, most uncoordinated boy and ask him to demonstrate an exercise. When the boy failed to measure up, Potts labeled him a bonehead or dummkopf, in Pennsylvania Dutch.

The worst for me was the ropes. Six thick ropes hung from the ceiling of the gym. At the sound of a whistle, he ordered us to climb to the top within thirty seconds. Most kids got about four feet off the floor and just hung there, unable to use their legs around the rope to push themselves up. Mr. Potts rolled his eyes and called us all girls that day.

Mr. Jones, our seventh-grade geography teacher, proved to be a case study in abnormal psychology. Kids called him Jonesy. A petite man in his forties and a dapper dresser, he was never without a jacket, vest, and tie. He'd stand at the door to greet us with a smile. When the bell rang, he closed the door and assumed his alter ego.

As he pulled down the shade to cover the window in the door, his smile faded. A sadistic military training instructor emerged. On the first day of school he stated, "Before you complete my classes you will know every country in the world." He held a long wooden pointer, unfurled the shiny Hammond wall-mounted world map and slapped it, "smack," with the stick to make his point.

"Furthermore," he said, "to help you in this endeavor, I employ a tool I made myself in our wood shop, called the convincer. It will provide you with the attention you may require to focus on your studies."

He then produced the biggest paddle I had ever seen. It

needed two hands to swing. He said, "Today, the first day of class, you'll receive a love tap from the convincer." Both boys and girls endured a not-so-gentle tap on the buttocks. It took a good minute before I could sit again!

I did learn all the countries by spring. The last day of class, Mr. Jones had the convincer cut up into hundreds of pieces. He gave each of us a section to take home to remember him.

When the bell sounded ending a period, Dr. B., our principal, entered the hallway opposite his office to supervise students passing. He was a lanky, large-framed man often seen carrying a Bible. We had a nickname for him too: "The Beak." He slicked his dark hair back severely, further revealing his thin, hooked nose, which made his face appear birdlike. We figured he was a deacon because he would often give a brief sermon on morality in assembly.

After I graduated from high school, I heard he had been convicted of embezzling tens of thousands of dollars from the school district to cover his Las Vegas debts.

Junior high offered several vocational arts programs in eighth and ninth grade. I chose print shop. For several hours a week I busied myself setting type and helping operate the bulky equipment. The multi-ton printing press fascinated me, how it would open and close its jaws, smoothly inking the type and producing the "piece." I would place a blank sheet of paper or cardstock in it, and, as if by magic, the press transformed it into a bulletin, invitation, or newsletter. For me, print shop was the coolest place in school. In my ninth-grade yearbook, I said I wanted to be a printer.

At home, discussion of my academic future occasionally turned to college. My dad said, "You should go to college, but you've got to pull up your grades." I had little concept of university except I thought it must be very hard, and you had to be very smart. It didn't appeal to me.

Then I found out that I would have Miss Moore for ninth-grade English; nickname: "Mammy Moore." Some kids already knew about Miss Moore. They described her as a fat, tall, elderly, snow-white haired, overly emotional teacher who loved to read Shakespeare's *Julius Caesar* aloud. She would literally cry so hard that tears would stream down both cheeks. It was the highlight of her class that students would joke about, and bizarre, because it was said that no one understood what she read.

As usual, I was assigned to a desk in the back of the classroom, grateful I could stay out of sight. All year long we waited for the time when Miss Moore would be reading from *Julius Caesar*. We weren't disappointed. She would ultimately tackle the job in the most theatrical fashion possible in her stark classroom. She rolled her head and pranced up and down the aisles between our desks, gesturing for emphasis. It was quite a performance. Some of the kids giggled and made faces behind her back.

One day, she spoke even louder than usual when she read. Tears formed and began to flow. Unlike some of the others, I didn't find it funny, but kind of sad. When I looked into her misty eyes, I saw something I had never seen in a teacher before, passion. I didn't know reading could affect you that way. She stopped near my desk and asked the class a question based on what she had just read. Time stood still.

Many students looked away to avert her piercing blue eyes as she looked out over her half lenses which were fastened with a shiny silver chain to her ears. She waited. For the first time that year, I raised my hand and told her what I thought.

The room went quiet. She just stood there mute, while glancing around the class at the kids. I began to regret saying anything.

Then, bam! She snapped her book closed and came closer. "Kenneth, that was excellent. I've asked that question for many years. You're the first person not only to answer, but to remind us that Shakespeare offered more than one interpretation for his audience. Wonderful. Did you hear that, class?"

I was so embarrassed. I slid down in my seat. I can't remember another thing Miss Moore said that afternoon. Her comments repeated themselves in my head even as I made my way home. What if I wasn't so dumb after all? No teacher had ever hinted I might be smart. From that day on, Miss Moore would beam at me as I entered her classroom. Somehow, she convinced me to change my opinion of myself and the importance of school.

There have been many times over the years I would think back on that day in English class while preparing for an examination. I never saw her again after I left junior high.

~

Those memories, and more, creep back as I thumb through my 1958 junior high school yearbook. It's hard to believe it's survived all my moves. When I finish looking at the photos, I'll turn once more to the inside of the cover and reread messages classmates and teachers wrote that last day of ninth grade. Some are fading, but Miss Moore's is clear: "It was a pleasure to have you in my class."

So, Miss Moore, it's time for me to correct my oversight. Even though it's hopelessly and inexcusably overdue, this missive is dedicated to you. Thank you for recognizing potential in me that no other teacher saw. Your words and caring smile enabled me to find a measure of confidence when I've needed it most. I've never forgotten you!

# Lady Ted and Beisbol

## *David Feldman*

In the 1950s, Tucson became a great town for baseball, especially because the Cleveland Indians arrived every year for spring training. But the real hotbed was 60 miles south, just over the border. The Mexicans called it beisbol.

The Tucson Cowboys played in the Class C Arizona-Texas League. To me, as a fledgling reporter, it proved fascinating for two reasons: A woman nicknamed "Ted" and a Cuban-born pitcher named Wenceslao O'Reilly Gonzales.

Ted, multi-talented, had been a journalism professor at the University of Southern California, a sports writer, and was a fierce protector of Papago Indian rights. (The Papagos are now called the Tohono O'odham people.)

She also helped a play-by-play radio announcer cover the local team by phoning in end-of-the-inning results on away games. The announcer then re-created the ballgame with sound effects and his dialogue. One of his favorite sayings, when someone hit a home run: "That ball's bleeding all the way to the fence."

Ted got her nickname (she was really Elizabeth) because women sportswriters were a no-no at that time. By using Ted in her newspaper byline, she got published. And she wrote as well as, if not better than, most of us males.

Ted's husband, who played second base for the Cowboys, was Indian — the first of his tribe to graduate from college. Ted spent many of her days driving through the sprawling Papago Indian Reservation outside Tucson, collecting handmade baskets and arranging for them to be sold at high-end shops, with every bit of the money going back to the basket weavers. She never took a penny. If she had been a Roman Catholic, I'd have nominated her for sainthood.

There are two towns named Nogales — one in Arizona, the

other just across the border in Sonora, Mexico. The first time the Tucson Cowboys played in Nogales, Sonora, it was a big deal. As a sportswriter, I was sent to cover it, and Ted was on hand to help re-create the game. Thousands of Mexicans turned out to see their team tangle with the *Americanos*. Special buses were run to the ballpark.

My wife, Betty, and I parked behind one of those special buses—far enough back so that we were legally parked. Come the end of the ballgame, we found that a special bus had backed into our beloved 1949 Chevrolet.

It was close to midnight, but we figured we'd better report it to the Mexican police. At the police station, with its single naked lightbulb hanging down, Lieutenant Jaime Urquidez took our report. Then we all went to the scene of the crime, where Jaime measured how high off the street our car was damaged.

He used his knee as the yardstick, proclaiming the damage to be "one hanspan and four feengers" above his knee. Strictly scientific police work.

Next stop, the downtown bus depot, where he planned to determine which bus was guilty. He used his flashlight and found scratches on a rear bumper that were exactly "one hanspan and four feengers" above his knee. He told the bus manager they were to blame, and that we were to be paid whatever it cost to fix the Chevrolet.

The car being drivable, we returned to Tucson. Next day, we had the Chevy repaired, at a cost of forty-six dollars.

A day later, we ventured to Nogales, Sonora, to collect our forty-six dollars. The main bus yard wasn't downtown, but four miles out of town. It seemed to be inside what looked like a volcano with the top shaved off, with the manager's office twenty steps up. Up we went, and showed the manager inside our repair bill. He looked at it, then—without a word—he climbed the next fifty-two steps to the top and disappeared down the other side.

"We'll never see him again," Betty said. "Let's just go on home."

I waited twenty minutes, then climbed to the top and down the other side. I spied another office. The manager didn't smile when he saw me, but I showed him the repair bill again. He counted out forty-six ragged American one-dollar bills and handed them to me. I thanked him in my halting Spanish, managed the steps up and then down, and we got out of town, thankful for the diligent police work by Lieutenant Jaime Urquidez.

~

Then there was Wenceslao O'Reilly Gonzales, the Cuban-born pitcher, whose name fascinates me to this day. He played with the Ciudad Juarez Indios, with his very first season, 1951, as his best. In those days, pitchers often went all nine innings, and there were a few twenty-game winners around. But thirty-game winners?

That first year, Wenceslao won thirty-two games.

We thought he'd be a natural for the big leagues. At 6 feet one, 165 pounds, he threw the ball incredibly hard.

Alas, Wenceslao O'Reilly Gonzalez pitched only two innings in the majors. He made it to the Washington Senators roster in 1955, and very early in the season he was called in as a reliever in the seventh inning. The Senators were being clobbered by the New York Yankees, 13-1. Wenceslao's season total for his two innings: He allowed six hits, six runs, and gave up three walks. That was it for Wenceslao. Back to playing in Mexico.

So he didn't shine in the majors. I prefer to remember him for his thirty-two win season, and especially for that wonderful name.

# My Regrets to the Heidelberg Class of '63

## *Robert Gilberg*

**Weather for Tiffin, Ohio, June 22, 2018: warm, humid and thundershowers.**

Gil, Gilly, Gilby! Why did I leave you and go down to Columbus? Simple, I had to get away from those nicknames that somehow followed me from New Bremen to Tiffin! Funny about that; I'm sure I never mentioned them.

But the truth is that Dr. Stinchcomb's physics classes and labs revealed that I liked electrical stuff: stuff like electrons, and magnetic and electric fields, and other sparky things. OMG, how did I miss that all through high school? It must have been the good doctor connecting with me in a way that our high school basketball coach/physics teacher, Mr. Shauck, never could, with his X's and O's approach to explaining atomic theory that had me wondering if it was a fast break or a carbon atom in that confusing diagram on the blackboard.

Or maybe he hated me for missing those game-tying free throws and it showed up in my test scores? Never figured it out— especially the physics thing. But somehow, thanks to Dr. Stinchcomb, I decided I should be an engineer and live with electrons and circuits and techy stuff, and OSU had engineering degrees. So, it wasn't you guys and girls, it was the call of science!

And I couldn't sing. Seemed everyone else at the 'berg could sing like angels. I had to slink away when some of you would break into a beautiful choral number and look at me, wondering why I wasn't singing. I'd slip back to my room and turn my little seven-tube radio on to some rock-a-billy station and hope no passing upperclass man would hear Jerry Lee Lewis's "Great Balls

139

of Fire" slithering out from under my door. What with Heidelberg's focus on choral and religious music, banishment was a real possibility. (Rock and roll was okay at Ohio State with all the lowbrows down there, though.)

Enough of my excuses. I just want to say that I remember the friends I made in one year at Heidelberg better than nearly all of those in my four more years at Ohio State. I'm not bashing OSU in saying that; it's just that the 'berg is a friendlier place than OSU's 35,000 (in the '60s) students ever could be. But the OSU football and basketball teams in those years were something else: Lucas, Havlicek, Bobby Knight(!!!), and Siegfried on the hardwood, and Matt Snell, Paul Warfield, and Bob Ferguson in the 'shoe. And Woody stalking along the sidelines! You'd all have to admit the Buckeyes were serious stuff compared to the 'berg's Student Princes athletic teams.

I want to remember two unforgettable characters from our times together. My roommate and drinking buddy Marv Jacobs is the first. I still remember waking up on most mornings to the "aroma" of Marv's first Lucky Strike cigarette of the day: Marv, sitting on the edge of the bed in his underwear, skinny legs dangling to the floor, wild hair looking like Nick Nolte's in "A Walk in the Woods" (without the beard), uttering his first curse words of the day.

"But wait, Marv, it could be a good day!"

But no, he was already into reviling Prof McKenzie for an insulting red line on his latest, genius paper for an — according to Dr. McKenzie — imaginary connection he'd made between Byron and Homer with some obscure, alleged Byron utterances only Marv apparently knew of. Or, on another day, it could have been his interpretation of a dispute between other giants of the classical world I'd never even heard of. And he was a freshman — like me — just out of high school?

Well, I can't tell you how surprised I was to recently find that he'd spent the latter part of his career at Ganado College, an unheard-of, minor school on the Navajo Nation in God-knows-where Arizona. And I had him figured for Harvard, or even Oxford. Go figure! Maybe he went there to reinterpret Carlos Castañeda?

140

The other classmate I want to recognize is Jimmy Beil. Jimmy was a music major who took me under his wing and lifted me out of my rock-a-billy world and flew me to his world of '50s/'60s modern jazz. From "Be-Bop-a-Lula" to "Lullaby of Birdland," so to speak. George Shearing and Errol Garner were his idols, and I never came back to earth after hearing "Misty" one night in his room. And Jimmy could play their music, too. I loved tagging along with him to various venues around Tiffin when he was playing piano for the bar and dinner patrons. I didn't know people like Jimmy existed in my ordinary-people world — and then I met you wonderful folks when I came to Tiffin.

Oh, I almost forgot, there is one more. My dear friend — how could I forget him — Mike Carnahan. I hardly knew him when we first found ourselves in the boys third-floor shower together. He was already showering when I walked in, removed my shower cover-up and joined him in the wide-open, fits fifteen — or more if we really liked each other — shower room. He looked at me, for the first time — fully naked in his presence — and exclaimed, "Gilly, what great legs you have!"

I didn't know whether to feel good about that or start worrying. "Ummm . . . thanks, Mike." Mike was a big guy . . . .

"I mean, you look like you're a runner. Are you coming out for track?"

*Whew.* "No. I've never run track, Mike. New Bremen didn't have track."

"Well, maybe you should come out anyway. You're got really good legs."

There it was again, *really good legs.* Did he have a leg fetish — or other? *I really wanted to take it as a compliment, but . . .* "Must be because of riding my bike so much in my high school years. You know that can do it, too."

"We don't have enough guys coming out for the team. Think about it."

"So, you're a track and field guy?"

"Yeah, but I'm a slug, so I run cross country because it's more endurance than speed. But I think you'd be good in the mile."

"The mile!" The thought made me want to throw up. I hated running. Hated it ever since my futile years on the basketball team

141

and running the steps throughout our three-story high school, or the gut-wrenching wind-sprints *after practice ended.* "No Mike, thanks for the suggestion, but I'm going to have to concentrate on my studies."

He looked at me like I was copping out—which I probably was—but he didn't let it bother him. Later that fall he even rode his bicycle back to Tiffin from Rochester ,New York, stopping by my home to meet my family, which added two hundred miles to his trip returning to school from Thanksgiving vacation. And he liked "my" legs?

Oh, and by the way, I think he did only care about my legs as runner's legs; as you probably know, he married his wonderful Heidelberg girlfriend.

I could go on and on talking about you exceptional people, but this would turn into a book rather than a little letter. So, I'll move on to some final memories I want to share with you. Freshman English Lit with Professor McKenzie and our first writing assignment: the one in the first or second week of classes when he asked for—demanded is a better description—a paper of 500 words—topic of our choice—due by the next Monday? Other than having had to write 500 times, *"I will never show dirty pictures to Linda again"* after getting caught in fourth grade doing just that with a *National Geographic* "centerfold" picture of a native African woman, I'd never written anything longer than five or six lines. With my crude cursive back then, which has only gotten worse with age—thank God for word processors—it took a whole pad of yellow lined tablet paper.

Pencil and paper were toxic stuff to me for the rest of my school years. Anyway, the paper Professor McKenzie returned to me looked like he'd used a three-inch paint brush to apply his comments. There was more red on my humiliated little three-page paper than lead from my scribbled Eberhard Faber No. 2 ramblings. I think his concluding comment was something like: "And what made you want to come to college?"

And that leads to the second memory I want to share: Remember the time we all had to take an "aptitude" test, administered by the deans of men and women, with follow-up interviews and come-to-Jesus moments when we all found out what we were really cut out for? I discovered—was told—that the reason I was placed on earth was that I'd be a really good *farmer*— or *auto mechanic*! In other words, "You'll never be an engineer or scientist—or writer. Forget it!" *Should I ask for my tuition back?*

I miss you all and am very sorry not to have been able to be with you on this occasion. Maybe another time—our 60th? In the meantime, read a good book: (Robert Gilberg Books on Amazon, or www.tamborrelwriter.com)

Bob (Gilly) Gilberg
San Diego, California

(PS: sorry about your weather for the class of '63's 55th reunion today, good people. I can assure you weather didn't have anything to do with my inability to join you—trust me.)

# What's in a Name…Second Generation

## Francisco Cota-Robles Newton
### *(Frank Newton)*

My mother not only passed on to me the rather dramatic (or melodramatic, if you will) family history of how she received her given name, she also related the curious circumstances that led to my own given name, Francis.

I was actually supposed to be named Peter, she explained; and indeed, the family referred to me as Peter until shortly before my birth. The choice for this name rests entirely upon the insistence of my older sister, Flo. She, in turn, got this notion from a rather laudable habit of my father.

When Flo and my brother were toddlers, my father made a point of reading a story to them at bedtime. And although I am sure my father would have much preferred reading a different story each night, Flo became absolutely captivated with "The Tale of Peter Rabbit." So night after night, when my father would ask "What story do you want to hear tonight?" Flo and my brother adamantly chanted "Peter Rabbit, Peter Rabbit!" Of course, my father would dutifully acquiesce.

As an aside, I have noticed over the years that this childhood quirk about hearing or seeing the same story incessantly was not unique to my sister. My own daughter must have watched "Little Mermaid" no less than 500 times; and now in the latest iteration, my little grandson must have watched "Happy Feet" 780 times until he finally moved on to watching "Cars" endlessly.

In any case, because of this curious obsession of my sister, when my mother became pregnant with me, and my father asked my siblings, "What should we name your new little brother?" it was virtually inevitable that they would insistently chant in unison "Peter... Peter... Peter." So it came to be that my given name would be Peter (ostensibly, I was to be the wascally wabbit of the Newton clan).

But then, fate played a hand, so to speak. It was mid-November, a month before I was due upon this earth, and the Newton family packed up and set out from San Diego to spend Thanksgiving with my mother's family in Tucson.

Now, in those days (the mid-1940s) no sane individual drove across the desert sands of El Centro, Yuma, and Casa Grande in the middle of the day. Because cars could easily overheat (even in the winter) crossing this arid expanse, all reasonably thoughtful and experienced drivers would only drive in the cool of night. And that, indeed, is what my father chose to do in that November of 1946.

Being such a long and tedious drive across the desert flats in the dead of night, my father would always play the radio to help keep himself alert. And as the family passed through El Centro and entered into the desolate dunes this side of the Colorado River, an urgent police announcement suddenly blared from the car radio. "A dangerous convict has just escaped from the Yuma prison. Motorists are advised to not pick up any hitchhikers along the highway!" And to add a bit of helpful information for wary motorists, the radio announcer said that the escaped convict's name was Peter Newton.

Well, as you might well imagine, that right there put a kibosh on any plans to name me Peter... anything but that! No felonious convicts would be allowed within the august Newton clan.

My father stepped in at this point to insist that he, himself alone, would choose the name of his incipient son. And as he was newly converted to Catholicism, and as his favorite saint happened to be St. Francis of Assisi, it was ordained that my name henceforward would be Francis...not Peter.

As a concluding footnote to this tale, right at this point across America the name Francis became painfully onerous to any little boy because of the release of a string of MGM wartime comedies starring Donald O'Connor and titled "Francis the Talking Mule." Suffice it to say, "Francis" has never been my preferred name; just plain "Frank" will do, thank you very much.

146

# The Pianist

## *Frank Primiano*

Cliburn is dead. So are Horowitz and Rubinstein. And I'm not going to be replacing any of them, despite my family's hopes and dreams. I can't say my parents didn't try to prepare me to assume the mantle of greatness, conspiring to force me to endure, in my formative years, endless piano lessons.

But I resisted, and successfully foiled the plot.

~

People say, and rightly so, that things were different in the old days — often implying a simpler, better time. As I recall my youth in the middle years of the last century, one situation that remains fixed in my mind as being different, but not necessarily better, was the ubiquitous presence of flies.

When my family lived in South Philly, milk was delivered to our door by a milkman in a horse-drawn wagon. Our trash, garbage, and ashes were collected in horse-drawn rigs carrying removable steel bins. Chunks of decaying debris and a stream of foul-smelling, grey liquid escaped the rusted-out bottoms and ruptured seams of these containers and found their way into curbside gutters, betraying the route of the garbage men days after the event.

Fishmongers pushing homemade, wooden carts with large, spoked wheels worked our block. They beheaded and gutted fish to order. Inevitably, heads and tails, and fins and scales, fell from the carts onto the same surface upon which we kids roller-skated and played stickball.

The open-air distribution of food, the use of animals for transportation, and the unrestrained roaming of canine and feline pets led to the chronic presence of decomposing organic material in neighborhoods of tightly packed row homes. The city cleaned the streets infrequently. As a result, flies were everywhere on hot summer days. Since we had no air conditioning, they entered our house through open windows ineffectively protected by removable screens, or past our screen doors when we opened and closed them.

Flies ruled our lives. As a countermeasure, twisted strips of sticky flypaper were suspended discreetly out of sight in upscale stores, but shamelessly out in the open in gas stations, garages, bars, and barbershops. The image of a shiny, tan, helical, paper ribbon, randomly covered with black bumps reminiscent, at a distance, of so many raisins, hanging over steaks in a butcher shop, is a vision of Americana not usually resurrected by the glorifiers of nostalgia.

Inside our house we dealt with flies in a more straightforward manner … with a flyswatter. But this had its downside. My mother revolted at the sight of a splattered fly on the refrigerator, or fly fragments mashed into the butter in its dish on the kitchen table. To accommodate her, Dad developed a way of catching flies by hand. I watched him and tried unsuccessfully to copy his technique.

At last he gave me a formal lesson. "Wait till the fly lands. Cup your hand slightly, and move it toward the motionless target. The fly'll take off if you move suddenly. But if you go ever so slowly, you can get within an inch or two of it." He was demonstrating on an unsuspecting quarry that had landed near his right hand.

"When you're that close, sweep your hand quickly over the spot the fly is on. At the same instant, close your hand. You'll grab it almost every time." His hand whizzed over the fly's resting place in a blink, and, sure enough, he nabbed the bugger. I smiled.

He went on. "At this point, you can crush it by tightening your grip—that's messy—or you can capture it alive. Slip the forefinger of your other hand into your fist to hold the fly immobile. Then you can open your hand. Use your thumb and forefinger to pick up the fly." My dad performed the second method as he described it.

"Your prisoner can then be squashed in a piece of paper and dumped into the wastebasket," which he did, before washing his hands. "The trick," he continued, "besides sneaking up slowly, is

148

to just graze the spot on which the fly rests, so it can't slip underneath as your hand makes its move for the catch."

"Okay. Got it," I said, ready to find a fly to pick on.

"Not so fast," he said, extending an index finger. "What I just told you is all well and good if the fly is on a nice, smooth surface like a table or a sink or a chair. But what if it's on something rough like cement, or on a pile of mushy garbage?"

"What?" I wanted to know.

"Then, brushing against what it's perched on can be painful, or, at best, messy. So, be careful and try to anticipate what might go wrong."

These last words were indelibly seared into my brain by an incident involving one of life's mandatory rituals—at least in our house. One that, eventually, I was deemed old enough to participate in, and which I learned to hate: music lessons.

~

My mother decided that, since we had a piano, I would be forever grateful to her in my adulthood if, in my youth, she provided me the opportunity to develop my musical talents. My two younger brothers, when they came of age, were, in their turn, also subjected to the opportunity to become grateful. The problem with this master plan, of course, was that it assumed that we had at least *some* musical talent to develop. Not so.

My creative cultural inclinations lie in art—to be specific, drawing—not music. I am convinced that I am tone-deaf, and I think my brothers are, too. I originally approached those eighty-eight keys with enthusiasm, as a challenge, spurred on by a desire to play as well as my mother. But all too soon the lessons, and associated practicing, turned into agonizing chores. I had very little ability and, consequently, less interest. The situation was exacerbated by the teaching style of my piano teacher, Aunt Josephine, my father's older sister.

Aunt Josephine was a professional piano teacher who subscribed to what I imagined to be the "classical school" of instruction. Whereas a friend up the street, who was also taking lessons, learned songs from the Hit Parade, I was forced to practice only chords and finger exercises every day after school, and on weekends. If nothing else, studying piano provided me a theoretical physics lesson in relativistic time warping. That is, how a fifteen-minute practice session can be perceived to last an entire afternoon.

My aunt was my piano teacher because she offered my father a deal he couldn't refuse: a one-hour lesson for one dollar. This had all the hallmarks of a conspiracy. The lessons were at my aunt's row house in South Philly. I went every Tuesday, all year round. There was no reprieve when school let out for vacation.

In the lingering twilight of hot, muggy, summer days, when I could be outside playing with my friends, Dad drove me to my aunt's after dinner. I think that no small part of his motivation for accepting her offer was a side benefit. He could watch Uncle Miltie and Bishop Sheen with my Uncle Paul on the eight-inch, circular screen of my uncle's Dumont TV. We didn't have a television at home. While they sat in the relative cool of the living room, I'd slowly drag myself upstairs to my aunt's sweltering, second-floor piano room to endure an hour of drudgery demonstrating my lack of virtuosity at playing unending repetitions of scales, and trying to read sheet music.

On one such exceptionally hot, stagnant evening, Aunt Josephine opened the room's solitary, screened window, raising the lower half as high as possible. A single, small, oscillating fan, turned on full blast, provided the hint of a breeze. As I sat beside her on the piano bench, I wasn't in the most receptive mood to have my musical horizons expanded. I looked for any way to distract my teacher from the task at hand. What came to mind was my old standby: casual inquiries about her health.

"How was your day, Aunt Josephine? How have you been feeling?" This usually killed about ten minutes. One of her joys in life was describing in detail, to anyone who would listen, her present and past, real and imagined, aches and pains.

"How's Uncle Paul doing?" Hearing about her husband's ailments was good for another five minutes.

Eventually, I ran out of my routine ploys. The moment of truth arrived. I had to start the lesson. As I struck the first note, flat of course, one of the several flies buzzing in slow arcs around the solitary ceiling lightbulb landed on the sheet music. My aunt

150

brushed it away.

"These flies are a pain, aren't they?" I was quick to create a non-musical interlude, no matter how short.

"Yes," my aunt said. "They're everywhere today."

A moment later, another joined my fingers on the keyboard. I shooed it. A more persistent one circled my aunt's head. She kept waving her hand back and forth to keep it off her face. As I struggled to spread my thumb and little finger across an octave, I noticed through the corner of my eye that, during a momentary lapse in her vigilance, the insect landed on the top of her head. I turned for a closer look. It was a large, shiny, blue-green house fly, sitting there, cocky as a rooster at dawn, staring back at me with both multifaceted eyes.

I said, "Hold still, Aunt Josephine, there's a fly on your head. I'll get it so it won't bother you anymore."

"No," she protested, "you'll squash it on me."

"I won't. My dad showed me how to catch it in my hand."

"I've seen him catch flies that way. You'll grab my hair and hurt me."

"Don't worry. I'll grab only the fly."

During this exchange, and my aunt's head-bobbing and weaving, hand-waving and protestations, the fly defiantly held its ground, unwilling to relinquish squatter's sovereignty.

Eventually, my repeated assurances wore my aunt down enough that she consented to give me a single try, probably because she realized I wouldn't focus on the lesson until I took at least one shot at the little nuisance. Even so, she kept whimpering, "Be careful. Please don't hurt me."

I stood and slowly crept behind her. I approached the target with my slightly cupped right hand, arm cocked for action. I repeated in a whisper, "Don't worry, I'll get 'im. Don't worry, I'll get 'im …"

My hand was within two inches of the brazen bug nestled comfortably on Aunt Josephine's thinning, gray, neatly curled hair. I swung with all my might, just grazing those few silver strands upon which the fly rested. I didn't hook my aunt's hair as she feared. Nevertheless, her head snapped to the side as I nearly yanked her from the piano bench.

She let out a scream and a hail of Italian profanity the likes of which I had never heard before. I didn't understand a word of it, but I knew it was major league, old-world fire and brimstone. Simultaneously, I let out a howl and some choice phrases of my own.

I caught the fly. But I didn't realize my aunt was wearing a nylon hair net. As I brushed the spot on her head upon which the fly was perched, my little finger snagged the invisible netting. My follow-through just about decapitated the poor woman. For my part, I almost lost a pinkie.

"What's going on up there?" my father and uncle called in unison from the parlor below. As I doubled over, grasping my aching finger with my left hand, still clutching the fly with the other fingers of my clenched right fist, I didn't know whether to grimace in pain, or start laughing at what happened.

I implored my aunt in a whisper, "Please don't tell my father. He'll kill me. I'm sorry. Really. Here, we'll finish the lesson. I'll be good. I swear. Are you okay? Let me rub your neck. Please don't tell him. Please. Please."

She considered me for a moment while turning her head from one side to the other. The realization must have dawned on her that she had me right where she wanted me. Pulling off the hair net hanging from her ear, rearranging her hair, and sitting up straight, she reclaimed her dignity. At last, she shouted downstairs, "Nothing happened. Everything's all right."

I retrieved the damned fly from my fist, wrapped it in a tissue, and smashed that sucker flat. After washing my hands in the bathroom, I returned to the piano room.

"Let me see that finger," Aunt Josephine said with no rancor in her voice. After a careful examination, we decided my chances of playing at Carnegie Hall hadn't been greatly diminished by this incident.

I finished the lesson feeling remorse and somewhat sorry for this not-quite-frail old lady, whom I could have seriously maimed. I felt nothing for the fly.

On the bright side, my aunt had an actual injury to chronicle to her neighbor ladies when they got together the next morning over coffee. As for me, I could count on an additional ten, or more,

152

wasted minutes during the preliminaries to future lessons.

Thus went my career as a pianist. The lessons continued. However, with my adroit maneuvering and skillful time management, they were completely ineffective. I finally quit when I was old enough, and brave enough, to stand up for myself.

But I continued practicing—not playing the piano—catching flies. I assumed my portion of the effort to keep their population inside our house at a manageable level. My father seemed happy to share his responsibilities as fly warden, but he never came right out and said so. He also never thanked me for saving him fifty-two dollars a year, with which, after a couple of years, we were able to buy our own TV.

# Solidarity

## *Ruth L. Wallace*

She had been told the drug would cause her hair to fall out. *How could I stand it*? she thought. *How could I BE? WHO will I be?* She had no wish to die. She had no wish to die bald, for sure. She had to take the drug.

She knew she was plain: her hair was her pride. It was red, a shade that glowed in the sun. She loved it pulled up, let down, and wound in a coil. Her hair made her who she was. *Without my hair, how will the other kids even know who I am?*

There were wigs, she knew. Red wigs, too. Red wigs that were straight, those with curls, long or short—lots of choices, she knew. But she just could not wear a wig. That was that.

The day came to go back to school. It was too warm for a scarf or a hat. With a slow tread and overwhelming dread, she opened the classroom door. First a shock, then a smile, then a burst of laughter. Her full heart melted and dripped out as a tear. All the heads in the room were bald! Bald was cool . . . she was who she was.

There is a certain enthusiasm in liberty, that makes human nature rise above itself, in acts of bravery and heroism.

—*Alexander Hamilton*

# Papa, Can You Hear Me?

*(In memory of my beloved father.)*

## *Dora Klinova*

My dear father, my glorious light, where are you? Where are your dark brown eyes that glittered with laughing sparks when you played with me? Where is your voice that said to me so many tender words? Where are your strong hands that threw me up to the ceiling so easily?

Where is your robust, graceful body? A cruel, unjust war took you away from me. You were only thirty-two and incredibly talented. Everything I can be proud of in my personality I received from your genes. You left for the war when I was a baby; I barely remember you. My daughter is now older than you were. Only your warm touch — the sense of comfort, happiness, and entire protection that radiated from you — are stored somewhere in my consciousness. My memory holds elusive feelings that I had something great in the very beginning of my life and lost this treasure forever. Subconsciously, hopelessly, continuously I still seek it.

Nevertheless, I am already a grandmother. I miss you. Somewhere deep inside, we, covered by gray hair and wrinkles, are still little children who long for caresses that we didn't receive in childhood. We carry this vague anguish for a lifetime.

The government never informed us that you were killed in the war. They just sent a letter that you had been reported missing. For a long time we believed that you were alive somewhere. When the war was over, I was a small child; I didn't remember your face. Longing for you, I did my own search to bring you back. I walked in the streets and followed every man in a military uniform who looked more or less like you, asking him if he remembered me, his little daughter. Without his family that the war cut off from him, one soldier was shocked and moved to tears when a little girl appeared near, looking with hope at him. He hugged me, kissed me, saying many warm words that he probably kept for his own baby. I felt sure that I had finally found you. I ran to Mama and announced that my search was successful and she should wait for you tonight.

Mama told me your story. Your commander gave you permission to escort us, your family, to the place where we were supposed to stay. You put us in a truck and we rushed away from the bombs. Suddenly we heard a loud shout: "Stop! Wait!"

Another truck overtook us, an officer from your military unit ran out, saying that he must go in our truck instead of you because his family was somewhere in a nearby city on our way. He had no written order. You believed him; in fact he was actually your friend.

Without a word you gave your place in our truck to him. With this you gave away your life, your chance to survive. You waved to us and left. You rushed back to the Army unit. You rushed to be killed.

That officer escorted his family as far away as possible. He was not in a hurry; he returned late with many excuses. At that time, he could find thousands of excuses. You came back to your military unit first. First come; first served. Instead of that officer, they sent you to the hottest place on the front.

Many years later Mama met that man. He told her about your sorrowful death. You were in a construction battalion that built bridges for the retreating Red Army and then blasted the same bridges to cut off the Germans. You didn't have any experience with dynamite. You were an intellectual, handsome man with a brilliant soul; blowing up bridges was not for you. You didn't have a chance to learn how to do it and were killed in the very beginning of your dangerous service. Your body couldn't even be found.

You were killed in 1941. We didn't have your picture, and I forgot your image completely. I thought that I never would have your photo. Almost sixty years passed before you came to me again. In 1999 when I visited Israel, my cousin Anechka, your sister Bronya's daughter, showed me an album of old pictures.

"Here is your father!" She held out a small, tattered picture to

160

me. The top of your head and half your face was pulled off and lost.

You see, my dear Papa, it just happened that more than half a century after your death, I flew from America to another part of the globe to find your real image, actually just a part of it. I brought this piece of your photo to the United States. Nobody would restore it. Finally I convinced one specialist: "If you have half of the face, the computer can make the rest. Try, please. I will pay you anyway even if nothing comes of this attempt."

The miraculous achievement of the computer's technique helped to restore the picture. They made you a modern American haircut with short blond hair. Your head looked like a hedgehog. I argued with the photographer. I told him that you had soft, silky, brown wavy hair. I remember the touch of your hair. When you put me on your shoulder, I grabbed and held it. Probably it was painful to you; nevertheless you laughed with me and danced.

The computer man changed your hair. I paid him well and was not sure who was in the photo. I have known only one living person who might remember you: your cousin Zhenya, who now lives in New York. I put your computer-made image in an envelope and sent it to Zhenya without any explanation. She called me immediately.

"Where did you find this picture? Nobody has it. Yes, it is Simon. Yes, it is your father."

"Did you recognize him?" I asked her.

"No, I don't remember him. I was 13 years old. But he looks exactly like all our brothers. It is he; I am sure."

So, you are with us now, my dear papa. I enlarged your portrait and put it in the bedroom in front of my eyes. When I awake, I can say to you, "Good morning!"

Your sister Bronya is no longer alive. She found her final resting place in a holy land, in Tel Aviv. I visited her grave and put flowers on it, in spite of a Jewish tradition that requires stones on the grave instead of flowers. I put some stones also. I respect traditions.

I cannot bring flowers to you, my dear papa. You don't have a grave. You blew up on a mine. I don't know your date of birth or death. I just put your name together with Mama's name in the

161

synagogue and I pray during the kaddish for your eternal peace.

Mama died in 1990. She had a hard life without you. Did you meet her in Heaven? If not yet, please, find her.

You were so thirsty for knowledge. In those hungry years in the Soviet Union when everybody strived for food, you studied and became a toolmaker. It was not enough for you; you wanted to deepen your education. You took a correspondence course at Leningrad's Industrial University. I am not surprised that in my mature age I still continue to study and cannot imagine my life without it. You gave me that thirst for knowledge.

Can you imagine, your little girl grew up, became a mature woman, had the nerve to come to America, the greatest country in the world, and dared to write stories in a foreign English language? It was hard to do what I did, Papa. I never would have been able to make it without help. Did you lead me? Probably you did; at least I know for sure that your genes pushed me to absorb knowledge endlessly during all my life and even now, when I should be retired.

Papa, I created many stories and made a book from them. American people like the book. Perhaps it came out really well. Please, welcome my book to the world and help the readers to find the most important essential thoughts I wanted to tell them. Papa, I also wrote two other books. In English! Yes, I did it! I do not know how, but I made it! I am definitely your girl, with your genes!

Please, lead my books in the ocean of American literature and don't let them be lost.

Again and again I look at your picture. I am not a young woman anymore; I am advanced in years; you are a boy; you can be my son, maybe, even a grandson, but you are my father. There is nothing boyish in your image except your ears. They framed your face with so youthful vigor that it seems they don't belong to you. Your neck is strong and solid and holds your head firmly. I have the same shape of face, only yours is smooth and mine is covered with wrinkles. My forehead, eyebrows, cheeks, chin, and lips with dimpled upper lip look exactly like yours. We both have wide lips. There is a belief that wide lips represent kindness. Yes, you were so kind; and you know what? I consider myself also

162

kind. Thanks to you.

I don't see young happiness in your eyes; they look too serious for your age. If I would meet a person with such deep-thinking eyes, I would trust him immediately. Your face looks so open and wise.

God, dear God, why should people like this boy in the picture be dead? Why are so many bad people alive? Who makes this selection between human beings? There is no answer . . .

Barbra Streisand sings the song:

*Papa, can you hear me?*
*Papa, can you see me?*
*Papa, can you find me in the night?*
*Papa, are you near me?*
*Papa, can you help me not be frightened?*
*Looking at the skies*
*I seem to see a million eyes.*
*Which one are yours?*
*Papa, how I love you.*
*Papa, how I need you.*
*Papa, how I miss you*
*Kissing me goodnight.*

No, it is not a song. It is a prayer . . . I would like to add to it:

**May the beauty of your life shine forevermore, and may my life always bring honor to your memory, my immortal beloved.**

Papa, can you hear me?

# Hawaiian Trilogy

*Yvonne Nelson Perry*

### *Ke Keiki*
### (The Child)

The woman opened her eyes.

She watched the long shadows cast around the one-room shack by a stand of bamboo outside the window.

Next to her, nestled in *tapa* cloth, lay her newborn child.

She reached out and caressed the top of the infant's head, the thin patch of hair black like her own.

"My *keiki kane,* my son," the woman said. "You are finally here."

Afterbirth pains in her belly penetrated her groin. She slid a hand down over the slack skin of her stomach and felt the cloth wad between her legs. Slipping several fingers under the padding, she pulled them back from the wetness.

She stared at her red fingertips, then wiped them on her coverlet, leaving dark streaks on it.

Now, she grasped a corner of the baby's blanket and moved the child closer. Folding back the soft cover, she looked at the infant.

"I have seen you before," the woman said, smiling. "You are your father."

She put a cheek against the child's.

"Wake up, little one," she whispered. "Let me look into your eyes and see your soul." She touched the baby's eyelids, closed under moth-like brows.

The infant did not rouse.

The woman remembered the stillness of this child in her womb. She placed a hand on her son's chest, to feel his life.

His skin felt cool, like wet stones after rain.

Propped on one elbow, the woman pushed aside the baby's covering and drew him to her. She opened her *pa`u,* squeezed the tip of an enlarged breast between two fingers and put the hard nipple against the child's mouth.

The infant did not take hold of it.

She cupped her son's head in the palm of one hand and pressed his face against her breast.

He would not suckle.

Exhausted, the woman fell back onto her *lau hala* mat and closed her eyes.

Wind through the bamboo sounded like murmuring water, far away.

### *Keiki Kane*
### (The man)

The first hours of the night came, dimming the day's light.

A man entered the one-room shack.

Standing over the sleeping woman, he stared at the dark smears across her coverlet, then at the child beside her.

Kneeling, he eased the infant toward him. He wrapped the *tapa* around the baby, now colorless and cold to the touch.

The woman did not stir.

The man gathered up his son, rose to his feet and went out.

A stark-white moon hung over the beach palms.

The man stepped out of the darkness of the grove and placed an armful of *lau hala* leaves on the sand.

After he broke off thin branches from a nearby *hau* tree, he snapped them into short pieces. Squatting, he laid them out inches apart. Then, he picked up long lengths of *lau hana* and began to weave them back and forth, over and under the *hau.* Soon, he had created a small platform of leaves and tree limbs.

Standing, he clasped the crude raft to his chest. The jagged end of a stick raked across his chin, drawing blood. He ignored the deep scratch and proceeded to the water's edge. There, he put the raft on the wet sand and reentered the grove. He emerged moments later with a *tapa*-wrapped bundle in his arms.

166

He returned to the raft and placed the *tapa* roll upon it. Then, he bent over the mound and turned back the dark cloth to reveal the newborn's face, ashen in the moonlight. With one finger, he stroked the baby's cheeks.

Gusts of wind rushed across the stillness of the bay, the tide receding.

Shedding his clothes, the man pushed the raft into the sea, following it on his knees. When the water reached his waist, he rose and continued to guide the small craft forward. Soon, the water covered his shoulders and lapped against his chin. The cut on it stung from the salt wash.

The shrill cry of a plover, flying offshore, pierced the night.

The man released his hold on the raft and watched it drift away.

*Lele wai e,"* he said. "Water, do it quickly."

He stood motionless in the moonlight, until the horizon swallowed the burial platform, until the dawn surrounded him. Then, he turned his back on the empty sea and returned to shore.

## Ke Wahine
## (The Woman)

Dressed in a sarong-like *pa`u*, the woman shuffled down the dirt trail toward the sea. Her bare feet raised clouds of gray dust that hung in the early morning air.

At the end of the path, she stopped and stared back at the shack in the distance.

A Kona wind whipped around her and lashed at the surrounding palm trees.

"You took our *keiki kane,"* she shouted. Then, she bowed her head and whispered into the wind, "You took our son away."

The cry of a stray dog caused her swollen breasts to throb. She touched them and felt the wetness of her milk.

Now, the woman descended a footpath that wound its way through lantana to the beach below.

Stumbling over dead seaweed along the high tide mark, the woman fell to her knees. When she rose, she covered her nose and mouth against the stench of the soggy mass.

She stepped off the low pile of kelp onto a narrow band of sand, smooth and warm beneath her feet. She faced the calm sea and watched a rippling wave slide across the hard-packed sand, then slip back out, leaving behind a filigree of foam.

The woman took several steps and stood ankle-deep in the white froth. Glancing over her shoulder, she saw her footprints vanish as an incoming wave spread itself out on the beach.

She moved forward until water came up to her knees. Under her *pa`u*, she felt the light touch of jellyfish tentacles encircle her legs. Then, biting stings. She sucked in her breath from the pain and waded further out into the ocean.

The woman went on until only her head remained above water. She tasted the salt of the sea, and her tears.

The sand shifted under her.

Her heart pounded like a beaten drum.

She untied her *pa`u* and watched it drift away. Reaching up, she unpinned her long black hair. It floated, weightless, a dark shadow around her.

"Wait for me, my son," she cried out. "I go with you."

Her words pushed against each other until they joined together. The mournful wail ended in silence as the woman disappeared into the sea.

> *Naha ke haule, ke hale o ke aloha.*
> Broken by loss, the house of love.
> —Old Hawaiian proverb

# My Dad

## *Barbara Stout Sirignano*

It was June 3, 1987, in Pasadena, California. It was a beautiful day filled with cool breezes, bright blue skies, and fluffy white clouds. From our living room you could look up into the majestic San Gabriel Mountains. I was a Registered Nurse and had been studying cancer treatments at the City of Hope Cancer Institute in Duarte, California. At lunchtime I thought I would stop by the house and see my dad, who had been bedridden from cancer for most of the past six months.

I sat down on the brown, wooden chair that was next to his hospital bed and tossed off my shoes. As I stretched out my legs, I looked at Dad and suddenly realized that Dad was talking and making sense. He was the dad of 25 years ago, the one I knew growing up—the dad of my childhood. For the past several months Dad had been confused and disoriented and quite difficult. All of a sudden, in this hour he was bright, focused, and loving again. The dad I remembered from childhood was back!

He talked about his life and asked about mine, and we laughed together. I will never forget looking into his gorgeous blue eyes. Dad's blue eyes were like the blue in blue violets or like the blue in the sky over the ocean just before sunset. I will never forget the gift of that day.

For many years I had worked with dying patients, and I knew that people often resurrect just before they die, but I didn't see it at the time. Three days later Dad died and it was only after his death that I began to really learn about the man who took care of me for my entire life.

Albert Stout was born on Christmas Day in 1906 in Marble Hill, Georgia, a small railroad town that looked like the ghost towns in old western movies. The family lived in a small shack on a patch of dirt at the edge of town. Dad was the fifth of six

169

children, all born within 10 years of each other. The oldest was Lillian and then came Frank, Ralph, Harold, Albert, and the youngest was Marion. Albert's dad, Finnis (Frank) Stout, was an aggressive railroad man, and after the track was laid in Marble Hill, he moved the family to Springfield, Illinois, where he worked in a railroad yard.

It was October 10, 1910; dad was four when his mother, Mary Stout, stood before a grand jury and confessed to murdering the father of a two-year old child. Newspaper accounts of the day said that she stood outside of his dining room window in the garden and shot the man while he was feeding his baby dinner. Many felt that Mary confessed to protect her husband. Some felt that Mary had been told to confess to the murder for no jury would ever send a mother of six young children to prison. The victim, however, was well known and held a very important political position.

I believe that Mary Stout lied to protect her children. In 1910 if her husband had been found guilty of murder, the children would have been separated and sent to the poor house. Since Mary confessed there was no trial, and the real facts never emerged. Some of these facts are very interesting. One was that Finnis Stout, Mary's husband, was accused of another murder ten years earlier that ended in a mistrial. It was also significant that he worked only one mile from the scene of the murder and was working at that time; and of particular interest is that Finnis Stout also worked part time for Al Capone, who was a known enemy of the man who died. In the end Mary Stout, mother of Lillian 11, Frank 9, Ralph 7, Harold 6, Albert 4, and Marion 1 was sentenced to nine years in Joliet Prison.

While Mary was in prison, her sister, Ida, came to take care of the kids and never left. Dad and his brothers hated Ida and blamed her for the breakup of the family. Their father divorced Mary Stout while she was in prison and married Ida. Dad sometimes spoke about his father, noting that he was very mean and kept a very thick belt on the doorknob in the bedroom and used it frequently.

Over the years, the five Stout boys became known as the children of a murderer. They hated their father and hated their

170

new stepmother, too. It was said that they ran wild on the streets and were often in trouble, and each left home early at 12 or 13. Like their dad, they, too, worked for Al Capone. In 2004 I spoke to Mary Stout II, the daughter of Ralph Stout, Dad's second eldest brother. She said in a telephone conversation, "I never had any children of my own; I didn't want them to turn out like the Stout boys did." She did have a point.

In 1919, Mary Stout, my grandmother, without a husband was finally released from prison. She settled in Chicago to care for the two youngest boys, Albert (my dad), now 13, and Marion, now 10. It was, however, too late to make much difference. The damage was done. Both boys were always getting into trouble. In the end, three of the boys — Dad (Albert), Frank, and Marion — would spend many years in prison because of it. Dad never told me anything about his years in prison as he was one of the "silent generation" that never tells secrets. All he ever said about that time in his life was, "I was out of the country."

Dad served almost 20 years in prison and was released in 1942 because the United States needed men to fight in WWII. For Dad it was a new beginning, and he became a very successful pipe fitter who worked on large pipes and helped to build Clark Field in the Philippine Islands. Dad used to talk about the Philippines; he also said he had many children there.

In March of 1954, Dad went to Las Vegas; and one night he was rather intoxicated and married my mother, who was also intoxicated. Nine months later, when Dad was 49, I was born. Unfortunately, my mother was a schizophrenic. She heard voices. Eventually, she left my dad and me. It was a loss he never got over and a hurt that he would never understand. He was left at the age of 50 to raise a 6-month-old baby girl (Barbara).

Life didn't get any easier for Albert Stout. First, it wasn't easy in the '50s for a man to raise a girl. I remember landlords that wouldn't rent to a man with a daughter but no wife; I also remember many mothers who wouldn't allow their children to play with a child that had no mother. Then to make matters worse, in 1957 he was hit by a drunk driver and was badly hurt. He was left with one leg shorter than the other by four inches. Forced to walk with a limp and a cane, but still able to work, Dad returned to the Plumber's Union, but they refused to allow him to work. In 1957 it wasn't cool to be handicapped. There were no special allowances made, and no special parking places existed. The handicapped, including Dad, were shunned, and many people simply did not want them around.

Without work, Dad was put on Social Security Disability and collected Aid to Dependent Children. There was very little money growing up, as his total income was only about $250 per month. Finally, Dad turned to alcohol and to bars and to prostitutes for his social needs. To try and make more money, he often gambled and was good at it. He would take me to Reno, and I would be put in the back room watching movies while he drank and played poker. Frequently, he took me to bars at night, and we stayed until way past midnight. I often read the signs that said "no one under 21 allowed," but somehow that didn't seem to apply to me. Most bartenders didn't want to mess with dad. He was aggressive and would fight someone anytime and anywhere. He wasn't the person you would want to meet in an alley.

With all of his amazing personality traits, Dad somehow managed to raise a daughter. Dad always loved Shirley Temple and wanted me to look just like her. When I was small, he would try to curl my hair around little, pink plastic curlers that he bought at the drug store. At school, if there was a problem, the teacher was always wrong, and I was always right. Throughout my childhood we moved many times, and I went to three or four schools every year until I was 12. We sometimes lived above a store, behind a store, in a basement, in a boarding house, or sometimes rented a room in someone else's house. During my life, Dad moved all of our belongings back and forth three times from Chicago, IL, to Long Beach, CA.

In Chicago, Dad always had problems in the winter, and walking home from the bar at midnight wasn't easy. Dad was very unsteady on his feet and frequently fell and hit his head. I remember the agonizing feeling of not being able to help as his bright, red blood spilled out over the clear ice and white snow on the sidewalk at midnight.

In 1960 Chicago was interesting. Unfortunately, Dad would frequently get stopped by the police. The officer would walk up to

Dad's window and say, "I need you to step to the rear of your vehicle please," and then walk to the back of the car. Dad would take five or 10 dollars out of his pocket and put it on the front seat. We would then get out and walk to the back of the car, and the officer standing with his ticket book in his hand would say, "I need to read your odometer." The officer would then check the odometer and return and say, "I have decided to give you a warning," and he would leave. It was interesting that by the time we reentered the car, the money was gone.

Dad drank a lot and had many DUIs. I will never forget being paraded in front of judge after judge while the attorney proclaimed, "she doesn't have anyone else." Amazingly, Dad was never put in prison.

In 1971 I started challenging Dad. One day after another DUI and another car accident, which are too numerous to list, I told him he should stop driving. After all, he didn't have a driver's license; he had been using his dead brother's license for the past 10 years, which unfortunately had no expiration date, and the man in the picture looked a lot like Dad. So Dad got mad and went to the DMV. They required a written test.

When Dad protested that the print was too small, they offered a tape recording. When he again protested that the recording was too hard to understand, they gave him an oral test. Finally, after several attempts, the lady just said, "Al, you know the laws, don't you? Dad said "yes" and passed. When he went for the driving test and stopped about 50 feet from the crosswalk because he wasn't sure where the red light really was and when he only went about 35 on the freeway, she said, "Well Al, you know how to drive don't you? Why don't you just get a little bit closer to the crosswalk when you stop and drive a little faster on the freeway? Dad agreed and they gave him a license! He took it home and put it away and pulled out the one he had used for so many years.

Dad had a loving side, but he rarely showed it to anyone but his daughter. He ended up penniless but with a daughter who loved him. He had a few old friends, but they only cared in his memory.

On June 5, 1987, Dad died in my home. I will always cherish the gift of talking to my dad three days before he died — the dad I used to have and will remember always.

# Family Secrets

## *Sandra Yeaman*

A Lifetime television program, *The Unexplained*, played in the background of the family room while Marie paged through a stack of old magazines before deciding whether to toss them. The subject of that episode: twinless twins. That caught Marie's attention. The focus of the episode: Elvis Presley. His older twin brother Jesse died shortly after birth, before Elvis himself was born 30 minutes later. The narrator reported that Elvis often mentioned feeling something was missing in his life, something he associated with Jesse's absence.

Other twinless twins described the sense of guilt they felt, well into adulthood, especially in cases where one twin developed and was born normally and the other either died shortly after birth, was stillborn, or never fully developed. The guilt came from wondering if the survivor caused the death of the other by taking more nourishment from the mother, depriving the other.

Marie knew the connection between twins was stronger than between other siblings. She was ten when her twin brothers were born. Her mother hadn't known she was pregnant with twins until then. They were a month premature, fraternal, not identical; they didn't look that much alike. Because they were premies, both spent weeks in the hospital before they came home. One was blonder and bigger than the other. He came home first. The other spent two more weeks in the hospital.

As they grew, they developed different interests. One went to college, the other to vocational school. But even from the earliest days at home, they seemed to think and act as though they were one. That connection began before birth, in the uterus. The older one often remarked that he felt his bigger blond brother kicked him out.

There were fraternal twins in her father's family, too. Uncle

Curtis and Aunt Bernice were several years older than her father. They lived in Montana so Marie didn't see much of them.

But Marie wasn't thinking of her twin brothers. She was thinking of her younger sister, Diane. Marie knew a family secret; or perhaps it would better be described as a secret from the family. It wasn't a hidden disgrace, just something she didn't think her sister knew. Because of something her cousin, Irene, had told her shortly after the twins were born, Marie knew her sister was a twinless twin, but until that moment, she didn't know the name for it. And she wondered if there might be more secrets like it.

When Thankgiving that year brought both Diane and Marie's families to their parents' home, Marie decided it was time for the secret to be revealed.

Early evening, after all the leftovers had been stored in the refrigerator and the dishes stacked in the dishwasher, Marie took a seat in one of the two rocking recliners in the living room. Diane settled on the sofa and picked up the book she was reading. Their mother sat in the other recliner. All three faced the television set with the volume low.

"I watched an interesting program on television a few weeks ago," Marie said, rocking slightly in the chair. "It was about Elvis Presley and how much he was affected by the fact that his twin brother died right after birth. They called him a twinless twin. Elvis said he felt his brother was with him and talked to him all the time."

Diane put down her book and looked over at Marie.

"They interviewed other twinless twins," Marie continued. "One said she felt guilty about surviving while her twin didn't, and another said she felt that her twin was always with her, like a guardian angel. She told a story of how she felt her twin telling her to pull over to the side of the road to stop just before a truck barreled through the intersection. She said her twin saved her that day."

Marie's mother began to laugh. "Diane, did you ever feel something was missing in your life?"

"No," Diane said. "Why would I?"

"You were probably one of twins. After you were born, the

176

doctor said he thought I had been pregnant with twins. He told me that because a few days after I brought you home, I had what seemed like a miscarriage. I never told anybody."

"Irene told me," Marie said, referring to her cousin. "You must have told your sister, Grace."

"And Ellen told me," Diane said, referring to her closest friend from the family next door. "So you must have told Mrs. Thomas."

The secret hadn't been much of a secret. Everyone who Marie thought should know knew, but each thought the others didn't.

But Marie still wondered. She had always felt the presence of a guardian angel, someone watching over her, keeping her out of trouble. She thought of the time she pulled over to the side of the road where she mistook tall grass for the road's shoulder, and her car began to slide until it rested against the only sign for five miles. That sign kept her car from rolling over. And the time when she drove more than 2,000 miles from San Francisco to Minnesota where her VW engine blew a piston just three miles from her destination.

She had hoped there was another family secret her mother would reveal. After all, twins did run in the family.

# The Storm

## *S. Johnson-Labertew*

The thunder clapped so loud her head almost went through the sagging roof of her mom's boyfriend's 1961 cherry-red Cadillac Eldorado Biarritz, effin' convertible. The roof leaked. Air flowed freely through windows that wouldn't quite close. Driving the deep-finned monster was like rowing a boat upstream; her arms throbbed from turning the oversized steering wheel, and her leg and back hurt like hell every time she had to stretch them to reach the gas pedal, which felt like it was in another county. Rain pounded the streets, and braking put her small-framed, seventeen-year-old body directly under the biggest of the multiple leaks in the hole-filled, fraying top.

What the hell was the old fart doing in the bank anyway. Robbing it? Jesus, hadn't he caused her enough misery screwing her every time her mother's back was turned. Now she had to sit in his mildewed old Caddy — waiting in the worst storm to hit the area in years, just because school had let out early because of the storm.

The talking heads on station KVSP, who for tonight were replacing her pop punk, were screaming their words, they were so excited to have some real news to cover. Trying to get people to go home or to the nearest shelter, while predicting some of the worst effing tornadoes in recorded history would be sweeping through town. DJs on a mission with something besides The Donald to talk about.

Anyway, she doubted the old man even had a bank account. What would he put in it? The tip money he took off her mom every night? That barely covered his booze and cigarettes.

Crap. She was damp and cold. The thunder and lightning were getting on her nerves. She really didn't want to feel the back of his hand, but this was getting creepy. There was no one anywhere on the streets that she could see. Heavy winds continued to blow gusts of rain in every direction. What if he and his worthless crony had forgotten she was out here?

Five more minutes; she was going to give him five more minutes, then she was going in to see for herself what he was up to. She tried to find some music on the radio, but all she could find were tornado alerts and some effin' preacher claiming the sins of his listeners were catching up with them and the end was coming and to send money to save their souls before it was too late. Big whoop. Her world ended the night her mother brought the old fart home after her shift at the bar. No amount of money for the Lord was going to save her.

She didn't know where the bastard got his stamina. He spent his time either effing or beating one or the other of them. She tried real hard to believe her mom didn't know about his daytime moonlighting with her daughter — but wondered, would she even care?

She had been tempted to tell her counselor but figured the prissy woman would probably throw it right back at her, or worse yet at her mom, who would then start yelling at her daughter for sneaking around her back and telling private family matters. Mom wouldn't relish spending an hour hearing from the hackneyed counselor how to be a better parent. No, better to shut up. All she had to do was get through three more months at the house of horrors that passed for a high school in this crap town; then she would be eighteen and graduated.

Hell, five minutes was up. She scooted across the torn leather of the bench seat and pushed open the Caddy's passenger door. It screeched like an old lady getting a bikini wax whenever it was forced open. Slamming it shut, she slogged through the torrent trying to miss the deepest puddles and shoved at the bank door.

Stunned by the sight that greeted her inside, she could only stand and stare — lifeless as a Barbie Doll.

There were three bodies on the floor. The old man, his crony, and Mr. Davies, the bank manager, father of John Davies who sat behind her in both English and math classes. It looked like they had shot each other.

Blood puddled everywhere. A backpack spewed money over the marble floor—lots of money. It looked to be stuffed full of hundred-dollar bills. What was a girl to do? She snaked between the bloody bodies and grabbed the bag and the old man's keys, then ran back out to the decrepit Caddy and roared out of town. She'd figure out how to get away with her heist later. Hot damn—nothing, not even a tornado, could stop her now.

# Leaving Town

## *Mardie Schroeder*

When Benjamin Harrison Johnson rode out of town, he left behind his partner and best friend, his badge, a salary, and a woman who told him no one had treated her with such a tender heart and respect.

One thing he knew for sure — he would not be back. He easily left behind the badge, the salary, and the woman. His partner, Virgil, was another matter.

How one man could change so drastically was something he would have plenty of time to ponder.

Years of working with a man every day, of riding together all day, sitting around a campfire, and sharing a bottle or two, you'd think you could predict what he would do from one minute to the next. Seems like you never really know what's deep within a man's heart.

Now Benjamin Harrison Johnson was alone, free to do whatever he wanted without thinking of anyone else.

However, it was hard to get Virgil out of his mind. BH could understand him wanting to stay put in that place. Virgil made steady money as sheriff. It was a town that showed promise now that the railroad had been built. But the woman was a whole different matter.

Virgil's woman had come onto Benjamin Harrison Johnson pretty strong, and he had had to push her away. In fact, she wasn't too careful who she flung herself at, as he had seen on numerous occasions. Besides, in a small town like that, everyone knew if you sneezed.

Virgil knew she had a roving eye, and when BH asked him what he saw in her, he replied, "She's pretty, she smells good, she takes a bath every night, and she plays the piano." That seemed to be enough for him.

Virgil didn't see BH leave town. He didn't see him tip his hat to the woman he'd spent the night with, to whom he'd given a gift as a goodbye token, although Virgil knew Benjamin Harrison Johnson would be leaving.

BH rode tall in the saddle. He was more comfortable sitting on a horse than sitting on a chair.

He had a long way to go and a long time to get there, and plenty of time to sort things out in his mind.

A canteen and lasso were tethered to his saddle. A bedroll wrapped in a well-worn slicker was tied behind it. His Winchester was secure in its scabbard.

A mule, trailing behind, carried supplies that could last two to three weeks if there were no mishaps.

Benjamin Harrison Johnson headed west. He would cross rivers, mountains, deserts, and prairies. He would encounter wildfire, Indians, mountain lions, and the most majestic palomino stallion he had ever seen. And he would win more than lose playing poker.

Late afternoon, BH stopped for the first time. He camped near a stream after he watered his stock and hobbled them in a nearby pasture.

Over a fire he put some beans in a small pot, adding a good amount of fatback. While they stewed, he stripped and plunged into the stream, leaving the dust and sweat to find their way downstream.

He sat stark naked, except for boots, on his bedroll and ate beans. He hadn't been able to let go of Virgil all day. How a man could be so indifferent to his woman flirting with other men was something he couldn't get his mind around. And it wasn't just flirting. She was not faithful to Virgil in the broadest sense of the word.

BH finished the beans, washed the pot in the stream, fixed his bedroll, and pulled on his long johns. He lay down and gazed at the stars. Lulled by the sputtering fire, the distant howling of the coyotes, and the occasional nicker of his horse, he slept.

What he didn't know was that he had an observer on the other side of the stream.

# Flying in Tibet
## *A Very Short Love Story*

## *Barbara Huntington*

I came to Tibet to die. Too recently I had watched parents, husband, and friends lose their dignity, bodies, and minds. Seeing them trapped and dependent on caregivers who, no matter how compassionate, might lose their temper over a third diaper change in the wee hours, I had vowed to stay healthy and fit. Despite yoga, hiking, healthy food, and daily brain exercises on my iMac, I knew something was broken. I meditated, but enlightenment took the form of cold car keys—the ones I couldn't find in my purse. There was no one else in the house to blame for their inappropriate placement in the refrigerator. After a series of tests, young Dr. Slater confirmed my worst fears, blurting out, "You know that people with female relatives with Alzheimer's have a greater chance of developing it themselves? Well, your mother..."

That is where I stopped listening and began to plan my last adventure.

One of the hardest parts of losing your life partner early is not having that comfortable person to bounce your ideas off of. A child of the Beatle's era, I had looked forward to traveling to our Isle of Wight and bouncing grandchildren on my knee when I was sixty-four. At some point I had begun to hate the Fab Four for their fantasy as I gardened and traveled alone. Life was unfair, but that's life.

Home from the doctor's office, I made my decision and ordered travel brochures online.

The catalog showed high snow-covered peaks and Tibetan prayer flags, but the picture of the Buddhist professor who led the tour was the deciding factor in choosing that company. I told myself it was because I wanted to learn more about Tibetan Buddhism, but Jim was tanned and thin, his gray hair held back in

185

a pony tail, reminiscent of the handsome hippies of my youth. I had been a faithful wife for forty years, but when a lengthy computer search revealed he also was widowed, I let my imagination go. Sometimes when I let my imagination go, it goes too far. No entanglements! It hurts to lose a loved one to death. No, I was doing this alone.

On that first day in Katmandu, our tour group stayed at a Western style hotel. I was at the opposite end of the long table from Jim, but noticed we were the only ones who had not been served. Then our meals arrived, lentil soup; of course, everyone else had meat.

That night Jim lectured on the history of Buddhism in Tibet, the immolation of monks, the escape of the Dali Lama, the bravery of students in the face of Goliath China. He brought up that, as the trip had come together, his Chinese-speaking student assistant had to negotiate to allow one of us to come on the trip. Years ago our fellow traveler had joined an organization to free Tibet, and the Chinese government originally denied the visa. His laughing deep blue eyes looked directly at me. I smiled back. I didn't know he was even aware of the snag that had almost derailed my plans.

That night, bundled in my down jacket, I sat on the balcony of my hotel room staring at the mountains and remembering an old biography I had read. It was about a Buddhist monk who carried the wisdom and karma of untold generations. In it, Tibetan Masters defied gravity and flew through the crags. Even though the book was eventually proved to be a hoax, and the author a plumber in London, that story had become the basis of my plan. As my thoughts flew, I heard soft guitar and whistling from the next balcony and recognized a folk song from my youth. I began to sing along:

> *In the land of Oden, there stands a mountain,*
> *One thousand miles in the air.*
> *From edge to edge, this mountain measures*
> *One thousand miles square.*
> *A little bird comes a wingin',*
> *Once every million years,*
> *Sharpens his beak,*

186

*And then he swiftly disappears.*
*Thus when this mountain is worn away,*
*This to eternity will be one single day.*

The whistling changed to a deep gentle male voice, harmonizing with my own. The song over, I crept back to my room under the soft quilt and dreamed of flying.

In the following days I lost my will to stay away from him. Walking at that elevation exhausted me, but I would amble a short distance from camp to meditate and then he would be there to sing, and talk of our gardens and grandchildren and the adventures and misadventures of our youth.

Our last two days were to be at a Buddhist monastery that hung precariously on a cliff. There were many caves around it and I had scouted out one I could reach with my wobbly knees—one that had a beautiful ledge for my taking off spot. That night, after singing I found my way up the cliff. There was no doubt about jumping. Alzheimer's would destroy any hope of "doing the garden, digging the weeds" from my Beatle's fantasy. Then a tender arm held me tight. I had been too involved in my reverie to hear him come up. Warm lips in the Tibetan cold. Comfort and love. He asked:

"Jumping?"

I nodded, "Flying."

"Alzheimer's?"

Another nod.

"Me, too."

Another kiss; then holding hands, we flew.

# Declaration of Love

## *Dora Klinova*

My love, my amazing sweetheart, I am writing this poem and YOU are its pearl. There is an endless amount of beautiful, magical words that I can tell you. I will try not to repeat any of them in the flow that runs from my heart.

I feel your soul; it makes the world around me colorful and radiant. All darkness, sinking feelings, unpleasant thoughts dissolve and disappear when I think about you. Now I truly understand the power of love.

My wonder, your brilliance puts everybody in seventh heaven. You are a soft cloud in the blue sky, the sun that gives warmth and light to the earth and to everything that exists.

Very often we use the words "honey" and "sweetheart" without thinking. We do not concentrate on their real meaning. Honey is the best product of nature. It gives relief when we are exhausted or down. So is love. "Sweetheart" means SWEET HEART, which will never disappoint us. Let us remember this when we use these fine words with our loved ones.

You have become an outstanding, very talented, and dignified woman. I sense your light and power, your every cell, every breath and pulse. Don't rush; let your life be like a dance. Remember, your every movement is full of beauty and grace. I know you are still growing. You are already glorious. You are priceless. You are beyond any competition.

You will have everything you want. All the abundance from the world, from the Universe, will come to you. YOU will see. You deserve this; you are unique. You will do whatever your heart desires. I promise you—I swear you will.

I will give you all my poetry, all the songs that I keep inside me. I will cherish you until my last sigh. Listen to my magic words. You are the brightest light in me, in my home. You are my juice, my inner song, my sun, my sky, my rosebud. You are my aroma, my essence; you give me the fragrance of life. You are a fast-moving stream, a flow of the clearest water.

You calm me down like quiet music. You set my mind to rest; you assuage my pain. With you, I feel relaxed and satisfied. You are my Mozart and Beethoven; you are my inspiration. You are deep as an ocean. You are a carpet of spring flowers, a field of green grass; with you I breathe as in a meadow.

You are a bonfire, a wind, a bird flying in a blue sky. You are a skylark, whose song awakens at sunrise; you are sunrise itself. You are a high mountain where we can feel the entire Universe. Near you, all thoughts disappear. You are appeasement, and you are a volcano, ready to explode at any minute.

I love you with all your best and worst qualities. It does not matter to me; I love you as you are. You are my unknown planet, a high ocean tide that can soar to the sky and go back into the deep ocean.

You are a ray shining through the leaves of the tree; you are the warmth in my home and the smell of delicious food. You are the best wine, sparkling champagne, a ripe apple, a grape full of juice. You are the best Parisian perfume.

You are a song I want to sing always. You were a tiny little seed, which became a gorgeous palm. You are full of mysteries and open like an interesting book we read over and over again. You are a princess I would like to dress in velvet, lace, and pearls.

You are full of treasures, a diamond shining with all the colors of the rainbow. You are a queen in your soul and by your blood. You radiate warmth that comforts everybody's soul.

It is a blessing to meet you; the person near you will be happy forever. I want to sink into your unforgettable bliss.

I will erect a monument to you, high as the sky, my beloved-forever.

# Four Bodies and One Spirit

## *Val Zolfaghari*

Sitting under a willow tree were four students, a book in each lap, preparing for their last examination. Their conversation and the movement of the English finches on the willow tree, under which they sat, had one thing in common: birds did not stay still, leaped from branch to branch, while the four students' conversation switched from topic to topic.

The minds of the high school seniors were bombarded with rational, irrational, practical and impractical ideas, concepts and desires. They rightly assumed that all four would graduate, take entrance exams, and be accepted at prestigious universities. Their lives had been agreeable in a disagreeable country. They came from well-to-do families from different religious backgrounds: Steve, Christian; Mohammad, Muslim; Benjamin, Jew; Anosh, Zoroastrian. They did not face the difficulties that most children encountered in the country. However, they understood reality, were unbiased observers, recorded unpleasant events accurately, and had many unanswered questions. For now, their conversations had taints of humor, cynicism, and stoicism.

The weather inched toward high temperatures. Birds stretched out their wings in the willow branches, relaxed, and conversed amid yawns. The students unknowingly followed the birds' behavior and began talking nonchalantly about the possibility of a war with a neighboring country and their involvement. As usual, Anosh expressed his opinion first.

"I am sure there will be war. Our history proves my point. Countries to our west, created by a colonial power, are united by a common religion and hatred of our nation. They managed to impose their religion by genocide, but were not able to wipe out our culture, identity, patriotism, and language. We eventually rose from the ashes to rule. They will attack us. I will participate in defense of our land. I have said enough. Let us hear Mohammad."

"I will state my case out in front: I will not take part in the war. Nationalism is against my religion. Our Western neighbors have the same belief as the majority of us. We should unite with them and fight infidels. After all, we are the servant of the same God, and the earth belongs to all of his servants. Benjamin, it is your turn."

"I am descendent of Moses and a member of the Chosen Club. All of you know where my real country is. If there is a war between my cousins and you, I will go where I truly belong. Steve, put in your two cents."

"I am not clear what I would do. My case is completely different from yours. I am an Armenian, but my ancestors were Zoroastrian and belonged to this land. I have dual citizenship, but I do not know what I would do if there were a war."

Planet Earth roamed, nonstop, two months and ten hours around the sun after the students' meeting. Then fireworks started. Planes circled the sky, anti-aircrafts fired, bombs were dropped, houses were flattened, and dust and smoke adorned the sky. The invited and uninvited war had descended upon innocent people.

Lunacy was celebrated by insane leaders, saying it was God's blessing. Meaningless speeches were spit out by truly despicable self-elected war mongers. They demanded sacrifices, promised heaven, hell, victory, martyrdom, defeat, and support of the prophets and saints who could not save their own lives. God's name was mentioned every nanosecond, but no deity was present to stop the madness of evil creatures.

Every hour scores of unborn, young, and old were crushed to death under the roofs which had previously protected them. The lost lives were amplified by deafening sound of sirens. Shamelessly, radios and televisions reported no victims.

Anosh went to the warfront as a volunteer and came back for a visit. Mohammad went to his native town and roamed the streets until his sister's death. Steve was smuggled out of the country to Armenia but returned against his parents' wishes. Benjamin spent most of the time at home reading books and going

192

through his family's papers.

Again, they met under the same willow tree. This time they were not going to prepare for their final examination or discuss the rumored war. Everyone, except Anosh, was there to declare his participation or non-involvement in the raging war. They were hesitant about who should start the conversation, so they opted for a lottery.

The winner of the first prize, Mohammad, stood up.

"Before the war started, I gave you the reasons for my non-participation in the rumored war. Today, my face stands as my witness that I have changed and aged many years in a short time. The wrinkles and furrows on my face are manifestations of the lava created by my inner volcanic eruption, caused by my sister's demise."

He stopped talking, bit his lower lip, heaved a sigh, and then with tearful eyes continued.

"One day the weather was sunny, and the official radio announced that it was safe to go out. My young innocent sister with her friends went to a public bathhouse. The enemy planes appeared from nowhere and bombed their bathhouse. We rushed to the site and started removing the earth with shovels and our bare hands. Suddenly, a mullah in a black turban with his large group of religious followers appeared with a bulldozer. We thought they were going to help us to save the victims, but it was not the case."

A lump in his throat choked him. Mohammad ground his teeth, clinched his fist, and murmured "Sons of bitches." And then he continued.

"The mullah ordered his followers to bulldoze the bombed public bathhouse. And they did. We protested, fought them, were beaten, arrested, and put in prison. The mullah visited us in the prison and said that the site had to be bulldozed to prevent the women's nude bodies from being seen by the public, which is a sin. In the prison, I realized what his foreign ancestors, who wore black turbans and ate lizards, did to my ancestors. I have come to say goodbye and will be on my way to the warfront early tomorrow morning. I have thrown my religious diaper into the trash and I am a free man. From now on, my name is Jamsheed,

193

which is my ancestral name."

Smiles of approvals danced on the faces. Then the winner of the second drawing, Benjamin, started his presentation.

"In our last gathering, I told you that I belonged to the chosen tribe in my God-given country, which is not the one I live in. Dropping of bombs, parading of dead bodies in the streets, and burial of innocent neighbors under tons of dirt shattered my idea of being elite. I started believing in 'humans are the limbs of one/the same body.' [1] I stayed at home and began soul searching. I roamed the rooms, opened every locked and unlocked box, and read all the personal letters. In a well-hidden old box, I found love letters written in German. My question was, "Why were they in German?" They should have been written in Persian or Hebrew. I found the answer to my question in my grandparents' daily diaries. My grandparents were German-Jews and this country was a country that accepted them with open arms and saved them from the Holocaust. The Promised Land to them was this land and it is for me, too. I will join the warfront."

All eyes stared at Steve. He was pensive for a minute, a smirk took over his lips, and then his mouth fired the word *"Gammas-gammas."* [2]

Loud laughter filled the air and an army of English finches flew out of the willow tree, mistaking the laughter for the firing of anti-aircraft. The birds completed their formation, laughter disappeared, and then Steve threw up both hands in the air and shouted, "We Armenians have repaired, gammas-gammas, half of this country's cars during peace time. I will be fixing, gammas-gammas, the broken equipment in the warfront."

They continued talking for a while, drafted a letter, and then left.

Eight years elapses. Now there is a single grave in a blooming cherry orchard garden. The grave's stone is covered with fallen cherry blossoms. Anosh, Jamsheed, Steve, and Benjamin are permanent guests of the grave. There is a glass covered frame next to the grave, supported by two wooden legs pinned to the ground. The glass cover is decorated with cherry blossoms, like Renoir's "The Garden of Essai." Inside the frame hangs the letter written by Anosh, Jamsheed, Steve and Benjamin.

194

A ten- year-old girl, Geety, runs toward the grave and reaches it with tearful eyes and shortness of breath. She bends over the grave, tenderly removes the cherry flowers, puts four roses on the stone, stands at attention like a soldier reporting, "You may not recognize me. I am that little brat who used to run around, dance over your books, and pull your ears and noses when you were studying for your examinations. Now, I am ten years old, mature, and even have small breasts."

She takes a deep breath.

"I am sorry for disturbing you so early in the morning. I sneaked out of the house and rushed here to be the first one to tell you that the war ended last night. At midnight people went to roofs, thanked you, sang patriotic songs honoring you for defending our country. It is a pity that you were not there to see it. Everybody told us that you, like Arash [3], fought with your souls and arrows and took back every inch of our land. I am sorry that I cannot stay too long, but I will recite your letter one more time from memory."

She closed her eyes.

"Today, all four of us decided to defend our motherland that has breastfed us with her crops, fruit and pristine water, and defended us against enemies unconditionally with its high mountains and deep valleys. Until now, we had four different religions. From this moment on, we will have one common religion—Love of Motherland. We understand that in a war bullets rain from the sky, not candies, and all of us could be killed by falling bullets and will have to be buried in the womb of our motherland. Our parent religions say that we must be buried in four different cemeteries. Our motherland does not discriminate against its children and does not agree with this practice. We follow our new religion 'Love of Motherland' and wish to be buried in a single grave.

Anosh, Steve, Benjamin, Jamsheed.

Geety salutes the grave, says in a loud voice, "All four families have changed their religions to yours." Then she runs away choking with tears.

"When I grow up, I will have four boys and call them Anoush, Steve, Jamsheed and Benjamin."

---

1 A poem by Saadi, a Persian poet.
2 Slowly, but surely
3 A hero in Persian folklore

# Chien Roti

## *Philip Shafer*

**Hanoi, French Indo-China**
**March 13, 1954**

I heard the gentle sound of his knock. Lt. Malcolm Deville stepped onto the balcony with me and said, "Excuse me. Major Torque, Sir." He glanced at my earphones, his face showing a barely visible smile.

I uncovered an ear. "Yes, what is it, Malcolm?"

"A letter from General Martinet — Your Eyes Only."

We exchanged a questioning look, but Malcolm hurried on, "And, Sir, I think the army's planning to send a reconnaissance-in-force, or something, south out of Hanoi in the near future."

"Oh?"

"The past week's interrogations. . .a curious pattern of . . ."

I raised a finger. "After the broadcast." I waved him away and cupped my palms over the phones, hearing squeals and then the background clatter of whumps, cracks, and shouting voices.

"CASTRIES CALLING FROM DIEN BIEN PHU. THE ATTACK GOES ON PERSISTENT AND FIERCE."

Damned static, but, yes, that's the colonel's voice, and in the middle of a fire fight . . . sounds like a 30 caliber and a . . . yes, 50 caliber machine gun, taking turns like a drum line competition, with those homemade Viet Minh hand grenades playing kettle drum, and . . . oh. That was big, and close. A Chinese 98 mm canon? . . . debris falling . . . and screams.

"EIGHTY WOUNDED THUS FAR TODAY, FOURTEEN — DEAD. TWO HUNDRED ENEMY DIED BEFORE NOON. THE NORTH

PERIMETER AT BEATRICE WAS BROACHED BUT QUICKLY SEALED. EIGHTEEN VIET MINH GOT INSIDE THE WIRE. THERE WAS NO RETREAT; ALL WERE KILLED BUT TWO, TAKEN FOR INTERROGATION."

Interrogation?

"OUR POSITION IS INTACT. THE MEN ARE PERFORMING SPLENDIDLY. I'M CONFIDENT OF VICTORY. WE NEED PLASMA AND RIFLE GRENADES. MAJOR ROUX HAS PARTICULARS AND COORDINATES FOR AIR SUPPORT."

Ha, the Colonel signs off the public broadcast with patriotic, martial music. Damned showman. Roux's static-laced voice drones on with details of medical evacuation, resupply, and artillery suppression — the bloodless data of carnage and death.

I picked up the letter and hefted it. I tapped it against the arm of my chair. Finally, I just studied the address: *Major Thomas Olivier Torque, Officer in Charge, Intelligence Unit #1.*

~

Why am I in Hanoi and not in desperate action at Dien Bien Phu? Is Malcolm right? A person can live a long life on just one kidney? Twenty-two years of service, but what chance to make thirty? What chance to make colonel?

Roux only has fifteen years' service. He's a fair-haired favorite.

Dien Bien Phu is going to make Roux and Castries famous — if they survive. Win or lose, gallant victory or tragic defeat, they'll be famous. Christian de Castries will be made general; Roux, the youngest colonel in the army. Promotion comes with stunning success, even glorious defeat, but always with sufficient slaughter.

Too much, too high a price. I used to brag, mission accomplished, no casualties. No glory in that. They retire majors like me — objects of feigned respect, whispered ridicule, and denigrating sympathy — failures, on mean pensions.

A sharp crack blanked my rambling thoughts.

Yes, the Viet Minh have brought in their big guns. Roux continued his litany of particulars. Distant, but carried clearly by the crackling electronics, came the rending scream of a man

198

abandoning bravery in realization of sundered body and un-imagined pain. Through the chaos of conflict, the cry pierced my heart, echoed across the years, and reverberated against Colonel Castries' words: "Two, taken for interrogation."

~

I sipped from my glass, shrugged, and sighed. I became aware of the steady side tone in my earphones and removed them. I turned the radio off, considering Malcolm, my second in command. Malcolm, specially selected for his medical knowledge, and . . .

Here I sit on the balcony outside my third-floor office in the old quarter of Hanoi, a watered whisky in my hand, Tonkinese and Chinese businesses, shops, and residences in a jumble of streets surrounding me.

A short block up from the Red River front, I like to sit here. The four streets angled together make an almost spacious intersection and give this army-owned building and me a broad view of the river and open country beyond.

The streets below are full of color and activity, vendors and shoppers. They remind me of Paris. The new quarter, three kilometers to the southeast and built over the past fifty years, is modern and Western, with broad boulevards and spacious elegance. Most of the French and European businesses and residences are there. The signs and the language one hears are French, but it doesn't feel like home. Home — a strange concept. Outside the army, I don't have a clear concept of home.

Malcolm reappeared on my little porch. "Sir, the courier said the letter should be opened immediately."

"Yes, yes, in a moment. But tell me about your intelligence suspicions."

"You know, part of our technique is asking about bogus projects or missions. I got a positive response six days ago. Building on that in subsequent interviews, I've got a strangely coherent picture. If such a mission is on, it's common knowledge on the street."

"You said, south. Where?"

"It's uncertain. Hué, Qui Nhon, Saigon?"

199

"Have you been to Saigon?"

"No, sir."

"Saigon's always hot and muggy. Here, in the north, the wet and dry cycles are more seasonal. March is delightful, still in the dry period with balmy days and cool nights."

I glanced up. The afternoon sun had reached my office perch, belying my euphemistic weather assertions. It beat down on us and the intersection of activity below. Aware of our sweat-soaked shirts, we each gave a grunting laugh.

I turned my gaze to the pastel sky of pinks, oranges, and blues arching above distant swatches of blended greens, yellows, and tans in sweeping curves with hazy edges. In contrast, sharp primaries, bold lines, and action pulsed in the streets with colorful activity.

"Change is coming. I'm not sure what." To Malcolm's questioning look, I added, "Write me a short memo." But my mind was still on interrupted thoughts — my unfulfilled life, the beauty of the day — all overlain with the just-beginning butchery. Regardless of the outcome — pain and pathos, havoc and gore, shattered bodies obscenely decorating a shattered landscape, all those beautiful young men, that beautiful land — destroyed. Changing the subject, I asked: "Where is home?"

Uncertain, Malcolm said, "Sir?"

I pressed. "How do we decide where home is?"

"I grew up in Paris. I lived here in Hanoi until I was nearly five, but we lived in Paris on rue D'Orsell below Sacré Coeur . . ." Malcolm smiled. "Home is where love is."

We held a long, thoughtful look, and then he left me to write his short memo.

I took another sip and let those rich, patterned hues and the vibrant panorama encompass me.

I should have been a poet or a painter. Humph. Never have I attempted to express those feelings with pen or brush — those appreciations for what I see and feel. I lack the talent. But the feelings are there.

A commotion in the street below drew my attention to a crowd gathered 'round the vendor who sold customers choice of fresh roasted young dog.

200

Ahhh, more thoughts of death? Anguish and pain? Or release from "this vale of tears." I remembered.

Nineteen thirty-two, a new sub-lieutenant was I when first I saw the small dogs die. My captain then, Ferraileur, explained to me:

*"Three parts make up the enterprise. They're often built where streets converge—three distinct experiences—sensual and emotional. A pet shop on one of the street—birds and fish, and glass front display, furry puppies, adorable, romping in their innocent play. The other street—hot crackling grease, golden carcass, rotating spits, aroma rich, nostril's delight, savor, each mouth-watering bite. Between, the dark, bar-restaurant."*

He took me there, my mentor and superior. Inside, clients imbibed their beer and watched the *Grand Guignol* appear. Selected dogs killed on the spot, beheaded, skinned and gutted hot, skewered, basted, rotisseried. We drank our beer and watched the slaughter.

*"Do you recall Odysseus?"*

His strange question surprised me, but, I played his game and answered, "Yes."

*"One-eyed giant eating his men, crunched whole and raw, screaming in death, disappearing down grisly maw. Cyclops complained. 'You Greeks are bitter, stringy tough.'"*

My captain cocked his head at me.

*"T'is true of all. Our flesh is charged as we're aware, whether it be fear and panic, or trustful bliss free of all care. Happy hormones, the chefs, you see, prefer viande felicité. Picked up, cuddled, four times each day, fed tasty treats and wrapped in love, these puppies dear, are tender sweet when death takes them quite by surprise."*

Six bottles each we had consumed. We didn't eat, but my captain—Ferraileur—observed the customers—all men. Shining faces, eyes all intent, as they observed the spectacle. He then began my lesson hard.

*"Our soldier's lot, kill or be killed."*

He paused and cast a kindly eye.

*"But knowing death enhances life. They flow as one, inseparable.*

*These people see immediate up close of life, then sudden death — the customers participate — anticipate — yes, consummate.*

"*Life is striving, death is not. In battle's ultimate contest, the visceral chill, I can't deny, the tingling thrill, I live while you die.*"

Again he asked, non-sequitur.

"*Do you have thoughts, fearful and dark, about the time before your birth?*"

I shuddered with uncertainty. He laughed out loud.

"*Nobody does. The painless bliss from which we come, is our reward when we are done. Dying is horrible only for the living. The soldier's secret advantage.*"

My captain smiled with distant gaze, speaking to some unseen spirit, perhaps himself, but not to me,

"*The ultimate prize, the gift of extreme, the giving of life as the giver dies. The vanquished cries. Exultation's peak you received from me. End struggle and pain; I'm finally free.*"

He never spoke that way again — Ferraileur, my mentor of philosophy, military. The terrifying stark rictus of death? The dead soldier's last laugh? Could that really be?

Well, I never went in that place again, nor stopped by fuzzy puppy's den. But an irresistible delicacy was *roti chien.*

I heaved a deep sigh, drained my glass, and opened the letter.

---

*Note: Grand Guignol* was a theatre in the Pigalle district of Paris from 1897 to 1962, with stage shows featuring the gruesome and horrible — madness, murder, torture, and gore.

# Sentence

## *Mardie Schroeder*

The cotton shift fell straight from her slender shoulders barely covering her bare feet. A blindfold prevented her from seeing anything. She heard the door open and the heavy footfall of boots stomp into the room and stop in front of her. She heard the door close. She heard the slap of a baton onto the palm of a hand.

"You know you have committed a crime." It was not a question.

"Yes."

"It is forbidden in our country to have any contact with an alien."

"I loved him."

"You know what happens to anyone who commits this crime."

"I do."

She heard the heavy boots walking away. She heard the snap of fingers. She heard the door open.

The bullet pierced the frontal lobe, disintegrated the parietal lobe, and blew out the occipital lobe.

She did not hear the door close.

Animals are such agreeable friends—
they ask no questions;
they pass no criticisms.

—*George Eliot*

# A Kiss For Good Luck

## *Sally Eckberg*

Things were going well in my training class, and I was quickly becoming an exemplary canine. Salem, who was my trainer, often singled me out to demonstrate the proper way to "finish," "down," or "come front." I learned that we were practicing for a specific event called a "Show." I felt that whatever it entailed, I could handle it confidently.

Some minor incidents occurred with other students while we were in class, notably a slight altercation with a yellow dog named Luna. I had a new duck toy that I brought to class one day. Luna found it where I had placed it carefully next to my personal water dish. She actually tried to play with it. What nerve! The minute I saw what she was doing, I rushed to grab her collar, and I might have growled a bit. Well, she actually bit me on my chin. I cried, and people immediately rushed to my aid.

There was a great fuss about the blood in my beard, which ultimately required extensive and painful washing. Luna's people were extremely kind to me and brought a new furry toy in an effort to make amends for the boorish behavior of their charge.

One preparation remained before the Show. The grooming went smoothly, and when it was finished, I looked terrific.

 In returning home from the groomer's, I made an interesting discovery. Left to my own devices, I decided to peek into Mom's purse as sometimes treats are available there. What I found instead were tubes of a wonderful substance called lipstick. I removed the caps carefully, although a little did manage to get on the carpeting in the car.

After testing each tube, I decided that the Red Berry was a bit too oily, but the Summer Coral was lovely. I did not apply much of it to my beard. I thought Mom went a little overboard in her reaction. Personally, I felt it enhanced my grooming.

Mom let me out in the backyard on the first day of the Show. She cautioned me, "Don't spoil your beautiful grooming by getting dirty." Of course, I had no intention of doing anything to destroy my perfect grooming.

Bailey, the neighbor's dog, was waiting for me. Something caught Bailey's attention, and she ran to the side fence and flushed something out of the vines. I ran to assist her. Imagine my surprise when I discovered it was a large barn rat. We chased it around the yard for a brief time until my natural abilities came to the fore, and I caught the wretched little beast.

The creature was wriggling and squirming, so I tossed it to Bailey. Surprisingly, she was able to catch it. Our revelry was interrupted when Mom called me, and I obediently went directly to her. Bailey continued to paw at the rodent, which wasn't even remotely into the game.

We did not leave for the Show immediately but walked to the coffee shop. When we arrived at the shop, a nice elderly lady sat at an outside table. I immediately tried to make friends by placing my paws in her lap. She and Mom had a brief conversation, and I stayed with her while Mom got her coffee.

While Mom was in the shop, the lady invited me to sit on her lap. This was a friendly gesture, so I showed my appreciation by kissing her on the cheek and ears. I might have gotten one good lick on her open mouth also.

Mom did a lot of complaining on the way home. She scolded me because of kissing the lady after the rat incident. She said it was lucky that the lady did not know about the rat. I rather wished she had told the lady as she might have been amused. But, perhaps not.

I came home from what was a grueling day at the Show with a Blue Ribbon in conformation. My interlude with the nice lady turned out to be a kiss for good luck.

# An Eclectic Look at Dog Handlers

## *Laurie Asher*

When you watch a dog show there are specific traits about the handlers of which you can be sure: The women typically wear an ensemble where both pieces are ill-fitting and far too tight. Watch as their derrieres are being squeezed from side to side as they run around in circles. Notice that the buttons on the jackets seem to be straining to stay fastened.

I am nervously waiting for one to pop, and in my mind's eye, I see the dog make an amazing jump into the air, all in slow motion, swirling in a full circle, and snatch the button. Does this add points, or detract? I see the crowd going wild, hooting and stomping, spontaneously breaking out in a dance to "We are the Champions" until the announcer begs them to stop and be seated. "Decorum," he barks.

And useless bras with no support are seemingly mandatory. If there is an abundance "up there," we miss every regal prance made by the pompous poodle and his bouncing bouffant.

The shoes—ugh! Apparently it is mandatory to wear unflattering flats that are worn out, making certain they don't match the skirt in color or style, with heels worn down on one side only, due to continuous circular motion to the left. Diabetic support hose seem to be a necessity as well—not that one has to be a diabetic to appreciate the snug fit.

If you're an avid watcher, after a few shows you start to notice that the handlers and the canine companions become virtually indistinguishable. This is particularly true of male handlers. Look at the expression on that English bull dog, and tell me that you don't see the exact expression replicated by his handler? Same wrinkles, same double chins, same body structure, same sagging jowls. Same wagging rear end. Is it a coincidence or simpatico?

One other thing I notice that breaks my concentration from

focusing on the fabulous Fauve de Bretagne, with its sweet little puppy dog eyes, is the habit of the handlers to tuck their dog brushes in their waistbands at their lower backs. Both sexes do it. I always worry about fleas and hope they don't migrate down into their bottom area. And I can't help visualizing the handler squirming and scratching, causing the dog to stop in its tracks, look up, and give them that "aha, now you know what it feels like" glance.

Let's take a look at the male handlers. They seem to have a theme of wearing vintage, sagging suits and old, worn out loafers — black with brown pants, and brown with black pants. If they wear a tie, we are assured it will not match their shirts or jackets.

Stripes go with plaid, and polka dots with argyle.

Notice, though, that the men typically stride, while the women seem to trot. On average, I prefer the male handlers, as they don't distract as much as the females when my imagination is in full play, as shared above. Nevertheless, the fashion-challenged handlers in contrast with their meticulously groomed charges are stunning.

Sometimes the handlers are also the owners, but oftentimes they are just the handlers. But *just* is not the appropriate word, as many of these handlers are the *most* prominent people in these dogs' lives.

Here are my suggestions for the women handlers: lose the K-Mart couture, ladies. Ask your daughters for help or hire a professional groomer, no pun intended. Wear sturdier bras, perhaps under wires for better support.

But I can forgive all that because dog handlers are some of my favorite people — genuine, loving, committed to their craft, and consummate professionals. They just march to the beat of their own drum, and the dogs seem to be the only ones that understand the beat.

And I know their pooches don't have fleas. They are, after all, America's finest dogs.

# Animal Magnet

## *Amy E. Zajac*

Growing up, our family always gave a home to stray cats, dogs, and critters. I always thought it was because my mother wanted us to have a pet experience and help us learn to love other species of life. It wasn't until I was about forty years old that I realized Mom is an animal magnet. Wherever we are together, or if she is alone, animals will find her.

Strays end up on the front steps or the back porch. Wild animals will hide in the garage or find a way into the basement. When they appear to her, Mom makes them her friend. It's simple for her. You see, she doesn't know how to show them anything but love. They are drawn to it.

I learned from her to feel compassion for any critter; she showed this to me my whole life. My feeling about animals is not a force like hers, though. Mom's is lovely to watch and anticipate how each instance will manifest itself into something special and sometimes amazing.

For the last several years, Mom has lived in the Georgia countryside, where there are small farms with barns scattered around. These barns house many cats of all shapes and sizes. Mom's had sadness invoked by the regular stream of stray and feral cats placing themselves in her domain. Many of them showed up for help as a result of accidents. Some were diseased or deformed from birth. She's not a vet and can't help them physically, although she does try. In those cases, Mom's efforts require her to capture them and have them euthanized — a heartbreaking task for her every time.

A couple of years ago, new neighbors moved in to the small farm/ranch next door. They added chickens to their farm offering and subsequently purchased a rooster to round out the grouping. The slightly distant rooster-crowing sounds every morning added

211

a new flavor for the neighborhood. After a few days, the rooster showed up in Mom's carport next to the cat food she set out for the stray cats. Surprised when she opened the door, he crowed, "Hello." The carport's extra-tall ceiling gave a loud echo effect, lingering only long enough to catch a second crowed, "Hello." She walked out to greet him, and he unexpectedly stood very still as if on cue.

The next day, she watched as the young farmer chased him around Mom's house twice; on the third time around, he grabbed the bird as he dove downward on the hill in the side yard. Covered in mud, he held the rooster closely under his arm, then he waved at Mom as he walked home. Relieved that neither of them was hurt in the process, Mom was grateful for a successful capture. To her surprise, and I really don't know why she was surprised, the rooster was back again the next morning. The neighbor and Mom repeated the move back to his farm daily over the next few weeks.

One morning, there was a knock on the door. Her neighbor came to talk. He told Mom he was going to stop trying to get the rooster to stay on his farm. "The time fussing with a bird that thinks he's home when he's here at your house is money lost to me. I will purchase a new rooster; one I'll teach to stay at my farm from the start. I'll block any paths and fence openings that promote curiosity at the onset. Do you have any friends on farms around the area that would take the rooster?" At that point, Mom said she did not.

For days on end, the rooster crowed and crowed at all different times of day, becoming a noisy nuisance. Mom asked around, "Do you know anyone who will take a rooster?" Weeks went by.

One day, one of Mom's granddaughters said, "I have a neighbor who has chickens; I'll ask her." Mom was hopeful. She endured another week of the noisy crowing before hearing that the rooster may have a new home.

A cage placed in the carport, the rooster's favorite spot, brought about a couple days of intense activity. The family who wanted the bird all arrived eager to take him home. The teenagers chased him and cornered him a couple of times, but he was clever

212

and quicker than they anticipated each time. Then several attempts were made by their parents, and exasperation was expressed that, "this shouldn't be so hard to accomplish! Did you see him jump? He's so smart, and he's keeping us just out of reach!" All agreed that they would come back one more time to try again. They left the cage and promised to return.

Overnight and the next morning, crowing kept Mom awake late and then woke her early. Mom saw the rooster in the backyard through the kitchen window, drinking at the birdbaths normally hosting finches, bluebirds, and cardinals, to name a few. Mom tapped on the window. The rooster jumped to the ground and looked at her. He jumped up on the window sill and crowed loudly. Mom slowly opened the window. He didn't jump away. She placed her arm over him and held tight as she grabbed his body, holding his wings close to her side. Mom walked to the door, opened it and stepped out into the carport. The cage door was still opened from the efforts the day before. Mom set the rooster on the floor in front of the open cage door, and he walked right in. She closed the cage and said, "Well, aren't you a good boy today."

Mom called the new owners, who lived about an hour away, and told them they could drop by anytime to pick up their new rooster. They were thrilled to hear Mom made it so easy for them.

Is Mom an animal-whisperer?

# The Monster Crows

## *William Barrons*

The downtown San Diego high-rise building I have resided in on the eleventh floor for twenty-three years formerly had lovely little birds fly into our backyard, for the spring and summer, to raise each and every year a charming brood of chicks.

Those beautiful mourning doves, ever-busy finches, tail-flipping blue jays, and a few songbirds, never come here anymore. Those birds or their descendants that were so faithful in returning to us each spring probably no longer exist anywhere at all. Why? I'll tell you why.

My apartment looks out on nice downtown scenery, including our backyard where those birds I mentioned used to proliferate. But a few years ago, a family of crows took up residence here.

Crows are said to be, by far, the most intelligent of birds. They even exceed, in brainpower, most non-flying animals. A bird research expert claims they have over two hundred expressions in their calls. That is truly an amazing discovery of their vocabulary.

Crows operate as families. That is, when it comes to caring for, feeding, and teaching of the new batch of crows each year, even the older brothers and sisters work to help them succeed in life. Obviously, that right there gives crows a great advantage over other birds who do nothing of the kind.

Well, as I said, that family of crows moved in. Each spring they chose one of several forty-year-old, and now very tall, pine trees in our backyard for their nest. Those pines overlook about every other nesting place a bird could find.

The mama, papa, big sister and brother crows seem duty-bound to all search for food for their new and ever-hungry arrivals in their nests.

Crows, being smart rascals, watch other birds fly into their nests to bring all sorts of food for their youngsters. So, being big,

215

bold, brainy, and without any morals whatever, they follow other birds as they fly into their nests and snatch their babies to take to our pine tree to feed their babies!

I was reminded of that bit of horror this very day as I write this true story when I saw a big black monster crow fly unusally fast into the tree picked to nest in this year. As I watched the crow take something — I didn't actually see what he or she had in his or her beak — into the nest, I saw a tiny hummingbird follow the crow right up to that tree!

It was as plain as could be. That teeny tiny little momma hummer was, from a few feet away, chattering away at that hundred-times-larger monster; that monster who had just seconds before scooped up her own baby from her own thumb-sized nest. The monster was right in front of her, feeding her baby to that crow family's baby!

Obviously, there was nothing that forlorn mother hummingbird could do but retreat to where she had lovingly tended to her now monster-devoured baby and weep the days and nights away.

The next time you see a crow or a flight of thousands of crows fly by, remember: yes, they are smart. But, in truth, every crow is a monster.

# Bella

## *Peggy Hinaekian*

I am a female gorilla in a large cage at the zoo. There is water streaming down from some rocks into a pond at the back. There are also some tiny trees strewn around in the cage. What is a gorilla going do with minuscule trees? Can't climb them, just eat the leaves, I suppose. The zoo management thinks they have created a suitable environment for us. They are greatly mistaken.

I am not alone in the cage. My mate, Coco, is with me. Whenever I give birth—it has happened only twice—the humans, who manage the zoo, take my child away from me after I have nursed him or her for a couple of years, and I guess they sell it to another zoo. Bad people. Mean people. Don't they know what it's like to be a mother? I would cry if I could, but I have no tears. Only humans do.

Being in a cage is no life. I am extremely angry and sad— gorilla anger shows in my eyes, they are not sparkling. I have a sad expression. Any sensitive person can see it, but no one pays attention to me, except Coco. I have no freedom to roam the forest, jump from one tree to another, drink from the stream, eat what I want, not the tasteless guck they serve us. I don't know how old I am, so don't ask me to give you day, month, and year. I have been in this cage as long as I remember. No, actually I changed cages when I was of mating age and Coco was introduced to me. It was love at first sight. He is such a great partner. I will never be unfaithful to him, not that I have the occasion or the inclination.

There is a poster next to the cage describing what a gorilla is. I know this because a curious kid, an intelligent kid, read it out loud to his younger brother one day. Here is a short version.

*A gorilla is the largest primate. 98% of their DNA is identical to that of homo sapiens. They are intelligent animals and can use tools and make 25 different sounds. They give birth to one baby every four to six years and they use baby talk to communicate with them. Gorillas in a zoo live about 10 years longer than those in the wild.*

Our names are also given: *Bella (female). Coco (male).*

I would much rather have a shorter life in freedom than a longer one in captivity. But no one has asked my opinion. I suppose I was captured in a jungle, but I don't remember when or where.

On any typical day, Coco is fast asleep at the back of the cage in the shade. He is not as curious as I am. He is much older than me and twice as big. I am of a curious nature and like watching the visitors go by. I like to watch their reactions and listen to their conversations. They don't know I can understand what they are saying.

Some visitors stop and gawk at us, while others just pass by eating ice cream or chips, and they are in such a hurry to see everything that they end up seeing nothing up close.

Some parents lose their kids and frantically call their names. If I could speak, I could tell them which way they went. I could use sign language but they would not understand.

They think we, the ape species, are dumb. We are not. They would know better if they just read the description posted next to the cage. It is quite an informative one. Or, they could look it up on Google. I know about Google from kids' conversations when they are in front of my cage. Don't parents know that they should always watch their kids? I have witnessed many mishaps during my long, boring life in this cage. Parents are not always vigilant. Human kids grow up much slower than animal offspring. They are dependent on their parents for years and years. How tiresome that must be.

Some of the adults walking by look at me. They scrutinize me, then laugh and say to their kids, "Look what *he* is doing with *his* hands, isn't that funny?"

*"No, it's not funny, you dope. I am trying to communicate with you in the only way I can, with my hands. Watch closely and maybe you would understand."*

Children always stop in front of the cage. I am huge, so they say, "Look Ma, *he* is enormous and *he's* ugly and *he* looks angry." "Gynormous," says another one.

218

First of all, I am not a HE. Second, if I could speak I would say, *"Look at your fatso mother, you bums. Her boobs hang lower than mine. And look at your ugly father with that beard full of crumbs, ogling the younger women in short skirts."*

Of course I look angry, because I am extremely frustrated. I notice everything and scratch myself and stare at them in anger — gorilla anger.

Some children laugh at my movements and want to throw food at me, just to be friendly. Some intelligent parents stop them from doing so because they have read the sign that says: "Do Not feed the animals."

I want to say, *"Yeah, don't feed us, we are fat enough with the food they give us — mixed with God knows what, genetically modified or some such thing — and not being able to exercise in freedom, we don't want your junk fast food to make us even fatter."*

Sometimes, curious children want to climb over the fence to come closer, but they are restrained. "Don't do that, it's dangerous," say the parents.

*"Yeah, can't you see I am foaming at the mouth, ready to pounce on your child and grab him?"* Just kidding, I do like children, but only smart ones. I want to say, *"I am not dangerous lady, I just look menacing. Don't be scared."* But no one would believe me. The glass partition at the back of the cage serves as a mirror and, when I look at myself, I get scared too. I don't look harmless at all.

One time, a little girl asked "Ma, why does he never smile, this monkey?"

*"I am not a monkey, child, I am a gorilla and I am a SHE. Can't you read the notice posted on the cage?*

Well, what do you expect from a child. Her parents don't know any better either.

How I wish I could break down these barriers and escape to the jungle with my mate. Where is the jungle anyway? I suppose I could ask one of these kids to Google it for me. Kids are smart with electronics, they have iPads now.

Some parents say such asinine things to their children. One day a couple with two young children walked by. They said, "Hey, Bobby, doesn't Bella look like your great uncle Charlie? The

219

one who sits in an armchair all day long looking angry at the world?"

What a stupid thing to say to a child. Now, whenever the child looks at Uncle Charlie, he will think of me. Well, in a way that is not so bad, at least I will be remembered.

The other day I was mistaken for a *he* again—extremely frustrating. The woman looked at me and told her children, "Look at the way *he* picks up the food with *his* hands and puts it into *his* mouth."

I signed back to her: *How many ways are there to pick up food? I am not a dog or a cat, I don't slurp from a dish. I am almost human. Haven't you heard of evolution?*

She walked away laughing at her own silly joke.

Some humans have not yet evolved enough to understand sign language.

# Samiwich's Short Story

## *Robert Boze*

My name is Samantha, but most people call me Sam. Well, everyone that is except my human dad; he calls me Samiwich.

Yeah, I know, kinda dumb isn't it? But you know what? Even though I get teased a lot, I love my nickname. Why? Because my dad loves me so much that he created a special name, just for me. It's even more special though because dad says that before he met my mom, he couldn't even spell C.A.T. Now, even though I wasn't his first cat, I'm his special cat. His special Samiwich. And there'll never be another Samiwich.

But, I'm getting way ahead of myself. Let me start over.

Hi! My name is Sam. That's short for Samantha.

My name wasn't always Samantha. For my first year and a half I don't really think I had a name, until I found my human parents. All I remember being called was "get out of here," "shoo," and when I was really small, "kitten." But there were dozens of get out of here's, shoos, and kittens so, maybe I was really kitten number eleven and a half, or something like that.

You see, I was born in a house that already had 53 cat brothers, sisters, aunts, and uncles.

When I was born, I was short, chunky and the people in the house said I was funny looking. One of them, the really old lady, said I was the runt of the litter. A few weeks later though, I heard the old nasty guy that lived with her call her an idiot for not seeing that I was inbred.

Inbred … that means my mother and father were related. I think they were actually brother and sister but in the tiny hoarding house I was born in, everybody was called a brother or sister. And, forgive me, but mating with any cat of the opposite sex that happened to be walking by was … well … common.

I remember life from the minute I was born. There were six of

221

us, four sisters and two brothers. We were all different colors and sizes and none of us looked the same. My face was broad and short, and my nose was kinda flat. My legs were really short, stubby they called them, and my body looked like a beer can … round.

My brothers and sisters … well, I never really got to see much of them. One sister and one brother only lived for a day. For some reason, Mom, our cat mom, refused to have anything to do with them. She just pushed them away and ignored them when they tried to feed from her. I got pushed away too, but another mom, who I think only had one kitten and she was born dead, decided to adopt me.

Anyway, she let me feed from her but that was all. Oh, and it was only when *she* felt like letting me. There were some days when I was lucky if I got a mouthful or two before she went into a rampage. I'm not sure but I think it had something to do with losing her own kitten. Why do I say that? Well, for two reasons.

First, a litter of one is rare, and then to lose your only kitten must have devastated her.

Second, one of the older kittens in the house told me much later that I looked like the daughter she lost at birth because of my mottled brownish sort of coloring. My favorite vet would later tell my human parents that I was a "Tri-colored Tortie." That meant that I looked like a tortoise shell that was three shades of brown, all swirled together. Isn't that cool?! I'm like a totally unique tri-colored tortie Samiwich! Yup! Definitely one of a kind!)

I must have been born in the winter, or perhaps the fall, because it was very cold. Two of my siblings only lived one day. My other three siblings wanted nothing to do with me. I think that was because I was inbred. Now, I don't want to act holier than thou, but if I was inbred and every cat in the house was related to each other, what the hell were they? Born from royalty?

My first year was spent pretty much alone. Nobody wanted anything to do with a round, short, squat, flat-faced kitten. Not to mention one whose coat couldn't make up its mind what color it was supposed to be.

The house we lived in was very small, and it was full of stuff. Aside from collecting cats, the owners collected all kinds of other

222

things. The room I was born and lived in until I was rescued was, I think, what you would call the living room. I guess that makes sense since there were at least 50 to 60 of us living in it, along with one or two humans on most days.

There was barely enough to eat, and we often went for days without food or water. Some days, when we were finally fed, we wished we hadn't been.

When I was one, it turned very cold again. Over the year some of my brothers and sisters kept dying around me. Every month there would be fewer and fewer. But then, someone would have another litter, and we'd be back to fighting for food and a warm place to sleep. That's when I started having breathing problems. Also, my teeth really, really hurt.

When summer came it got unbelievably hot. More of my family kept dying all around me, and I had to fight to stay alive. I promised myself I would not die! No matter what, I was only 18 months old, and I had so much I wanted to do. While fighting for everything in my life, I also realized that I wanted to be loved. I needed to be loved, and I had so much love to share.

Finally, one day the rangers from the Humane Society broke down the door. "Ah, air!" I could hardly lift my head but I pulled in as much air as I could, just as a young woman picked me up, snuggled me and told me, "You're okay. I've got you and you're safe."

The next time I woke up I was on an operating table. My throat had a slit in it and a tube hanging out, but I could breathe. The vet said I had an upper respiratory infection, and it had almost turned into pneumonia. He also told the nurse helping him to schedule an appointment with the dentist because almost all of my teeth needed to be pulled. That's when I passed out.

Two days later, I woke up in someone's lap. They were bottle feeding me, and I felt a thousand times better. Oh, and I could breathe! When I started to purr with happiness, I scared myself. I sounded like a lawn mower run amok. But the girl whose lap I was in just laughed. "You are adorable, Cassie. Cassie. That's what we named you by the way." I smiled at her, laid my head against her chest, and when she kissed me on the head I purred even louder. Then I went to sleep.

The next week was kind of fuzzy. I remember the girl coming in two or three times a day to check on me, hug me, and make sure I was okay. "You are such a fighter," she said one day. That's when she told me that over 50 of my brothers and sisters had died, and only four of us had made it out alive.

But now, I had my own super large crate, all the food and water I wanted and someone who loved me and came to check on me every day. How lucky is that!

My crate was on the bottom row in the cattery and I had to stretch my neck to see who came in whenever the door opened. One day, I looked up and saw two people standing with the girl who had named me. "I have someone I'd like you to meet," she told them. She eased me out of my crate, kissed me on my head, and handed me to the woman next to her. I looked into the woman's beautiful eyes, glanced over at the cute guy with her, and I knew I had found my parents!

*I need to let them know I'm theirs*, I told myself. I did a gator roll in her arms, laid my head against her chest, and cranked up my lawn mower purr to full maximum.

The woman looked at the cute guy and said, "She's picked us, you know."

"Yup, I figured that out before she ever got into your arms," he said, scratching my head.

I never went back into my crate because my new mom carried me in her arms while my dad filled out the adoption papers. An hour later I officially had my new parents.

On the way home, I looked over at my dad, who was driving, then up at my mom. I thought back to a year ago and realized how lucky I was. That's when I made myself a promise that I would never let a day go by without letting them know how much I loved them.

As we pulled into the driveway, Dad turned to Mom and said, "We already have a Cassie, so what do you think about naming her Samantha? We can call her Sam, for short."

"I like that," my mom said.

Dad's eyes looked into mine. "You okay with that, Samiwich?" My mom chuckled but I was in shock. All I could do was let out a tiny squeak. Oh . . . My . . . God! I had my own nickname! Up until the shelter, I didn't even have a name. Now, I had a name, Samantha. A nickname, Sam. And now, my very own super special nickname, Samiwich! Me! I was Samiwich! The one and only Samiwich!

I meowed at Dad, licked my mom's hand, did another gator roll in her arms, and snuggled as close to her as I could get. No matter what was inside the house in front of us, I was home. These were my parents, this was my house, and I was in heaven.

As soon as we were inside, mom introduced me to Cassie, a big blond lab and shepherd mix, and Yoda, a brown swirled Sokoke cat. Yup, I'd met a Sokoke before, and they were full of themselves. Yoda was no exception and he wanted nothing to do with me. Ha, we'll see about that!

As I watched them, I realized that Yoda and Cassie were a couple! He was her "Boy Toy!" Yup, she would clean his ears, he would purr and lick her nose, then clean her ears.

Wow! How do I deal with this? I'd never met a dog before and had no idea how to make friends with a dog-cat couple.

Every once in a while though, Cassie would get fed up with him, grumble and bark in his ear because he just wouldn't leave her alone. That was my opening. I'd console each of them separately, always being careful not to favor one over the other.

Sam Note: Cassie was always friendly toward me, but I had to butter up Yoda for 10 years before we finally became friends … sorta.

~

Well, I'm now almost 14 years old. Time has flown by. I love my family more than anything in the world, and right now they need more love than ever before.

You see, in August, Cassie had some kind of a stroke. She collapsed, and Mom and Dad scooped her up and rushed her to the emergency vets. But she never came home. Well, only her ashes came home—a week later.

Then, in late April, Yoda, who was now over 16 and my bestest friend, kept getting weaker and weaker. Finally, when he couldn't eat or drink any more, Mom and dad had the vet come to the house and put him to sleep. Just as he crossed over the rainbow bridge, I gave him a kiss on the nose and told him that someday I would see him and Cassie in heaven.

Little did I know that day might be closer than I thought. Two days later I was diagnosed with breast cancer.

Three weeks ago, I had a radical mastectomy, but I'm getting better every day! Thanks to the love, thousands of hugs, and extra special care I get from my mom and dad. Oh, and everyone at the vet's office too.

You see, no matter what, I will never forget how lucky I am. Nor will I ever stop returning all the love my parents and everyone else gives me. That's what's made me who I am. What makes people love me and me love them back. With all my heart.

---

Author's note: Samantha/Sam/Samiwich has no idea how unique, and very special, she really is. It's impossible to describe how much joy she's brought into our lives and the lives of everyone in whose arms she does her trademark "gator roll." She truly is one of a kind! Is she spoiled? You bet! But deservingly so — as she tells us daily with her lawn mower purrs. And yes, she's recovering well.

# Someone New in the Neighborhood

## *Sally Eckberg*

My family and I moved into our new house with tons of space for exploring. It was the perfect place for an animal of my stature and sophistication. I am a Doberman Pinscher of exquisite conformation. My coat is jet black, my ears are perfectly pointed, and I am of a commanding size, one hundred ten pounds of muscle. My name is "Diego The Nightmare Sanchez."

Now the little secret is, that although I look like I could tear up a bear in minutes, I am sweet tempered and prefer to spend time with my head in someone's lap. However, I have yet to find someone with a lap large enough.

That doesn't mean that I don't guard the yard from foreign varmints. The Fancy fluffy chickens depend on me to keep order, but I have learned to stay away from their wicked clawed feet. Nasty dispositions, those chickens. They have caught me helping myself to a few eggs. Good grief! Talk about getting your feathers in a bunch.

Okay, truth be told, I was not exactly polite to the chickens at first. Unfortunately, the El Primo dog trainer, Salem, was called to prevent me from tearing the chickens apart. He used an electronic collar. After a few shocks, I wanted nothing more to do with the chickens. I am not saying anything about the eggs.

Then there are the cats, Mozart and Pythagoras. Mozart is a fairly gentle creature but, Pythagoras is a large black feline with the worst temperament in the west. Even the chickens try to avoid him. He has no manners whatsoever. He is constantly snarling and spitting when anyone comes near him.

I patrol the perimeter of the yard in the early morning and in the evening. I have had to assert my guardian skills. Usually, it is enough to show my large white teeth with just a low growl to make any varmints go skedaddling.

Lately, I have heard some scratching under the porch in the front yard. This usually takes place in the late evening. I have made my mind up that I will use all my stealth to find the intruder and destroy it.

When my human mom and dad went in to have dinner and watch some moving lights in a box, I lingered outside in the front yard. I was starting to yawn when I heard the scratching start. It moved around under the porch. Who knows what evil intent this creature had in mind?

I decided I would surprise it. I crept quietly up to the edge of the porch. There was a little light from a window. I waited until my eyes adjusted and searched carefully all around the area under the porch. There! I noticed a slight noise and movement over in one corner. Strange, the thing seemed to be coming toward me. I could make out shiny little eyes and a nose. At first, I thought the animal must be a crazy possum with a death wish. I thought that until the animal turned his black-and-white-striped back on me, and I got a swish of what I thought was poison gas.

I got out of there as fast as I could, yelping all the way to the back door. I was not greeted with words of love and sympathy but with words I had never heard before.

Sleeping in the house was out of the question. I rolled in as many weed patches as possible and a few flower beds also. Finally, I fell asleep near the back gate. A severe penalty awaited any uninvited guest. They would receive a complete rub down and a nip to go with it if they resisted.

Morning arrived with Dad getting out a very large tub, scrubbing brushes, soap, and something called Odor Away. I got the picture quickly and tried to slink off behind the chicken coop. Dad found me and quite harshly pulled me back to the tub which was now filled with water. I endured three scrubbings and as many rinses. I didn't resist because I was making myself nauseous from the smell.

No one is perfect.
That's why pencils have erasers.

— *Anonymous*

# Chapter 7 – Home Base

## *Richard Peterson*

### *Prologue*

*A reluctant accomplice, Chicago detective Roy Dobbs, helps kidnap a woman (Colette) from outside a Boston museum. Dobbs' companion — mystery man Elleston — believes she has information vital to their pursuit of Sergio, an elusive Haitian criminal/killer. To complicate matters, Colette has two thugs with her, and the kidnapping has gone awry. Elleston ends up commandeering the woman's SUV; he speeds off with Dobbs and Colette having collapsed onto the back seat, with Dobbs gripping her in a clumsy front-to-back bear hug. (Note: As part of a space alien experiment, Dobbs was given a "gift" of being able to read people's minds. He can turn this ability on and off at will.)*

"Scully, we're going to Home Base. I repeat, *we.* Important cargo on board. I need a distraction for end phase." Beats of silence, then, "Fine, just like in Morocco. But take it down, uh, two notches. Out."

*Scully?* thought Dobbs. *And maybe he's Fox Mulder?* Dobbs shook his head, amused. *Probably the British gal.* He wished he could turn around and probe Elleston.

*Just like in Morocco?*

But he was still wrapped around the woman, both of them facing the rear of the vehicle.

She was much quieter now, apparently tired of thrashing and trying to finger-rake his face. Now he searched her jumbled thoughts.

"It won't be long, old boy," said Elleston. "We'll wait for Scully to finish her preparations. Should be about twenty minutes."

Dobbs had to hand it to the man. Even in this neutral situation, he didn't break character.

Minutes passed. Dobbs's three-quarter length brown leather jacket wasn't much protection against the cold. He wished that Elleston would turn on the SUV's heat, but speaking might agitate the woman. So he tried to ignore the chill and kept scanning her thoughts.

Her fear-riddled brain kept flashing pictures of an older woman — thin long nose, short haircut, a mole on her left cheek. Within this kaleidoscope, highlights appeared: playing cards, the interior of a lavish casino, and stacks of multi-colored gambling chips.

"Very good." Elleston, on his smartphone again. "We will be at base in ten minutes. I'll call when ready."

Elleston kept making turns — probably, Dobbs figured, to minimize encountering stoplights or signs. After all, he and the woman, clinched, made a suspicious-looking sight. Finally, the vehicle slowed. Dobbs wanted very much to look out a window, but didn't dare shift his grip. The vehicle stopped. Elleston got out of the SUV and pulled open the rear door.

Dobbs slipped a hand free. He gave the other man the classic forefinger-to-lips gesture to be quiet.

Elleston, in a low voice, "Will she make a fuss?"

Dobbs carefully disentangled himself. "I need a couple minutes with her," he whispered.

Elleston was carrying the woman's pearl-gray handbag. Just past him Dobbs could make out clusters of masts and the superstructures of boats. *A marina?* "We're going on one of those?"

"Right you are," said Elleston. "Don't take too long." He moved away and left the door partially closed.

After the woman sat up, Dobbs spoke in a slow and soothing tone, attempting to convince her that theirs was a rescue mission, not a kidnapping. Of course she refused to give her name. But after repeated questioning, he caught it: *Colette*.

"You know this woman, don't you?" He described the woman with the mole on her cheek. Again, repetition yielded a thought-

232

scan result. She was Colette's aunt. Carefully Dobbs fashioned the skeleton of a story while monitoring her mental reaction to his words and altering his narrative, as needed.

At one point— "Y'all say she hired yuh," said Colette in a honey-thick Southern drawl, "but how can she afford yuh? Aunt Frederique doesn't have the money."

"That was true at one time," said Dobbs. "But she hit it big. She won at the, uh" —digging hard into memory— "on one of those riverboat casinos. A great deal of money." He took a stab at it. "Poker? Isn't that her game?"

The reaction burst clearly in her mind. *Wrong.*

"No, no, that's not right," he quickly added. Then he had it. "Blackjack...yes, that's what she said."

Colette didn't reply. *Got it.*

He continued. "Your aunt is very concerned for you. That's why she hired us...to help you get out of your situation." He remembered several of her thought-fragments. "You're not happy with your boss, are you? You feel threatened."

She was quiet for a moment. "And yuh know this how?"

Dobbs said, "We can talk about it on the boat. Out there." He nodded toward the marina. "Your aunt is onboard, and very much wants to see you."

Colette said nothing, but he could tell she was excited at the prospect. She and her aunt had a strong bond.

"Did she bring her cat, Winston?" she asked.

Dobbs paused, scanning her. *Clever girl.* "Not likely," he said. "There was a dog on board, but she insisted that it be removed. She's allergic to animal hair."

That tipped the scale. Colette was still unsure, but wanted to believe.

The detective got out and shut the SUV door. He hunched his shoulders. The air felt chillier. He walked over to Elleston, who had just finished another phone conversation.

"We need to establish trust with her," said Dobbs. "Have you checked her bag?"

"Of course. No weapons, just the usual female bric-a-brac. ID documents, no doubt counterfeit."

"Okay. Give it back to her," said Dobbs. "And keep those

special glasses. Speaking of weapons, are you carrying any?"

Pause. "Why no, old boy."

*Liar.* Dobbs asked again. Elleston, clearly irritated, denied being armed.

"Here's the deal," said Dobbs. "I know you have a stun gun in your inner coat pocket, so let's not waste time arguing. I found the woman. You *owe* me. I only want to borrow it."

Elleston leaned forward. "How the *bloody hell* do you know this?"

Dobbs held up a calming hand. "All right, I'll tell you. But only *after* we're done with the woman. Her name's Colette, by the way. Right now, though, I need to borrow your stun gun."

Clenching his teeth, Elleston turned his back to the SUV and handed Dobbs the object, no larger than a pack of cigarettes.

With Elleston leading the way, Dobbs and the woman walked to a grid of tall steel bars that formed a security gate. Elleston used a plastic card to buzz them through, then they proceeded down a ramp and onto one of several concrete walkways. Dobbs paid little attention to the sailboats and yachts around them, but kept checking the woman's thoughts for signs of flight or panic.

The quiet marina was dark, with tall lamps along the walkways casting small pools of light. Water softly lapped against the boats, and the cool air smelled of salt water and diesel oil.

They hadn't gone far when Elleston brought his phone to his mouth. "Proceed," he said softly.

Dobbs readied himself. He had been scanning Elleston as well and knew what was coming.

Five seconds later — *crack!crack!crack!*

Colette flinched and cried out. A series of small bursts had shattered the stillness, on their left and at the far end of the marina.

"Keep walking, people," Elleston urged. "Let's go."

Another few seconds — *crack!crack!crack!crack!crack!crack!* A string of rapid-fire bursts now, clearly firecrackers, from the same area.

That brought excited chatter from the boats. A few people were coming outside. Then a few shouts and whoops — more *crack!crack!crack!* — and laughter. Unmistakable: Probably teenagers acting up.

"Just a little distraction for our neighbors," explained Elleston. "Hurry along." After a few more yards he made a sweeping gesture with his hand. "Here we are. Let's get aboard."

Dobbs glanced over the craft: a yacht with a dark hull and a gleaming white superstructure. He was poor at making estimates, but the vessel was clearly huge. After they climbed the eight-stair access ladder, Elleston led them through sliding glass doors and into a large salon.

Plush beige sofas, walnut flooring, bamboo-design wall panels. Black, closed blinds covered several floor-to-ceiling windows. Gazing around the room, it occurred to Dobbs that this was what the VIP lounge at a major airport might look like. He detected a pleasant odor of vanilla. Most likely, he figured, from some kind of scent dispersal system.

A handful of questions came to mind, but they would have to wait.

"Whose boat is this?" asked the woman. When neither man answered, she snorted with disgust. "Okay then, where is Aunt Frederique?"

The salon had two sofa clusters, each with one long sofa perpendicular to a shorter sofa. They wouldn't do for Dobbs's purposes. At one end of the room sat a modern, kidney-shaped desk with two chairs in front of it. *Perfect.* He gestured toward one of the chairs. "Please, Colette, have a seat. My colleague will go get your aunt." He raised his eyebrows and nodded at Elleston.

Fortunately, Colette was moving toward a chair and didn't notice Elleston's scowl. But the man quickly recovered and played along. He firmed his lips, squared his shoulders. "Quite so. I'll be back in a flash." He hurried off.

Dobbs took Colette's coat, then draped both it and his leather jacket over a sofa. She had her bag now and placed it on the floor beside her chair. He moved the other chair so he could face her.

"As I said, Colette, this is a rescue. Please understand, your Aunt Frederique has your best interests at heart."

He needed more time to build a rapport, but then Elleston abruptly returned. He had removed his suit coat, revealing a light blue shirt with a white coat of arms on the breast pocket.

Dobbs frowned slightly. *Mr. Dapper.*

"She'll be here straight away," Elleston said, clapping his hands together. Broad smile. "Now, I've spoken to the chef and asked him to prepare us something." He bowed slightly. "Miss Colette, would you prefer roast beef or salmon?"

At first Colette seemed puzzled. But Dobbs's scan told him that she was hungry; apparently stress had activated her appetite. Then her face brightened as she made her decision. Both she and Dobbs ordered the salmon; Dobbs also asked for some hot cinnamon tea. Elleston went over to the desk and used an intercom inlaid into its teak surface to place their order.

Dobbs pushed himself out of his chair and began pacing. Elleston settled into a tall-backed executive chair behind the desk.

"You see, Colette," said Dobbs, "in exchange for bringing you here, all we want is information. Nothing more."

He looked over. Elleston was leaning back, adjusting his rectangular-framed glasses. Thought-scan: The man was both amused and curious as to what Dobbs would do next.

"And since we need to be honest with each other," continued the detective, "I'm sorry to inform you that your Aunt Frederique—although I'm sure she really *does* care about you—is *not* onboard."

Colette's cobalt-blue eyes flared with surprise. Dobbs stepped behind her and pressed the stun gun into the right side of her neck. Her body convulsed.

He grasped her shoulders to keep her upright, then met Elleston's surprised look. "I know a cop in Chicago," said Dobbs. "She's top-notch undercover, and once told me, 'Sometimes, to get out, you have to go deeper in.'"

# The Little Shit and the Ghost Lamp

## *David J. Schmidt*

The Little Shit had been really getting on Desiree's nerves. In the dozens of times she had led this tour of her college campus, she had never dealt with anyone as obnoxious as the Little Shit.

Of course, Desiree realized that it wasn't very Christian to think of a high school student as a "little shit." She knew her old youth pastor would not approve of the word's presence in her internal monologue. At her home church, you used softer words if you were mad at somebody. "Little jerk." "Little turd," maybe. Or "little piece of crap," if you were really upset. But you just plain weren't allowed to say "shit," not even in your head.

Not to mention, this kid probably went to church himself. Heck, for all Desiree knew, his dad might even be a pastor. That was the most common way high schoolers got plugged into these campus tours: through their home church. It was Desiree's job, as campus tour guide, to convince these high schoolers that this particular private Christian college — Point Loma Nazarene University — was a good fit for them. The Little Shit was one of those prospective new students. Desiree had to be nice to him.

*But darn it,* Desiree thought, *he is a little shit, all the same.*

Desiree knew that she didn't like the Little Shit from the very beginning of the walking campus tour. She was showing the high school students and their parents Mieras Hall, one of the historic buildings built by the mysterious sect of the Theosophists at the turn of the century.

"They had a very unique architectural style," she told the visitors. "Madame Tingley, the Theosophists' leader, designed this building herself. Notice the strange purple orb on top of the building, which looks kind of like a turtle's shell. The building itself is even shaped like a turtle. As legend has it, Madame Tingley wanted to be reincarnated as a turtle because she believed…"

"Aw, that's gay!" came the Little Shit's voice from the back of the crowd.

Desiree was thrown off by the comment: violent, angry, and entirely stupid. *What is "gay" about a turtle? Or about reincarnation or Theosophical architecture, for that matter?*

As the tour went on, Desiree quickly discovered that the Little Shit's comment had nothing to do with the historic building — he found everything on campus to be "gay." The cafeteria was "gay." The palm trees at the entrance to campus were "gay." The synapses in the Little Shit's brain appear to be firing entirely at random. "Aw, that's gay," was not exactly a comment; it was more like a spontaneous, involuntary reaction. Desiree recalled a relative who suffered nerve damage and whose arm would twitch constantly.

At first, Desiree tried to include the Little Shit in the conversation as she led the tour group around campus. When they passed the tennis courts and the gym, she asked the Little Shit if he enjoyed playing any sports.

"You tell me," the Little Shit responded with a self-satisfied smirk on his lips.

What Desiree said was, "I beg your pardon?" But what she thought was, *Are you on valium, kid? How am I supposed to tell you what sports you like?*

Two of the Little Shit's friends had come on the campus tour with him. They laughed at all his "jokes." When he called something "gay," the two of them would snicker. When he pulled down the hood of a boy's sweatshirt, they guffawed.

Desiree took a good look at these two boys, each of them a head shorter than the Little Shit, as the group walked down to the dorms nearest overlooking the ocean. A long, grotesque parade of Hollywood bullies marched through her mind. First, she imagined the blond kid from *Harry Potter* — Draco Malfoy — and his two goons, Crabbe and Goyle. But no, Crabbe and Goyle were much taller. These kids reminded her more of the old holiday film, *A Christmas Story*, with "Ralphie" and the Red Rider BB gun. Desiree thought of the red-haired bully from the movie, who always hung around with his toady.

238

*Yeah, that's the right word — toady. These kids are toadies: little yes-men who, if they're lucky, might grow up to be big yes-men and spend all their lives kissing the ass of some corrupt business exec.*

The Little Shit and his toadies spent most of the tour giggling uncontrollably. They spat on the ground. They gave each other the finger. After any statement Desiree made, the Little Shit would say, "*Wha-a-a-a-a-a-a-at,*" long and slow, like he'd suffered a stroke. He grabbed every piece of paper he could find and crumpled it into a ball to throw at his toadies. The first time Desiree saw him do it, she asked him to please not throw trash. Rather than apologize — or claim it wasn't him, or make an excuse, or say *anything*, for that matter — the Little Shit just pointed at another high schooler in the group. He pointed and shook his head, non-verbally, like a baby.

When Desiree took the students through the Crill music building, the Little Shit grabbed a piece of coffee cake from a catering tray. By this point in the tour — which was, thankfully, nearing its end — Desiree had resigned herself to thinking of him as the Little Shit. She could ask God for forgiveness later, on Monday morning, during the chapel worship service. For now, she needed some kind of release, even if it was only in her mind. Thinking of him, silently, as the Little Shit gave her just enough inner catharsis to keep her head from exploding.

Desiree reached one of the last stops on the tour — the theater. She used her staff key to open the front door and ushered the tour group into the lobby.

"Stay close by the doors here," she told her guests. "I need to go in and get the lights turned on."

Desiree tried the house lights, but they weren't working for some reason. Luckily, the Ghost Lamp was plugged in. It glowed dimly on the stage.

"Okay, this happens sometimes. Gather around, everybody," Desiree said. "I'm going to ask you all to stand here in the lobby and close your eyes for a few seconds, to adjust to the dim light in here."

She pulled the front door shut and everyone stood in silence with their eyes shut. An observer might have mistaken it for a prayer meeting. After half a minute, they opened their eyes. They

239

could just barely make out the rows of seats in the theater. Beyond the seats, on the edge of the stage, the Ghost Lamp bathed the theater in soft, warm light.

"What's the deal with that lamp up there?" one of the students asked, pointing at the solitary bulb atop the bronze pole. No lampshade adorned it; nothing but a minimalistic lamp standing sentinel in the darkness.

"That's an old theater tradition," Desiree answered. "It's called a Ghost Lamp."

Normally, during this part of the tour, she would only mention it in passing. Here in the dim light of the empty theater, however, everyone seemed to fixate on the Ghost Lamp. Desiree slowly led the group forward, allowing them to file past the edge of the stage and get a good look at it.

"So what's it doing up there on the stage?" another student asked.

"The theater staff always keep it turned on in here, when there is a show going on," Desiree responded. "It's a tradition in a lot of theaters. They say it 'keeps the ghost happy' during a production. People call our theater ghost 'Irving.' You have to appease Irving, they say. If you don't keep the lamp on … bad things might happen. Costumes might go missing. Someone might even get hurt."

Desiree paused for a second, for dramatic effect. A couple of kids smiled nervously.

"Of course, this is a Christian college. And personally, I don't believe in Irving," she clarified. "It's just a fun little superstition."

"So why not just get rid of the lamp?" asked a mother with a Baptist-church-bake-sale-organizer look to her.

"Well … I think sometimes it's just better to leave well enough alone. And so far, so good. Irving hasn't ruined any productions yet." Desiree smiled. A voice rang out in the dark theater, one she knew all too well: *"Wha-a-a-a-a-a-a-a-at?"*

"I'm sorry," Desiree said between gritted teeth, staring at the Little Shit. "Did you have a question?"

"That's so gay!" His two toadies chuckled. Desiree tried to ignore them.

"Well, folks, I think we can move on with the …"

"It's gay!" the Little Shit groaned again. "This is so stupid! Nobody believes that crap. This is the gayest school ever! I'd never come here! Your stupid ghost stories and your ..."

The light bulb exploded.

In one brilliant flash of savage white light, the entire crowd was cast into darkness. A voice screamed out in the dark. Desiree couldn't tell if it was male or female. The dry, nervous sound of feet shuffling. Someone fumbling with their keys in their pocket. The unnatural silence of twenty people holding their breath at the same time. The air felt congested, dense, almost solid.

Desiree rushed to get some light into the place.

She jogged up the aisle between the seats, feeling her way along, and opened the front door, bathing the crowd in faint natural light. Slowly, they shuffled towards her in single file. A couple of parents whispered quietly.

"Umm ... sorry about that, folks." Desiree herded the tour group towards the exit. "I don't know what happened in there. First time for everything, right?" She chuckled nervously.

The visitors regrouped in front of the theater and Desiree proposed that they continue with the tour. Then she noticed — somebody was missing. She did a quick head count, trying to remember all of the high schoolers, parents, families with children, two grandparents, and suddenly realized: *It's the Little Shit. He's the one who is missing.* Desiree propped the door open and walked back into the dark theater. A dark shape stood at the very back, in a corner by the stage.

"Hello?" Desiree called out. The shape didn't move.

She approached the figure slowly, cautiously. It remained motionless. At first, she thought it might be a prop from the play. Finally, when she was just a few inches away from it, she heard shallow breathing. It was the Little Shit.

His head hung low, staring at the ground, oblivious to the shards of broken light bulb scattered around him. Still as a statue.

"Come on, buddy," Desiree encouraged him. "Why don't we go outside?"

He didn't respond.

"Is everything all right?"

There he stood, stock still, staring at the ground.

241

"Let's go join the others, all right?" Desiree repeated.

She started walking backwards, urging the kid towards the exit. He slowly followed. His feet dragged mechanically, eyes staring at the ground, hair hanging over his face. Even after they came into the bright sunshine, he didn't look up once.

His head hung down for the rest of the tour, avoiding eye contact. Nobody had any idea what happened to him during the two minutes he spent alone inside that dark theater. He didn't speak a word the rest of the day. All Desiree knew was this: when she said goodbye to him at the end of the tour, she really *did* feel bad for thinking of him as "the Little Shit."

# Window Shopping

## *Marcia Buompensiero*

Standing outside, looking in, my reflection on the car dealership window smiled back at me. Beyond the glass, the fire-engine red BMW on the elevated platform turned slowly, a super-model showing off every metric inch of German-engineered perfection. I held my breath. I sighed. The sexy sports car winked at me—I'm sure.

"She's a beauty, isn't she?" said the woman who had just walked up to the window and stood next to me.

"She sure is," I said, sighing again.

The woman tilted her head just slightly. "Don't you feel a little guilty when you think about trading in your old faithful, reliable car for something like this—a flashy new model?"

I chortled, thinking, *I should, I suppose. Still . . .*

"Yeah," I said, suddenly feeling that little pinch in my gut that I knew was my conscience.

We both stared in silence for another moment. Then, she said, "Do you think that's what a man thinks when he strays?"

We both laughed.

I turned to make a pithy comment. That's when I saw the black and whites pull up. Four uniformed officers jumped out and headed toward us. One had his hand on his holstered weapon.

"Mrs. Wagner?" he said as he got within earshot.

My companion turned and smiled. She stooped down and laid a gun on the pavement. Then she pulled herself up and raised her hands in surrender.

# Bonding

## *Val Zolfaghari*

He was not an Englishman but had an English accent. As a boy, he was sent to England to be educated. Kids in school called him "Bloody Foreigner." He longed for friendship. Some days for fun, he dressed like a Middle Eastern imam, four girls pretending to be his wives walked behind him and made fun of him. Some days, he dressed like a French Chevalier, declared war on English boys, fought them, and signed a peace treaty. Whatever he did, kids did not bond with him.

When he graduated from high school, he was given a new title, *"WOG."*[1]  He did not mind the new moniker and said, "Anything is better than being a dirty Englishman." He moved to the land of opportunity to bond.

Sundays were special. He felt no rush to leave his cozy bed. He threw his cold, hot-water bottle out of his bed and rolled around. He jumped out of bed and had a nonconventional English bath. Instead of wetting a small towel and cleansing his body, he filled the bathtub and immersed himself in it and read for a long time while singing, "She loves you, yeah, yeah, yeah …" After his imperialistic bath, he was ready for a good breakfast.

He had discovered an English restaurant, Crown, close by, and some Sundays enjoyed his greasy bacon breakfast and humorously announced to the owner, "I believe animals should have equal opportunity to be slaughtered."

One Sunday, Wog desired greasy bacon, put on his best suit, leisurely walked towards Crown, and craved to bond with someone. He encountered an old, friendly gentleman wearing a yarmulke [2] . They smiled, swapped *Shalom*, and then the gentleman asked Wog," Are you Jewish?"

 Bonding overwhelmed Wog and his sense of humor bloomed. "No sir, my ancestors were damn lazy and joined the line too late to be chosen."

The gentleman laughed. "I wish your damn lazy ancestors had joined the line earlier and we had bonded. You have lost a lot."

Wog made a funny face. "I know, sir."

"What have you lost?"

"Do you really want to know?"

"Of course, we may discover we have something in common."

"At birth, they cut off part of my important thing, too."

The old gentleman changed into a teenager and shouted, "Dude, more than the right amount?"

Wog nodded, "I don't know."

They high fived.

The gentleman said, "Measure it before the next time we shalom."

Wog said, "Dude, I will."

The gentleman laughed. "Dude, at the age of 87, I have the right size but it is no good."

They said goodbye and walked in opposite directions. The gentleman resumed his old age, admonished himself for being silly, and hoped that there would be no more encounters between them.

The following Sunday, they met, exchanged shalom, and the gentleman changed into a teenager and said, "Dude, what is the number?"

Wog gave a number written on a piece of paper to the gentleman. The gentleman took out a calculator, put in Wog's number, punched a few more buttons, and shook his head.

"Dude, five percent difference? Too much. I am sorry, we cannot bond."

Wog pleaded, "Dude, five percent is not much."

The gentleman shook his head. "Five percent of that thing means a lot."

"I have a suggestion."

"What is it?"

"Let us bond five percent."

The old gentleman shook his head. "I am sorry it is impossible. Goodbye," said the gentleman and he walked away.

A month later, the old man walked into a local coffee shop and saw that Wog was sitting alone with a sad face. Humanity took hold of him, he reverted to a teen and walked to Wog.

"Shalom, how are you?"

"Does not my face tell you how I am?"

"It tells me you are miserable, but you will have a happy face in seconds."

"Why?"

"I was wrong, five percent error is acceptable."

"You mean we can bond!"

"Yes."

Wog became happy and shouted, "Finally, I have a friend. Waiter, waiter, hurry up. My friend is ready to order."

"Shalom."

---

1 WOG: Westernized Oriental Gentleman (a derogatory title)

2 Yarmulke: Jewish cap

# Spoiler

### *Anne M. Casey*

Thief sneaks 'round in the night
with sleight of hand
and pellet bright,
turns a dream
into fright.

One spare sip,
another down
changes laughter
to a frown.

Down......down
to Oblivion
I slid

One door opened
another closed
Motel dark
we hid.

Pain and **pain**
ripped into me.
Strangled gasp
I tried to flee

Pushing, tearing
He hammered me
eyes squeezed tight
I couldn't see.

A final thrust,
a ragged groan
he tore away, fell off of me.

Goodbye, goodbye, plans informed.
Farewell senses
all transformed.

We write because we believe the human spirit cannot be tamed, and should not be trained.

*—Nikki Giovanni*

# Law and Disorder

## *Harry. W. Huntsman*

I had heard that if anyone testified in court against a bad guy in Searcy, Arkansas, my home town, they would never do it again.

While at a service station, my wife and I, and several other people, watched a scrawny young man, whom some of us knew, obviously drunk, walking past. A police car raced into the station and a large officer, well known to most of us, jumped out, ran to the young drunk, and dragged him to the police car. He opened the back door and easily threw the man onto the back seat. But when he tried to close the car door the young man blocked it with his feet.

After two or three more efforts to close the door the officer began beating the drunk's legs with a black jack. A moan of protest went up from the group of witnesses, and they inched toward the officer. There was so much anger I thought they might attack him in spite of his club, gun, and size. After he drove away with his prisoner the crowd got larger and angrier. Several said they would go to court against the policeman.

My wife and I lived just a few blocks away. Afraid there might be a riot at the jail, we hurried home, and I called the state police. By the time they arrived the crowd was dispersing.

By the day of George Parks's trial, for public drunkenness and resisting arrest, the story circulated that city firemen and police officers sold whiskey out of the fire department and that George, a fireman, had not shared the money from some of his sales. Officer Bollen was to collect the withheld money and punish him.

I was the only witness to testify at the municipal court hearing, though there was a large and angry audience.

I was asked only one question. "Did George Parks resist arrest?"

"He tried to keep officer Bollen from closing the car door," I said.

George was given the minimum fine of $50.00.

I was pastor of three country churches and worked part time at an appliance store.

The morning after the trial I parked near the store, and the chief of police pulled in behind me. While I fed coins into the parking meter he lectured me. "I don't understand a man in your position going to bat for a man like that."

"I don't understand why you hired a man with his reputation for brutality," I said.

"He's a good officer."

"Some business owners in Heber Springs told my dad they ran Officer Bollen up Heber Mountain at midnight in front of their pickup trucks, without his pants, because he beat up high school students. The kids called him "Blackjack Bollen.""

Chief Clark was beginning to shake so I turned and went in the store. After he left I crossed the street to the courthouse to talk to the judge. "Why can't we get better men as our police officers?" I asked.

The judge became rather upset. "Because the taxpayers won't pay enough to get good men."

The following week the City Council fired "Black Jack Bollen."

Bald Knob, a town in the same county, hired him as city Marshall.

Within a year Chief Clark faced brutality charges before the City Council after almost killing a man by stomping him. Since he was within a year of retirement, a divided council stripped him of gun and billy club and let him check parking meters.

# Heading up the
# Holy Roller Sisterhood

## *Terri Trainor*

### Fort Myers, FL  1982

Stephanie feels her face smiling before she even opens her eyes—today is going to be her day! After years of tolerating taunts and Polack jokes, today, at her church, the new priest, from Poland, would be serving the mid-morning Mass. Under a Polish Pope, imagine!  And today is the day of the elections for the Women's Club leadership positions. She had been nominated for President.

The woman who nominated her (Lilith, the incumbent) did it as a joke, but so what? She knows that they think she didn't notice their snide little asides, but it offers her an opportunity to practice humility. Lord knows, that was a grace that did not come easily to her. Besides, joke or not, she fully intended to win.

All month she had been preparing, diligently knitting warm wool booties for the nursing homes in the area. Bright red, yellow, blue, green, and purple ones, as well as the standard brown and black ones—she wanted to bring joy as well as warmth.

Whenever she thought of the cold feet of those poor old creatures in the overly air-conditioned nursing homes, a tear would spring to her eye, and her hands would knit a little faster. Not on her watch! There would be no cold feet in Fort Myers tonight! There would be no cold feet in any nursing home on the Eastern Seaboard should she get to lead the Women's Club.

She gets out of bed and surveys the large box of matched pairs of booties in the living room with satisfaction as she goes to make her morning tea. Eighty-five flawless pairs of booties! All perfectly matched up and buttoned together by the heels.

She thinks about the outfit she selected: her lime green and peach short set, with a cute new pair of sandals. It would be hard to miss her in those colors! She could be forgiven a bit of vanity around her feet; she was a retired foot model for Filene's in Boston, after all. Her girl, Uma, at the nail salon even painted little flowers on the big toes. She looks down and wiggles her toes in delight.

She closes her eyes as she takes that first sip of hot, sweet tea. As the warmth fills her mouth and belly, she offers a little prayer of gratitude for the new day. She pops an English muffin into the toaster and begins to scramble an egg. Her doctor recommended that she pay attention to increasing her potassium levels, so she dutifully places a banana next to her breakfast plate. Who says breakfast can't include a sweet dessert! She pops in her teeth and smiles to herself. When everything is ready, she sits down and says grace before eating her meal.

As she finishes, she glances at the clock. She has her weekly 8 a.m. appointment with her hairdresser this morning. Looks like trimming the roses would have to wait until later in the day. She washes and dresses in a hurry and packs some yarn and needles to take to her appointment. While under the hair dryer, she might be able to knit one more pair of booties.

Her hairdresser greets her with a warm hug as she walks in.

"Stephanie!" Sarah gushes. "I love the lighter blonde on you! What do you want to do today?"

"I'm really liking it, Sarah — good suggestion. Shampoo, and style, please. Oh!" She reaches into her purse and teasingly pulls out a baby blanket.

"I brought a little something for your new niece..." She hands it to Sarah.

Sarah gasps and unfolds it to admire the craftsmanship. Stephanie looks on proudly. It's beautiful, she admits to herself proudly, soft frothy white with raised pink and yellow roses.

"Oh Stephanie — you shouldn't have. It's so fancy! How did you make the little roses? Thank you!"

Stephanie looks down modestly. "Oh you know, a little this, a little that — glad you like it." Stephanie might have made an even one hundred of the booties if she hadn't knit the blanket, but

Sarah was like family. It was worth it. She doubted anyone else at the church made 85 pairs of booties.

"Like it? I love it, love it, love it!!! Just in time for the christening. Thank you soooo much!" Sarah bounces in delight and sing-songs, "It's so pretty, it's so pretty, soft and fuzzy…"

"Stop—you're making me blush!"

"You're going to join us, aren't you?"

"I'm sorry, it's the same day as the Nursing Home Ministry."

Was that presumptuous? She hasn't actually won yet, she might actually be available and it would be rude not to go in that case. But 85—no 86 pairs of booties—surely that was enough to win, right?

"I'll save you some cake, then. Let's get you shampooed…"

Stephanie finishes up the second bootie, just as the timer on the hair dryer pings. She crochets a quick loop to fit around the knit button of the first bootie. Sarah rushes over to escort her to the styling station. Stephanie smiles in satisfaction as Sarah makes her hair even prettier than usual. She talks about the election, careful not to say anything too catty about the woman, Lilith, who nominated her. Can't be too careful. She's told too many of the ladies about Sarah and they may now be clients.

Sarah finishes with a flourish of hair spray and a "looking good, Mrs. President."

Stephanie flushes. "Let's not count our chickens…"

She glances at her watch and notices that she's right on schedule. She should be able to carry her box of booties to the meeting hall before any of the other ladies arrive and get into church with time to light a little candle.

As she kneels and lights the candle, she thinks of her little Jimmy. Had he not peeled and consumed so much lead paint off the wall beside his crib, he might have grown up to be a priest. Instead he's spending his life in a residential facility for the severely retarded, unable to feed himself. Her heart pangs with guilt, even as she reminds herself of her circumstances—the Depression, the small apartment, the second baby's colic, the increasing violence of the 2-year-old boy.

For a moment, she's back in Boston—nursing her baby girl, while her boy climbs out of his crib and starts hitting the

257

newborn... She sighs. Her poor beautiful Polish boy — her first-born — her heartache. And now her grown daughter finds Stephanie an embarrassment. God knows, she just wanted her little girl to be educated, play the piano, know etiquette — all the things she had wished for herself. The lyrics to her favorite song dance across her mind, "I beg your pardon, I never promised you a rose garden ...."

Her daughter, Anne, grew up refined, cultured, educated, worldly. But Anne also chose to marry a violent man... no one's life is perfect. She glances up at the Virgin Mary, who gently smiles back down at her. Mother Mary understands — you can't live your children's lives. You can't protect your babies from experiencing tragedies of their own. She thinks of Mary sobbing over her baby boy, grown and suffering on the cross, and feels part of a community of mothers reaching back thousands of years. The thought offers comfort — the catholic, universal experience of motherhood.

Maybe this Polish priest, Tim, will come to stand in her heart for the Jim that might have been. Deep down, she knows that's why today's important to her. She wants to see if this new Father will also feel like a loving son... She glances up at Mary. "Is it wrong to want this?" The statue's half-smile offers a compassionate benediction.

Stephanie dries her tears and stands to find her seat. She settles herself into her pew near the front. She glances at the Mass program and notes with pleasure that her favorite songs are part of today's Mass and lets herself dream of her future victory, when they count the booties — then count the votes, hoping her diligence will sway some of those who have yet to accept her. Before she knows it, the opening strains of "Onward Christian Soldiers" call her to stand. She smiles, thinking of how her little grandkids mock-marched to this song when they attended church together last. She thought them naughty at the time, but now it made her smile. God, it's hard to think of them as teenagers already.

She turns to see the processional. Ah, the new priest has blonde hair and blue eyes, just like her Jimmy. She grins in pleasure as Father Tim's eyes dart her way and his mouth twitches almost imperceptibly. Ah yes, they would get along just fine. Thank you, God!

As Mass ends, there's a bit of a rush to the front patio to be among the first to welcome the new Father. Stephanie hangs back a moment. Maybe it's vain to think so, but she knows she'll be noticed without having to beg for attention. She heads out once the rush abates and stands on the fringes, thinking of what her daughter would do in this situation. As the ladies begin to drift towards the community room, she walks up to the Father and introduces herself.

"Welcome, Father, I'm Stephanie O'Leary. I'm looking forward to working with you in the Women's Club."

"Thank you, Mrs. O'Leary, please call me Father Tim—Irish, are you?"

"O'Leary's my married name, I'm Polish, just like you…we're very glad you were chosen to lead our parish."

They walk together towards the community room. When they get there, Stephanie immediately notices something is off. Her box has been opened, and it looks like over half her booties are no longer there. She glances around and notices smug looks on some faces and angry, guilty looks on others. She glances at Father Tim and decides to remain silent.

Lilith steps up and takes Father Tim's arm to lead him to his place at the center of the Women's Club officers' table up front. The ladies take their seats. Lilith stands and clears her throat. Everyone quiets down to listen.

"First order of business, we've selected the Rose Garden of Fort Myers Nursing Home as our charity home this month. We have a contest for knit booties going on. The winner will go with Father Tim to deliver them on Saturday." Turning to him, she adds, "We hope you'll do the honor of counting the entries."

Father Tim grins. "Of course, ladies, I'd be delighted. Where do I start?"

Rose shyly pulls out a small paper lunch bag full of booties that she's tied into pairs with some yellow ribbon. "Let's start small, shall we?" she says as she hands them to Father Tim.

Everyone titters politely as Father Tim counts out five pairs of booties.

"Now there are five people who will sleep with warm feet

Saturday night. Well done."

A few more ladies present their offerings. Father Tim notes each of the unique forms of connectors between the pairs. Some had matching yarns tied into bows, some had safety pins, some had ribbons, even paper clips.

Father Tim reaches for Stephanie's box and begins counting. Stephanie keeps her head down. There should be eighty-six beautifully matched pairs in there. Where did the others go?

"Ah, this reminds me of home, look at how they are connected."

Stephanie had made a knitted button on one of the booties and a crochet button loop on the other. "My mother used to make them just the same." He counted 36 pairs of booties. He looked over at Stephanie, impressed. "A fine haul indeed for cold feet."

With fifty of them missing, that left less than half of her hard work in the box, Stephanie thinks to herself. She feels hurt and confused, but she holds her tongue. Her face must register some of her sad puzzlement, however, because Father Tim looks at her for a moment before continuing.

Next up is one of Lilith's best friends, Carole. As he counts, he notices some of the fasteners are different. "Looks like you had a little help from a friend here," as he holds up a pair fastened by a white ribbon and a knit button pair. Carole blushes and mumbles, embarrassed, "Some of us are more talented and generous than others."

Stephanie does her very best to keep her face neutral through this "aha moment," but she can't help but glance at Father Tim. He gives her a subtle nod. Her lips twitch as she glances down at her hands. That nod encourages her to keep the faith — and her silence.

A few more of Lilith's friends get treated to variations of "who gifted you with this fine set of booties" and "funny, the ones with the buttons are a lot more colorful than the others." Carole looks ready to speak up, but Lilith and some of the others give her the "glare." After some moments of struggle, while the counting continues, Carole finally slides over a couple of seats to sit in the empty chair next to Stephanie. She puts her hand on Stephanie's arm, leans in and whispers: "I'm sorry." Stephanie pats Carole's arm and tries not to tear up. Kindness is often harder to bear than cruelty.

Lilith wins with a bootie count of 50 pairs even. Less than half of which were knitted by her hands. Father Tim congratulates her and "the anonymous donor of the larger quantities of footwear." He continues that he was looking forward to delivering the booties with Lilith the following day. Everyone claps politely.

The next order of business: the elections. Ballots pass from hand to hand. Father Tim would be counting the votes. Some of those feeling upset about the bootie situation glance over at Carole, who inclines her head towards Stephanie. Small nods aimed in Carole and Stephanie's direction emerge from all over the room.

Stephanie wins by a landslide. Lilith appears stunned that she lost her leadership role. Stephanie gratefully looks around, avoiding Lilith's angry eyes. Father Tim announces a new policy: the Women's Club President would be welcome to attend any visitations going forward. Stephanie could join him and Lilith on tomorrow's visit, if she chose.

In closing, Father Tim mentions that he'd be in the confessional for the following two hours, as was customary for a Friday. "I welcome the chance to put hearts at ease."

As Stephanie gets up to leave, Father Tim walks up to her with a stoic face and dancing eyes: "I look forward to working with you, Mrs. O'Leary."

Stephanie blushes, "Thank you, Father. Please call me Stephanie."

As she walks to her car, Stephanie allows herself a smile of satisfaction. Oh yes, a new day has dawned.

# Spirit Rises to the Challenge

## *Ty Piz*

A dust storm whips across the desert. It showers waves of dirt and rocks, tumbles sun tarps, and tosses folding chairs, even knocking over motorcycles. Shouts for help echo through this race paddock. Folks run for shelter. Families are separated, and tears stream down a young girl's face as she worries for her daddy's safety out on the race track.

The whirlwind shakes the van with such intensity that we worry that it will roll us over. We huddle in, riding out the storm, giving thanks that we're finally together. Brenda and I try to take the girls minds off the storm. We play a game of Old Maid.

After an hour the weather calms. From inside the van we can barely hear the announcer's voice over the loud speaker, "Riders meeting at the tower in ten minutes."

"Thanks for lunch," I tell Brenda and the girls. "The game of Old Maid was fun. I'm going to the riders' meeting. Love you!"

I start for the door, then turn, "One of these days I'm going to beat you girls at this card game!"

Racers and crews gather beside the tower. Club president Chuck speaks, "We've lost a lot of time due to the wind and dust. Maintenance crews are sweeping the track, and traction is not great. We've decided to combine the expert and amateur classes to get you as much practice as possible."

Chuck's eyes scan the group. His face is serious. "I can't stress enough that this is Saturday practice. The race is tomorrow, so take it easy out there."

It's good that Chuck continues to remind us that it's a practice day. We're all racers, and mostly we just want to get out there and blaze as fast as we can.

Walking to the van I talk with Ray, a stocky expert racer from California.

Ray says, "At Willow Springs the wind howls a lot. I've been there when the wind hits so hard you can't see anything in Turn-Eight and Turn-Nine."

I nod, "That's wicked scary. Last season two guys collided in Turn-Eight at 120 mph. One guy is paralyzed. The other passed on."

I bow my head, "Godspeed to them."

Ray says, "You've gotta ride from memory. If one person shuts off, it's dangerous for everyone."

"I agree. During the last session, I kept it twisted on and stayed leaned over as I looked for the edge of the track."

Ray brushes his hair out of his face, "Have you seen the road signs by Bonneville Salt Flats?"

"What signs do you mean?"

"The signs that say: 'In case of dust storms, slow down safely, do not stop on the road.'"

I nod and give him a half smile. "Yeah. Good message."

Ray becomes increasingly agitated. "A few years ago at the World Grand Prix at Laguna Secca, on the cool down lap as racers headed toward the Corkscrew, a rider stopped to do a burn-out for the crowd."

I shake my head in disbelief, knowing what show-off hijinks can lead to at those speeds.

"Two riders traveling side by side, still doing 70 mph, did not expect to see this racer stopped. One of them collided with him."

My hands cross my heart. "Oh crap."

"This racer is famous in America. He was injured so badly that he may never race again."

Ray looks away. I place my hand on his shoulder. "I'm sorry for him and his family."

"Thanks, Ty. I was at Laguna Secca with my family when that happened. It changed everything. We went from the energy and thrill of watching a high-speed ballet, to shock, then sorrow! It's something you never forget."

We reach the van. My girls are playing cards. The sounds of their laughter remind us that this is about family and fun. If we stay alert out there on the track, it will be.

I recall 1999, while racing the Baja event in Mexico where most of the race was ridden in heavy dust conditions. The high speeds across the desert made it extremely dangerous.

Ray heads toward his trailer. I tell him, "Ride well today!"

He turns and gives me a thumbs-up.

"Girls, I'm in the second practice session. This is good, the track will be mostly cleared off before I go out."

Contemplating today's track, speeds will be slower than usual. This extra time will give me a chance to make some adjustments to soften the suspension for these conditions.

I complete my mechanic duties. The announcer calls my group to the pre-grid area.

With helmet in hand, John and Michael already have the bike fired up. I ask, "Hey, did you add fuel?"

John smiles. "Yes, enough for full race distance and a bit extra."

We're all getting revved up now. The girls are excited. They shout, "Go get 'em Pops."

Sharing high-five's, we all smile.

~

The track goes live. I head out with a pack of racers.

It's 10:30 a.m., and already the track is cooking hot. There's a light layer of dust, and I cannot lean the bike over like normal. I'm holding onto the handlebars too tight. I remind myself to breathe and use a light-touch on the levers.

After four laps the dust has cleared off. As Sye, a fast local rider, begins to let it hang-out, I stay tucked into his hip pocket. This is such a rush. My shoulders soften, and, as I relax into the ride, the energy force builds inside me.

As I set up for each turn, the first movement is initiated from the core. With a slight twist of my hips, legs press down, bringing chest, shoulders, and head inward. Eyes search far ahead for the next reference point while my hands become pliable. Riding at speed onboard my Yamaha TZ-250, nicknamed "Isie," feels like ecstasy.

We burn a few hot laps. Conditions are primo. We set up slower riders and pass them with little effort. Still watching every movement Sye makes, I'm going to school on his lines. In this session, he is the professor and I am student.

We ride the last section of turns. Sye carries a lot of momentum through the twisties which sets our line perfect to rail the front straight-a-way. This burst of power gives me a few more miles per hour at the top end. In my gut, I know this shaves a few tenths of a second off my lap times.

Tucking in at 142 mph to stay out of the constant wind, my chest vibrates on the gas tank as everything beyond the asphalt surface blurs. Yellow bugs splat against the windscreen as we exit Turn-One and set up for Turn-Two at 115 mph. It's the same location where earlier the Dust Devil nearly knocked me off the bike. Licking my lips, my hands clinch the grips. Isie swoops left. She swerves right, I twist the throttle on.

"What the hell!" I nearly collide with a slower rider that's weaving side to side.

Shocked. From inside my helmet I shout, "Squid, what are you doing?"

Riding away, my hands tremble on the grips and knees shake uncontrollably against the tank.

Tentative in the next few corners. With conscious effort I work to slow my breath to recapture focus on the racing lines. Several turns go by, and the rhythm of the ride returns. By this time, Sye has checked out.

The very next lap in the fast, sweeping section known as The Carousel, there's another rider going so slow he's almost parked in the middle of the track. Shaking my head. He doesn't have a hand up to warn riders approaching from behind that he has a problem with his bike or that he's exiting the track. I ride around him, then tuck-in as I dial Isie up to full speed along the main straight. The checkered flag comes out to signal the end of the session. Thank you, God.

As I make the cool-off lap to cool off the engine and ease down the adrenaline pumping inside my body, I ease my pace and continue toward the pit lane. Thoughts of my wife and kids flash through my mind. I look up and see my girls standing beside the van wearing their TEAM PIZ racing shirts, holding the stop watch and clipboard. I know they were in the grandstands watching this practice session.

266

Still trembling from the near miss on the track, I set my helmet down and remove my ear plugs.

John strolls over. Together we lift the bike onto the stand. I put my leathers away. I'm still shaking.

Michael walks up. "What's going on?"

"This squid almost took me out. Wait here, I've got talk to the race director before someone gets hurt out there."

Steamed, I head to the tower and find Chuck. He's a former racer with a family of his own. I know him well. Unintentionally I get very close.

"Chuck, this is crazy."

Chuck motions with his hands to settle down. "Ty, what's going on?"

I'm trying to calm down, but the dangerous maneuver that just happened on the track still has me steaming. "You cannot put us out there with the amateur class."

"What happened?"

"Towards the end of the session, the lines were cleaned off so we were flying. I was chasing Sye, and all of a sudden this guy starts weaving across the track like he's on a Sunday cruise through the canyon."

Chuck nods his concern. He lifts his hat and wipes his forehead. "It's a fast track today."

"Man, with all the different bikes and mix of skill levels it's dangerous out there!"

"Look, Ty, you're the experienced racers. You guys should know how to get around them."

"Chuck, this is not playtime on some open track day. Some of us train really hard, and our sponsors have spent lots of money to get us here so we can prepare for the national race next weekend."

"Okay," Chuck says. "I see the problem."

I think he does get it. I dial it down to a simmer and step back. "Look, cut our sessions short if you have to. Just run us separately so I can get a few clear laps to dial-in my bike."

Chuck nods. "Okay. I get it. I'll talk to other officials and see what we can do."

I'm glad the distance back to the van will give me a chance to cool down. I head back to update the girls. I don't want them to see me upset. I certainly I don't want them to worry. By the time I walk to the van, the wind has picked up again, but I'm calmer.

This is a chance to hang out with my girls. Hugs all around. I listen to their excited banter about the trials. We talk about the whirlwind that hit earlier and how the entire paddock went crazy. Brenda had tried to calm the girls fears, but I could tell she had been worried, too. The wind is whistling, and I see the girls' eyes dart around. It's making them uneasy again.

"Gee, Daddy, it shook really hard before!" Cireen says. "Is it going to get bad again?"

She's nervous and wants out of the van. In her perky seven-year-old voice, "Daddy, will the wind carry us away like that tarp?"

Brenda, trying to ease their minds, "No, we're okay in here."

Alicia concerned, "Dad, are you still going to race?"

I hold her in my arms, "Yeah Little Buddie, when the wind calms down I'll go out. It'll be just fine."

Jessica, always in take-charge mode, grabs a deck of cards, "Let's play Old Maid?"

That works. The girls faces light up.

Brenda says, "Okay, girls, does anyone want cold drinks before we start?"

I pull out the cooler with ready-made sandwiches and cool-aid. We have lunch and play cards as we wait for the storm to leave. John and Michael are in their pick-up beside us; they seem fine.

Time passes. The wind has a mind of its own. We wait. Finally, it is time. We head to the track.

~

Emotions let up as the weekend of speed ends safely. We pack up the kids, the bike, and we head towards Phoenix. Nighttime settles in. From the desert, peering eyes glare at us. Coyotes dart across the highway. Countless stars fill the sky.

We arrive home and carry the girls to their bedrooms. It's summer vacation; they will get to sleep in after another lengthy weekend at the track.

The night hours slip quickly by, and the quiet of the early

268

morning before dawn erupts with the sound of my alarm ringing. Five-twenty a.m. A shot of instant oatmeal. A splash of orange juice.

I drag out the mountain bike and prepare for the eight-mile pedal across the desert to the campus. For this session I'm instructing Clinic Three, "Motorcycle Transmissions and Final Drive Systems."

Twenty-two students, the norm at this prestigious technical trade school, await. Another funky Monday arrives after an amazing weekend at the track. Striving to adapt my energy buzz and fit into the company dress code. Pressed shirt and slacks, hair cut above the ears and off the collar.

Shivers course through me. My hands shake as I draw a transmission chart on the white board. My voice cracks, words come out in a stutter. I grab a glass of water on the table beside the podium. Emotions skitter through my brain as a flash of yesterday's race drifts into my presentation.

I am standing stationary behind the podium. Behind me, the whiteboard is blank. All eyes are on me. Panic rages within. I switch gears. In my mind, I'm out on the track. The weather conditions are windy. Dust storms threaten. Focus. Focus. I focus on the track. In my mind, it is clear. I have assessed the risks and decide to go ahead and race.

My hands grasp the podium to prevent tipping over as I accelerate by the racer in second place. There's open track ahead, and I begin to chase after Sye. He squares off the exit while spinning his Ninja Warrior to redline, he blasts ahead. I hold Isie pinned. Side by side at 145 mph. My heart pounds, yet the soothing tai chi breath inside me remains calm. The world is silent.

Suddenly, the checkered flag flies. We slow our pace for Turn-One, then reach over and give one another a handshake. On the cool down lap, I reflect on the events of this day. A first place trophy in lightweight Gran Prix class, and now a second place trophy in middleweight Gran Prix behind an amazing racer and fantastic person. A great race weekend for certain.

A familiar voice shocks me back to the present.

"Ty?" Michael is speaking. "The large splines on the main

shaft, do they face the ignition side or the clutch side of the engine?"

Suddenly, I'm back in the classroom with a bunch of gearheads. I am safe in my element.

The class turns and glares at Michael. Then another student says, "Hey, I was at Vegas yesterday. It was cool, Michael, seeing you pushing Ty's race bike to the starting line."

Michael is quiet. It's not his style to bring attention to himself. Suddenly, the class makes the connection between Michael and my race team. I sense the admiration for Michael. That somehow makes me brave.

I forge ahead with my presentation on transmission parts. Then time for a break arrives. During break, John and Michael come forward along with three other students. They ask questions about the track. About my race bike which is usually in this room, but today it's at home waiting to get new pistons before the national race next weekend in California.

We talk racing. John races snow machines in Minnesota. Michael will start road racing motorcycles as soon as he graduates MMI. These other students race moto-cross. They all seem to understand the buzz of competition.

Class resumes. My earlier jitters gone, I feel confident in the knowledge and experience I have to share with these mechanics.

~

There is no comparison between the thrill of the next race and teaching in the classroom. I am still pulled toward the track, eager for the challenge. Somehow, I have discovered a compatible connection between competing and teaching. It's the cycle of life that continues to thrill. It completes this sequence. It's not everything. It's just enough.

# When Emailing Becomes Ridiculous

## *Laurie Asher*

Okay, you email someone asking for explanation.

And they reply with a suitable answer.

Feeling compelled, you email back, "Thank you."

They reply, "You're welcome."

Now you type, "Wow, great customer service."

They respond, "That's what makes us #1."

Feeling warm and fuzzy, you reply, "That's why I keep
returning."

And their response is, "What a wonderful testimonial!"

You tell them, "Well, it's true."

They inquire, "Can we use your comment in our next online ad?"

"Of course, you can," and ask, "What do I need to do?"

"I will email you a form for your Photo Release and Disclosure
Agreement forms."

"Wait, a disclosure? What am I getting into?"

"For legal purposes, you will be required to relinquish all
ownership rights, sign a full disclosure rights affidavit, provide
your driver's license and social security number, auto vin number,
blah, blah, blah..."

Nobody remembers the original request. They'd have to scroll up about 2.3 feet to get back to the top.

But, hey, thank God for email. Otherwise a 2000-year-old Sequoia, $7.50 in U.S. postage, gasoline, mail truck maintenance, as well as carrier's wages could be lost.

So I guess it's a pretty good deal—if you can somehow keep your fingers from doing the talking.

# Grassroots

## *Gary Winters*

politics for the stay-at-home mom

get involved at the grassroots level

you want to play by the rules & such

form a grassroots political group

collect some funds for a nonprofit

political action committee

okay grassroots moms get ready now

fill out the lengthy IRS form

then detail every aspect of your

personal life & that of your cohorts

including facebook & twitter too

don't forget the content of their prayers

pay the fee & then wait donkey years

all the while wondering if perchance

you forgot to include the brand of soap

or toothpaste you might prefer because

if you leave anything out they call

that omission perjury — lying to an

independent government body —

that can take your house & car & watch

# The Legacy

## *Mary Louise MacIlvaine*

*This blood-dimmed tide is loosed, and everywhere*
*The ceremony of innocence is drowned.*
**W.B.Yeats, "The Second Coming"**

Allie has knocked over her mother's houseplant, torn a leaf, and got wet potting soil on the carpet. Mama mutters, "Bad girl" and grabs her chubby arm. Allie twists out of her grip, bangs her head into her mother's head, and Mama's had it. Allie sees her rage, shrieks, and Mama cries, "Nobody needs this!"

Allie's screech gets louder. "Stop it!" her mother shouts and then screams, "Stop it!" to make her point. Allie contracts. She slams her stomach with her fisted forearms. She tenses her neck and chest and face, stopping and starting with jolts and gasps, blubbering and snuffling, pulling herself together. She stiffens to a stifled standstill, barely breathing, her little tummy hard. "And look at your diaper! Ugh! Why did I ever want you?" Allie whimpers in submission, but soon Mama softens in guilt: "Oh, Allie Ballie Sally, you know I love you."

### Freezing

Mama has issues, so it's up to Allie to get along. She tightens up to be good, but it's wrenching. It hurts and she cries. She armors her baby sweetness to hardness as she must, holding herself back with muscle power. The more coming at her, the stiffer her defense.

### Coping

And what of Mama? Does she say, "Only babies cry," which deadens emotions? Does she say, "Dirty, dirty," which alienates the pelvis and all its functions? "Mustn't look," which dulls seeing? "Don't be a pain," which shames excitement? Whatever

275

slips out of her mouth, these ancient lines have their impact.

## Attitudes
I can't tell you the backend of Allie's flowerpot fireworks, what sense she'll make of this and other run-ins. Maybe, "Mistakes are horrible," "I must never get mad," or "Always submit." Maybe, "Mommy won't love me if I cry," "Exploring is dangerous," "I have to be on guard," "I mustn't want with my eyes," or "I don't dare reach out with my arms." Maybe, "Dirtiness is horrible," or "Potty mistakes are nasty." Or maybe, "Life is hopeless," "People can't be trusted," "Love always hurts," or "I'm just bad." Perhaps, "Women are cruel," or "Good mommies are mean." Or then again perhaps, "Hurting other people is good," "I gotta get even," or "I'll do anything not to feel this way." What will it be? What character? What personality? One or more of these will become a roadmap for Allie's life, anchored in her mind and musculature, distorting seeing and thinking.

## Mama's Problem
Mama's suffering too. She can't relax and enjoy her daughter with warmth and love, charms she once wanted. She snaps, and anything not her way is wrong. "This has to stop. How'd I get such a bad baby? Why me?" She knows tyranny too well, the tireless flogging, and she's done taking it. Now she mutters, "Get to know me, Sweetheart, 'cause you're not gettin' past me." She's got moves no one can parry, angles you never see coming. She says, "I don't pretend I'm a good person. I yell and I'm mean, but I'm toning it down." Yet she wedges her life-hostile attitude into every glance, every comment.

## Warrior
Mama can't feel, can't tolerate, and can't enjoy the natural life still urging up inside Allie. She's waging war with nature. And she's training Allie to her own standard: "Don't get suckered by desire. Freedom is a lie. Do as I say, and don't think." Armor is the way of life. No one dare deviate.

276

## Hatred

Mama was a child not long ago and learned what it takes. She toughened and never noticed what was missing, not until later, later faced with her love vanishing so quickly into anger, faced with the hardened heartbreak of helpless hatred: "Is love even real?"

## Lack of Love

Now as she lies awake, no lack makes her as miserable as this lack, the lack of mother comfort with her child, the lack of love in her bedroom, the lack of someone to understand. This lack attacks her at every slack moment, a black reminder of her unspeakable genital misery, the painful emptiness, the heavy death of hope. The ache of the lack lingers longest when she longs for love, her last chance to redeem her pain. She cannot bear this lack, this void, this rack. She has to make it stop and go away. She has to never see it more and never know it, murder truth in broad daylight. Armor forms, seeing dulls, and life is heavy.

## How Serious is It?

Run-ins teach Allie where dangers lie. She braces herself in her limbs, her face, her mind. Mama rationalizes as she chastises, "What choice is there? She'll never remember." With the flower pot, Mama eased her heater and prettied her brutal words with sweet, but if she could have looked with unarmored eyes, she'd have seen her baby was still tense, cowering, and afraid. Allie didn't bounce back. The body doesn't forget. Moments of shock shore up sheets of muscle armor against the same again. Allie's enrolled in Mama's master class. Mama doesn't mean to, but she's ensuring Allie will be uptight, harsh, and mixed-up about love all her life.

## Allie and the Video

Allie is three now and Mama says, "Mommy's online. Watch your video." Allie doesn't want the video, but Mama plays her off by twisting reality, "Look what Dora's doing! Isn't it fun?!" Allie didn't think so, but she can't fight the con. She scrunches her face,

277

confused. She can't think it in words, but she feels sour and achy. She can't know what she likes or doesn't. Her mother nixes her gut instincts. Her insides go dark. Facts are not real. Reality doesn't compute. She pretends to watch Dora, but it's no good.

### Allie's Attitude Aftermath

More and more, Allie deadens her senses and depends on what Mama says. Her body feels wrong, but she must trust Mama. It's how it is, even though Mama's unnatural guidance dooms Allie to bent beliefs, clouded thinking, and muddled motivation for learning. It bleeds dry her drive to feel out the world. She sits glassy-eyed, holding her breath. Her instincts are thwarted. Spontaneity dies. Life within suffocates. Her best shot is to stay on guard, mirror Mama, think as she's told, and get used to it. From perpetual restraint, Allie will block and distort the basics of life, hardly seeing, sensing, feeling, breathing.

### Deadening with Muscle

Attitudes are but half her problem. You know as I know that she will use her muscles to not hit when she's mad; to tense up and not cry when she's sad; to puff up and act brave when she's afraid; to dim her eyes and not see when Mama looks mean; to hold her breath when she's angry; to freeze and not touch her privates when she might; and to block her throat and not let out sounds of suffering. Even at ten months she slammed her stomach, steeling herself against misery. And the muscles she uses to block feelings and perception don't get strong and flexible like you might hope. They get spastic. Not just her body, but her face will get rigid. She might have nice features, but her expression will be unpleasant. Yes, Allie will get through these crises and grow up, but the muscle armor she lays on will get in the way of love and learning for all her life.

### Fullness

Like a wolf caught in a trap and chewing off its paw, Allie is losing something vital. She's losing her inner sense of herself. She's losing freedom, clarity, ease, and flexibility. Like the wolf who chews off its paw, she can survive without the fullness of life.

278

She can make do. Like a she-wolf, she can live to give birth to a new generation with new chances, but the hidden backstage of her life will conceal a wasteland of crushed hope. Only her descendants who fight for a cleaner life will live to redeem her longings.

### The Dog's Fur Coat

Allie's mother dreamt that her own mother took away their childhood dog's fur coat and hung it up in her bedroom where no one could touch it. Do you see it? Can you sense it? The dream expressed her helplessness at her mother's interfering with nature and not being able to abide natural warmth, comfort, and pleasure, which should be our birthright as human animals.

### Prohibition against Desire

It begins with bans on desire. Allie wanted to check out the houseplant. She wanted to touch it, feel it, and get a sense of it. With desire dangerous but denying it safe, she shies away from wanting to learn. She holds back, maintains her restraint, and avoids reaching out to the world. Giving up pleasure, she resigns herself to unpleasure. Desire for satisfaction must be put down. Her mother beat it down, and now Allie takes over. She must, even though it maddens and dulls her. The rules are cemented in her mind and muscles: Don't give pleasure an inch. Stifle it. Stay away from excitement. Keep your nose to the grindstone. Delight is for fools. Save fun for secret getting even.

### Unpunished Rapture

Someone once said, "If I were to begin life again, I would devote it to music. It is the only cheap and unpunished rapture on earth." Of course, rapture is the rising up from the weight of life to heavenly bliss. Music can lift the spirit, unburdening it from armor. It can liberate pleasure in a way that passes for innocent. But when full pleasure is abhorrent, we adapt. We allot our living bit by bit.

### Impulses and Armor

This is Allie's heritage. Many find it impossible to accept that infant run-ins matter, but the misery in Allie's eyes is visible to those who can bear to see it and feel its brunt. It's right there. Blocking of pleasure impulses is the mechanism of armoring, the ill legacy passed from parents to children and grandchildren. And armor is the mechanism of our sorrows and destructiveness.

# Hot Chocolate

## *Gary Winters*

I don't like coffee

black white or muddy

never did really

but I managed to

guzzle tanker loads

of the cheap drab drug

before I stopped cold

after a lifetime

devout coffeehouse

habitué type

and I don't regret

one nanosecond

but I have moved on

to new rituals

now the sassy black

coffeehouse barista

smiles when I walk in

hot chocolate, right?

she goes and I nod

nonfat milk no whip

extra chocolate

# Solicitors Get Some Credit for Developing Creativity

## *Joe Naiman*

One of the impacts of the mortgage and financial services crisis is that I'm not receiving as many solicitations for home equity loans, refinancing, and other such services as I've received in the past. I don't know whether it's because some of the companies are no longer around to offer the loans, whether they're cutting back on mailing costs to speculative customers, or whether my previous correspondence has taught them a lesson.

When I receive such offers, their disposition depends on a couple of factors. If there's an expiration date listed, I'll discard it after the expiration date. If no expiration date exists but listed stipulations would make me ineligible, those will also be discarded. If there is neither an expiration date nor a disqualifying stipulation, I'll put it in a file just in case I ever may actually need such quick money.

In some cases I receive merely a postcard addressed to me, and those can be recycled. If an application form or personal number is included, I take steps to prevent identity theft. A two-sided solicitation is torn into tiny pieces before being put into an envelope with other mixed paper and subsequently dropped into a recycling bin. A one-sided solicitation with sensitive information extends the time between my trips to purchase toilet paper.

Once in a while, some condition exists which prevents ordinary secure disposal. One such company issued me a plastic card which couldn't be torn into pieces. My action was to return the card along with a cover letter. I noted that I normally had two options; I could dispose of the letter or I could apply for a loan and put the soliciting company through the expense of rejecting me since some South American governments have better credit than I do. I informed them that because the plastic card prevented simple disposal, I had no choice but to apply for a loan.

I informed them, however, that I didn't want to take on too much additional debt and was therefore applying for a loan of $20.00 to treat my friend to the local Italian lunch buffet. I never heard back from them.

Subsequent situations requested a loan to treat my brother to the lunch buffet or asked for a loan of $25.00 to cover the increased price but I haven't heard back from those lenders, either.

Perhaps one of the reasons I'm in such financial distress is that I usually don't take advantage of African inheritance proposals which from time to time are e-mailed to me. One such situation, however, merited a response.

This particular one was from Zaire, and the sender mentioned boxes of something. I'm sure the guy didn't realize that I'm a professional sportswriter, but in the early 1970s it was popular to hold heavyweight boxing matches in international venues and the first thing which comes to my mind about Zaire was the 1974 fight in which Mohammed Ali defeated George Foreman to recapture the heavyweight title. The combination of Zaire and boxes was too good to resist.

I was also providing high school football reports for The Coach on XTRA Sports at the time. I thanked the African for the information about the boxing match and told him I'd be coordinating with the radio station to try to attend. I also let him know that I'd be contacting the US State Department to try to secure a passport for the fight. I'm sure that's not the confidentiality he requested in his e-mail letter, and although I've received subsequent African inheritance proposals I've never received another one from Zaire.

It's too bad I didn't know then what I know now about Ken Norton's fight in Caracas after which the Venezuelan government wouldn't allow the boxers or their managers to leave until all income taxes derived from the fight were paid. I could have told him I'd be in touch with the Zaire tax authorities to ensure that such an incident wouldn't be repeated. He'd probably be sweating more than the boxers I've seen from ringside seats.

California's "junk fax" law stipulates that any unsolicited faxes must include a toll-free telephone number the recipient can call to be removed from the list. Most of the time a legitimate number is provided. One phone number was toll-free, but after I provided my fax number the automated voice indicated that they would attempt to fax me a confirmation, after which I'd receive no further faxes.

First of all, this is in violation of the junk fax law, since it would provide a subsequent fax. More importantly, my number is a fax/modem line, so a fax won't be sent if I'm using the Internet. After receiving subsequent faxes with the contact information to respond affirmatively, I came up with an alternate plan.

I wrote a letter informing them of their transgression. The fax solicitation included a toll-free number to fax them if I was interested in their service. So not only did I fax my letter to their toll-free number, but I informed them that if they wanted to get into a fax war I would not only incur charges on their toll-free number and use their paper receiving my faxes, but that my faxes would prevent their customers from faxing their acceptances. That was the end of faxes from that company.

A subsequent unsolicited fax also carried a toll-free number which indicated that they would attempt to fax me a confirmation. This fax, however, spawned some additional creativity on my part.

The junk fax law includes an exemption for businesses with whom the recipient has had a previous business relationship, which at this point was their only legitimate defense. The truth is that there was no business relationship, but the truth also is that I've been mentoring someone who is working on a historical fiction book, and I'm working on a novel in which Irish Republic founding father Eamon de Valera is one of the main characters. The unsolicited fax was on behalf of some financial services company, and one of the questions on the application form was whether I have an IRA.

It was actually Michael Collins rather than Eamon de Valera who formed the Irish Republican Brotherhood that evolved (or devolved) into the IRA, and I noted that in my faxed response, along with a caveat not to confuse Michael Collins, the Irish independence leader, with Michael Collins the astronaut since Guinness and Bailey's Irish Cream can't be used as rocket fuel. I explained that their mention of the IRA in conjunction with my research on Eamon de Valera constituted the previous business relationship which made their fax legal, and I informed them that if they faxed anything else to my number I'd fax them substantial material on Eamon de Valera, Irish history, decentralization, and other related matters. I even followed my signature with "P.S. Don't drink too much. Redheads are sexually arousing."

I never heard back from them. I hope they're not wasting any Irish whiskey on trying to build a rocket ship.

Solicitations can be a nuisance, but they can also stimulate creativity. I'll at least acknowledge their role in generating creative thoughts. But for some reason, creative people don't seem to be the customers they desire.

# Compliments Add Value to Relationships, Right?

## *Tom Leech*

Once upon a time, when I was a recent high school grad, I worked as a reservations agent for American Airlines in Chicago. This was a few decades ago, before high-tech, computer-based systems for handling reservations were yet to arrive. The Chicago office was on the second floor of a commercial building across from the legendary Palmer House.

At any time during the day about 75 agents would be seated in two long rows, on the phone talking with customers to arrange for flight reservations. Of those, only about 10 of us were male. While we were often busy, we had a fair amount of camaraderie, swapped stories about Chicago nightlife, even shared back rubs, etc. If we had some lighter traffic moments, some of the agents would break out photos (real paper then, no smart phone screens) of family, pets, and other activities in their lives, current and previous.

During a break moment, several of us were sharing stories about current and earlier worlds. I was particularly enjoying a chat with a woman agent, Christine, who was a couple of decades older than me and whom I had gotten to know. She had done some on-stage work before and showed me a photo of herself in a dress-up costume. I gave it a good look and complimented her about her appearance. She nodded appreciatively and shortly after that our conversation faded as we had to head back to our agent duties.

A male colleague (with two college degrees) also was a recent hire-on. He was just getting a taste of hands-on employment and likely quickly moving upward to management positions with the airline. As we were getting ready to head back to our work spots, he pulled me aside. "Tom," he said, "You just made a mistake when you commented on Christine's photo." That was a surprise comment to me as I was obviously being a nice guy. He continued: "Your maybe-true statement about her looking good 20 years ago could easily be interpreted in a negative manner."

What? Was there something wrong with my clearly-complimentary message? I had said "My, you were really good looking then."

And my advising friend replied: "So you mean that she's not so good-looking now?"

Oops. OK, lesson learned.

A decade later, I had left the airline business, gone to college, took on employment and was doing a bit of romancing on the side. I and a female pursuit were heading toward the beach wearing our swim duds. I was taken with her eye-catching physical shape (this was in early bikini time) and told her she looked 98 percent perfect — that's clearly a compliment, right?

She gave me a look and said "OK. So what's the two percent not so right?"

Choosing my words carefully, I gave her some likely useful information: "Well," I said, "Your fanny sticks out a bit too much."

She even thanked me for my astute observation. Sad to say, that was our last date; I never knew quite why.

# The Bachelor

## *Peggy Hinaekian*

Philippe De Gros was of French nobility.

He was 51 years old.

He was an imposing man, tall and broad-shouldered.

He had a pale complexion, thinning blond hair, and piercing, ice-blue eyes.

He lived in a luxurious condo on Avenue Montaigne in Paris, next to the House of Dior.

He was an only child, extremely wealthy, and had never been married.

His parents owned a dilapidated chateau in the Haute Savoie region of France.

He spent a lot of money renovating it.

His parents still lived there, with six employees taking care of them and the chateau.

~

Philippe de Gros realized he was getting on in years.

He wanted to find a woman of marriage material, soon.

He wanted an heir to his fortune.

He liked women.

In fact, he fawned on women.

He liked them earthy, sexy, and witty, in that order.

He also liked breasts more than a handful and ample, wiggly hips.

He had been looking for a wife for the past five years.

He was invited to numerous matchmaking parties in his aristocratic milieu where he met eligible candidates.

Philippe de Gros met his friend Patrick at their usual hangout on the Left Bank one Friday evening.

"I don't particularly care for single women," he said.

"What do you mean?" asked Patrick.

"They want to absolutely hook a husband, that's why," he retorted.

"What's wrong with that? And you absolutely want a wife."

"How will I know whether she really loves me?"

"You have money, so you'll never know."

"Listen to me, Patrick," he continued. "Divorced women are a better bet."

"You know that they have been at least desired by someone else."

"Whereas unmarried ones, well, they are unmarried because maybe no one has desired them."

"Not really. Divorced women are used merchandise, as far as I am concerned," replied Patrick.

"And why are they divorced in the first place?"

"Maybe they were impossible to live with."

"Maybe they were too possessive and controlling."

"Or maybe they did not like sex anymore."

"And, the husband was always begging to get laid," he continued.

~

Philippe de Gros knew he was a good catch.

He had met scores of women among his aristocratic circle.

He had had several short-lived affairs.

He did not find their company uncommonly exhilarating.

The sex had mostly been good, though.

But, none of them did he even consider as a wife to be.

They put on too many snobby airs, talked with an affected accent, and tended to be too thin.

They starved themselves to death, to be à la mode.

No flesh to grab.

He preferred sexy women of humbler stock.

They were more effervescent.

He had met a limited number of the latter, unfortunately.

~

Philippe de Gros was in a hurry.

290

He thought his time was limited.

He had the conviction that older men's sperm was not as potent as younger men's.

He had to find a wife rather quickly and make her pregnant.

A beautiful young woman.

A gorgeous woman that his friends would envy.

With her looks and his brains, their son would be perfect.

A perfect heir.

It did not dawn upon him that she might beget a girl.

~

Philippe de Gros was looking for the impossible-to-find partner.

He looked all over Europe but he did not look in Germany.

He did not care for the German language.

It was too harsh for his ears.

Philippe de Gros then met Nathalie Nescu, one lucky, memorable evening.

He met Nathalie at a cocktail party given by Patrick.

"Philippe, I would like you to meet my interior designer, Nathalie. Nathalie, my best friend, Philippe."

Nathalie was from Romania.

She had that subtle come-hither look, almost imperceptible.

She was beautiful, well-educated, witty and, above all, desirable.

She had long raven hair, an hour-glass figure, and a sparkling smile.

They had a banal conversation while sipping champagne at the bar.

"Have you lived in Paris all your life?" Philippe asked.

"No, my parents moved here when I was seven years old."

Nathalie had been married before.

She had not had children.

Even better, as he could not and would not deal with another man's offspring.

He dared not ask her why.

Was she sterile perchance?

All these questions were going through his head during their conversation.

He was fixated on her luscious pouty lips.

He yearned to kiss her.

A faint perfume emanated from her and he liked it.

She had very little makeup.

She did not need too much.

Philippe de Gros cast a furtive glance at Nathalie's voluptuous body.

He was unmistakably attracted to her.

He wanted to find out more about her.

He wanted to get her in his bed.

Like a peacock, he put out all his masculine charms.

He looked straight into her bottomless black eyes and asked. "Would you have dinner with me sometime?"

"*Avec plaisir*," she replied with a coquettish smile.

~

Philippe took Nathalie to lunch and dinner dates and to the theatre, of course.

They finally ended up in bed.

It was most pleasurable.

He came to the conclusion that she was *the one*.

He broached the subject of marriage in a rather offhand manner.

They were at a posh hotel room in a French ski resort.

They were sipping red wine in front of the fireplace.

"What do you think about getting married?" he asked.

Nathalie was slightly taken aback.

She accepted the proposal and gave him one of her bewitching smiles.

She had been expecting this.

~

Philippe de Gros was ecstatic.

"He is so unromantic," remarked Nathalie to her friend Danielle.

"But," she added, "he will be a good husband and good for my business."

"So, this is a business deal rather than a love match," remarked Danielle.

"I don't love him, but I do like him a lot."

"He has charisma and a good sense of business."

"He is also rather eccentric, and I like that."

"And, he is very knowledgeable about antiques. I am learning a lot from him," she concluded.

"You shouldn't marry a guy you don't love," said Danielle. "You still have time. You are only 33 years old."

Nathalie did not heed Danielle's advice.

She had made up her mind.

~

Philippe de Gros was a happy man.

He had finally found a suitable woman to be his wife.

He was very much in love.

He had never been in love before, except for a brief crush on his history teacher at the Lycée.

Nathalie reminded him of the history teacher.

Coincidence.

He desired and lusted for Nathalie.

~

A date was set for their wedding.

The future of his lineage was almost guaranteed.

*But can she bear children?* Philippe de Gros asked himself.

Could he perhaps ask her to take a fertility test?

No, he could not.

But with hips like hers, he was almost sure.

293

# Aim to Please

## *Frank Primiano*

In the car, six-year-old Isaac's father tried to reassure him. "This is only a checkup … to make sure you're healthy. Maybe one needle, but it shouldn't hurt much."

"Yes, Daddy." The boy was subdued at the prospect.

"We'll go for ice cream afterwards."

~

The doctor finished questioning, palpating, and measuring. He said to Isaac's father, "I'll need a specimen," and, to Isaac, handing him a small, plastic cup, "Take this to the bathroom and try to fill it."

The look on Isaac's face betrayed uncertainty. His father said, "Urinate in the cup, then bring it to the doctor."

The boy's eyes widened with understanding. He marched through the bathroom door, closing it behind him, leaving the two men to chat while they waited … and waited. At last, Isaac's dad stepped to the bathroom, looked inside, and was confused by what he saw: Isaac, his back to the door, standing in an expanding puddle.

"What happened, Buddy?"

Isaac's shoulders slumped as he turned. "I'm sorry Daddy, but it's really hard to get it in there from up here."

That's when Isaac's father noticed the almost empty cup on the floor and Isaac's last futile squirts in its direction. Stifling a laugh, he reached for the tiny receptacle. "You did fine. Zip up."

As his father presented the sample to the doctor, Isaac asked, "How was my aim?"

It was good enough … and the results were normal.

He had a chocolate sundae.

Every secret of a writer's soul,
every experience of his life,
every quality of his mind,
is written large in his works.

— *Virginia Woolf*

# Contributors

**ASHER, LAURIE** — Growing up, Laurie acquired her formal education on the boardwalk at Venice Beach, California. As a product of the California Public School System, she never did quite master grammar or punctuation skills and will always require excellent editors! She has written one currently unpublished children's book in honor of her nephew, and is working on two other novels. She started writing after retiring from a career in real estate. Her favorite literary quote: "Everything stinks until it's finished." — Dr. Seuss. Laurie has been published in the SDWEG anthology since 2016. She currently serves as Secretary to the SDWEG board of directors.

**BARRONS, WILLIAM** — "Having been born on the coldest day in February of 1926, in the coldest city in Michigan (Cadillac)," Bill says he somehow survived the Great Depression. He joined the Marines quick at 17. Served 2 ½ war years, including in the Pacific, got out, got married, went to college and had kids. Bill rejoined the Marines in 1949 as a Public Information Officer. He had great joy writing for newspapers and TV. Became a 2nd Lt. Platoon Commander, a position he really loved. When his wife got sick and nearly died, Bill went on inactive duty to care for his family. He became a telephone equipment engineer in Chicago, then designed and sold home remodeling for 22 years. Retired at age 69, Bill did research and wrote full time. So far, he's written a dozen books and at age 92, he says he plans to continue writing, "until I'm 100!" Bill's published detective/mystery books about the San Diego Police Department's Homicide Detail include: *.22 Caliber Homicides; Nude Beach Homicides; Coldest Cold Homicides; Forever Homicides; Red Hot Homicides; Homeless Homicides; Rawhide Homicides;* and *Hellish Homicides.* He's currently working on *Holiday Homicides.* When not solving homicides, Bill works on his memoir *Marine Corps Daze* about his service in WWII and after.

**BEEBY, GERED** — Gered is Past President (2003) of the SDWEG and remains on the Board as a Director-At-Large ("Official Greeter"). His suspense-thriller novel of industrial espionage, *Dark Option* (2002), was nominated for a PMA Benjamin Franklin award in the category, Best

New Voice — Fiction (2003). He has written two screenplays. "The Bottle Imp" is a deal-with-the-devil story based on Robert Louis Stevenson's 1892 classic tale. Gered has also written "Dark Option" for the screen. He has contributed short stories and essays to *The Guilded Pen* anthologies since its first edition in 2012. A registered professional engineer (PE), Gered serves as a Subject Matter Expert for the California Engineer Licensing Board. In this capacity, he performs detailed analyses for the Board's technical advisory unit.

**BENSON, JENNA** — is a substitute teacher and freelance writer currently living in El Cajon, California. She moved to California two and a half years ago to be closer to her family (and the beach), and to focus on her craft and passion: writing. Jenna is originally from Las Vegas, Nevada, and graduated from the University of Nevada – Reno in 2014 with a bachelor's degree in English (Writing) and Sociology. She has been writing creatively in different facets for over a decade. Her writing includes poetry, fiction, non-fiction, technical writing, short stories, and columns on a variety of topics published in newspapers. Jenna has been a member of the San Diego Writers and Editors Guild since May 2018 and has already learned so much from the community. Her hobbies consist of reading books from her ever-growing "to be read" pile, binge watching the latest shows, working on her upcoming novel, practicing yoga and meditation, and attempting to train her beloved cat, Oliver.

**BERKELEY, ALIA** — is a San Diego native. She has been a Registered Nurse since 2011. She has a BA in Literature, with an emphasis in creative writing from UCSB, College of Creative Studies (graduated 1998). Alia's literary heroes include Jane Austen, Lewis Carroll, and Charlotte Bronte as well as Kurt Vonnegut, Jr., Iain M. Banks, and Neil Gaiman. She has written unfinished stories and poems throughout the years, but really got serious about writing five years ago and enjoys writing a mix of fantasy/sci fi and general fiction. Alia is currently involved in querying agents for an Alice in Wonderland-themed manuscript for adults, *The Unreality Tourist*. She has been working on the project (and a sequel) for five years. Her future projects include a story loosely based on the time she lived in New Zealand and a story about being a carny.

**BOZE, BOB** — Bob is a diverse author with four published books: his autobiography - *Love is a Pretty Girl with a Cape to Share Your Dreams With* and his romance trilogy, *Horses of Tir Na Nog*. In progress is another romance novel, *The Beach Pool*. His writing partner, Casey Fae Hewson, another romance writer and administration trainer, lives in New Zealand. Together they are co-authoring a romance novel, *Light My Way,* and collaborating on a business book, *How Not to Fail in Business Without Really Trying,* dealing with how to successfully open and operate a small business. Originally from New York, Bob is an avid reader, reviewer, beta reader, and guest blogger on several web sites. His travels have covered most of the world, and he has lived in London, England; Istanbul, Turkey; Houston and San Antonio, Texas; Los Angeles and Paso Robles, California; before finally calling San Diego home. Bob's education includes: Studies in Creative Writing, Literature, English Literature and English at NYU, William and Mary, University of Maryland, and the University of Delaware. He holds a dual BS degree in Electronic Engineering in Systems Design and Development and Project Management from Northrop University. Bob has volunteered and mentored at the San Diego Zoo for over 25 years, is an active member of the San Diego Writers and Editors Guild, San Diego Professional Editors Network, and participates in local writer's events, such as the San Diego Festival of Books fair and the La Jolla Writers Conference.

**BUOMPENSIERO, MARCIA** — is the author of *Sumerland,* winner of the 2017 San Diego Book Award, Best Published Mystery. Writing under the pseudonym "Loren Zahn," Marcia also publishes the Theo Hunter mystery series: *Dirty Little Murders* (2009/2017), *Deadly Little Secrets* (2015), and *Fatal Little Lies* (2018). *Deadly Little Secrets* received a "highly recommended" rating from the SDWEG Manuscript Review Board and was a finalist in the 2015 San Diego Book Awards unpublished manuscript division. She writes non-fiction magazine articles about the history of San Diego's Little Italy. Marcia is the SDWEG Treasurer, serves on board of directors, and has been the managing editor of *The Guilded Pen* anthologies since 2013. SDWEG recognized her efforts to further the impact of the Guild in the writing community and honored her contributions by presenting her with a *Rhoda Riddell Builders Award* in 2018. She is the founder of Grey Castle Publishing: www.greycastlepublishing.com.

**CARLETON, LAWRENCE** — Larry is a former academic and former jazz trumpeter and currently amuses himself and, he hopes, others, by writing short stories with interesting characters in unusual situations. He's contributed to several anthologies, including all SDWEG *The Guilded Pen* anthologies since 2012. Larry is particularly proud of his new book, *I'm Not Roger Blaime and Other Curious Phenomena,* which contains twelve of his best stories. Facebook: Lawrence Carleton.

**CASEY, ANNE** — Which came first, the writer or the reader? For Anne, the desires to read and to write seemed concurrent. She created the usual child's pencil squiggle stories on envelope backs which were related to her doll house family and paper dolls on long winter days in Ohio. She continues to write on paper scraps which rival in number her book collection. Anne has contributed to the SDWEG Anthology, has written training manuals, and edited college theses. She is past editor of, among others, the Writers Guild newsletter, and served as an at-large member of the SDWEG Board. Her current writing projects are the long in-process Hungarian recipe book, "First You Steal One Chicken," a memoir, "The Juniper Street Lemonade Stand," and a poetry book tentatively titled "Myriad." Following retirement from UCSD as a medical/scientific secretary, she finally obtained a degree in Literature/Writing at UCSD. She and her fluffy white cat Marlin live in San Diego with family very, very close by.

**CONVERSE, A. J.** — a New Englander by birth, a Navy brat, a Navy Officer, a financial expert, and an entrepreneur, has traveled extensively in his lifetime. His short story, "Warrior's Stone," appeared in *The Guilded Pen* (2012), where he published short stories "The Marble Game," "Drippy Pants," "The Woods," "The Wake Up," "A Rose for Mrs. Delahante," and "One Soldier" in the following years. "Old Kim," will appear in the 2018 anthology. His first novel, *Bitch'n*, set in a 1959 beach town named Coronado, was published in November 2012. In his second novel, *Die Again*, a college student's life changes when he catches a serial killer. *Boston Boogie* is an adventure thriller set in 1963 Boston. The *Baja Moon* influenced his fourth novel of the same name. In February 2016, he released *News from the East,* an action adventure set in 1974 with some modern themes. Early in 2017 he completed *Flagship*, based on his experience in the Vietnam War. *Hornwinkle Hustle* will come out this fall.

**COY, JANICE** — is the award-winning author of four suspense novels, each addressing a different theme. Her first novel, *A Grave in the Vegetable Garden*, explores the idea of justice; her second, *A Table on Kilimanjaro*, considers success; her third, *The Smallest of Waves*, examines freedom; and her fourth, *North of Eden*, delves into whether the truth should always be told. A former journalist, Coy has always been curious about people's motives. "Now I get to create motives for my characters," Coy says. "Although, often, they surprise even me." Coy is a SCUBA diver, a hiker, a runner, and an animal lover — all elements that enrich her stories. *The Smallest of Waves* was a suspense finalist at the SDBAA. *North of Eden* has received the Indie Reader stamp of approval. Her books can be purchased through her website www.janicecoy.com or Amazon.

**CROTHERS, BARBARA** — Barbara has been a story teller for many years, and finally, with a few published short stories and poems to her credit, she continues to edit journals kept during travels adding detail to memories of events, interesting people, and amazing places in Mexico, Guatemala, Spain, New Zealand, Fiji Islands, and Alaska in her own beloved homeland. She graduated from University of Redlands and is a Fellow of the Whitehead Leadership Society. Barbara has contributed to all the editions of *The Guilded Pen* since 2012. She has served on the SDWEG board of directors and continues to assist in special projects when she desires or is requested to do so.

**CROTHERS, FRED** — is currently retired and living in San Diego. Fred has published short stories in every edition of *The Guilded Pen* since 2012. He is currently working on more of these short stories gleaned from personal memories of operating a tavern in Carson, Washington, from 1975 to 1980. Fred says it seemed an easy task to write about these many events, but he has spent many hours in rewrites and editing to present them in the best possible light, to ensure their truth shines through. He hopes that many others will enjoy this glimpse of reality from yesteryear.

**CURRIER, C.H.** — aka, Scott Currier, was born in 1954 in Pasadena, California. He attended Blair High School, and Pasadena City College. At age 22 he moved to San Diego. In 1979 he attended Cal Poly San Luis Obispo where he graduated with a Bachelor's of Science in Ornamental Horticulture. He returned to San Diego and worked in both the landscape and nursery industry for 40 years until retiring in 2015. His wife, Lynne, and he have two daughters. Scott is currently completing his first book titled, *Where the Ashes Fell*. It is a historical novel based on stories his grandfather, Spencer Otis, wrote in 1933 about growing up during Reconstruction after the Civil War in Northern Virginia. Scott has been a member of The Writer's Connection of Rancho Bernardo for three years and owes any successes in writing largely to their tutelage and encouragement. He also thanks his mother, Liza; she could turn a yarn. Scott's passions are traveling, politics, and classic cars. He owns a 1966 Jaguar XKE and a 1967 Alfa Romeo Duetto.

**DOUBLEBOWER, BOB** — Bob was born in Philadelphia and raised in the southern New Jersey town of Lindenwold. He attended Villanova University, where he received a Bachelor's Degree in Civil Engineering.

He began his engineering work with Bechtel Power division in Washington, DC. His career has taken him to Colorado, Arizona, Virginia, and California. He now maintains a consulting engineering practice, Regional Shoring Design, in San Diego county. Bob has been published in *The Guilded Pen* since 2012 and is currently working on a horror novel, *The Circling Bench*. Bob is past-president of the SDWEG board of directors and currently serves as vice president.

**ECKBERG, SALLY** — "I was born and raised in a mortuary, I had to learn to play only quiet games. Therefore, I became quite addicted to reading and drawing. This, I am sure, had a great effect on my career choices." Sally's first major in college was Speech Therapy. After working in a clinical setting for a short time, she decided to get teaching degrees in both regular and special education. She started out teaching multi-handicapped children and then decided to concentrate on deaf education. Sally's love of reading and storytelling greatly affected her teaching. She tried to make her lessons in English, reading, and history as creative as possible. Her students wrote and acted out historical scenes. They also wrote alternative endings to stories as well as taking on the persona of literary characters to act out scenes in a book. Sally says she has always loved to make up stories and her students were the perfect audience.

**EDGE, CHLOE KERNS** — Chloe holds a degree in Lit/Writing from UCSD. She published in *Birdcage Review (1982)* and *Maize, Vol.6 (1983)*. *Tattoo (1988)* was published for women in prison. Chloe has been published in *The Guilded Pen* since 2012. She writes poems, nonfiction, and is currently working on a memoir. Chloe has been teaching an ongoing Creative Writing Class for four years at Oasis in Escondido.

**FELDMAN, DAVID** — Dave spent 30 years as a copy editor at *The San Diego Union-Tribune*, 55 years working as a reporter and editor on newspapers, including *Stars & Stripes* in Europe and the *Honolulu Star-Bulletin*. He has taught journalism in colleges for 34 years. For the past six years, Dave has faithfully copyedited *The Guilded Pen*, and has been published in it since 2012. Dave served on the SDWEG board of directors and is currently fighting retirement although he still tinkers with classic cars. In 2018, Dave published his autobiography, *Irreverent Forever, True Tales from a Newspaperman's Outrageously Rewarding Life*. It is a candid look at some of the world's zaniest people — newspaper men and women — and their tales from the old days, filled with rapscallions, inebriates, and a few decent souls. Dave blogs at: www.feldysworld.com.

GILBERG, ROBERT — Bob was born in New Bremen, Ohio, in 1940. Graduated with BSEE from Ohio State University in 1964. Post graduate studies at Wright State University in 1965/1966. Thirty-five years in micro-electronics design and manufacturing at NCR, Burroughs, Linkabit, and General Instrument. Multiple patents in VLSI design and shared in an Academy of Television Arts and Sciences Emmy Award for video anti-piracy and security technology. Worked with the teams that invented multi-channel, digital satellite and cable television systems and digital High Definition TV, developing key micro-circuits well before available from the general industry. Author of four books: my memoir, *The Last Road Rebel and Other Lost Stories*; novels: *Alice Chang, Twists of Fate,* and *Starvation Mountain,* (all with 4 and 5-star reviews). Married to my wife, Nikki, of Binghamton, New York, for 51 years and father to a continuous line of Cocker Spaniels, Fox Terriers, and parrots since 1967. Retired in 2000 as Associate Vice President, VLSI Design, Motorola-General Instrument. rgilberg@san.rr.com; tamborrelwriter.com; kirkusreviews.com/author/robert-gilberg.

HAFNER, JANET — Janet talked before she walked. Under an apple tree, she taught neighborhood children how to read. She loved language. Her involvement with language was a progression. First, she taught how to use language to achieve goals. Later, she used language to get grants to develop programs. Her professional career included teaching English as a Second Language and Spanish at Palomar College, training teachers in effective techniques for second language acquisition, and coaching corporate managers and supervisors to overcome linguistic challenges. She co-created *Conversemos*, a televised Spanish course offered throughout the United States. Now she uses language to entertain, young and old. She is a member of The Society of Children's Book Writers and Illustrators. Her children's novel, *Eye of an Eagle*, aims to show how easy it is to misjudge people. Janet's memoir essays appear in anthologies, and she has been published in *The Guilded Pen* since 2015. She is a member of Writer's Ink and has published essays in the Oasis Anthology 2017. Janet is a sometimes charcoal artist, a sometimes ballroom dancer, but an all-the-time optimist who loves to laugh and knows the value of tears. Visit: jrhafner.com or jrhafner19@gmail.com.

HARMON, MARGARET — Just before her fifth birthday, Margaret decided to become a writer — and was expelled from kindergarten for reading during naptime. School improved, and she began writing for publication at sixteen. She's best known as a modern fabulist and humorist. Fables from *The Man Who Learned to Walk In Shoes That Pinch:*

*Contemporary Fables,* and *The Genie Who Had Wishes of His Own* aired on National Public Radio and are taught in literature and oral interpretation classes. Ray Bradbury described her fables as "Fantastic!" In *A Field Guide to North American Birders: A Parody,* birders discover their own species. Over 300 of her essays, features, humor, and Op-Eds have appeared in national publications. Awards include "Best of the Best San Diego Writers" on NPR. Her website: www.margaretharmon.com.

**HINAEKIAN, PEGGY** — Peggy is of Armenian origin, born and raised in Egypt. Her paternal grandfather owned the largest private library in Egypt and introduced her to books in three languages at a very young age (English, French, and Armenian). Raised in a cosmopolitan environment, she became an avid reader and kept a journal since age twelve. She was editor of her high school magazine and wrote short stories. Her short stories and essays have been published in the SDWEG anthologies since 2016. Her debut novel *Of Julia and Men* was included in the New York Times Book Review Magazine under "Discover New Titles — Great Stories, Unique Perspectives." The novel is almost entirely fictional except for the international settings, which Peggy drew on her lifetime of world travel. Peggy is an internationally recognized and well-established artist, living and working in the United States and Switzerland. The illustration on the cover of her book and the 26 images inside, are her own artwork. View it on www.OfJuliaAndMen.com. Visit www.peggyhinaekian.artspan.com to see Peggy's art and bio.

**HUNTINGTON, BARBARA WEEKS** — Barbara has been a civil rights worker, teacher, computer mail order house CEO, technical writer, marketing analyst/consultant, and director of a university program to assist underrepresented students as they enter PhD programs. She retired in 2013 as Director of Preprofessional Health Advising at SDSU and is co-author of *Writing About Me: a Step-by-Step Guide to Developing a Powerful Personal Statement for your Application to Medical School.* She has a BS in Zoology from SDSU and an MBA from UCLA. Barbara lives in Chula Vista with her dog Tashi, surrounded by a drought-tolerant garden where she grows her own organic vegetables and walks her labyrinth of rocks and succulents. For several years she has published poems and stories in *the San Diego Poetry Annual, A Year in INK,* and *SDWEG Anthology.* Her selections in this anthology are from her unpublished memoir, *Laughing Just to Keep from Crying...and Rattlesnakes!* Her blog is: https://barbarahuntington.com.

**HUNTSMAN, HARRY** — Harry was born in 1925 on a farm in Arkansas, the oldest of nine children. None of his family, neighbors, or Sunday school teachers had more than an eighth-grade education. After service in the Navy, he attended college and graduate school on the World War Two GI Bill. After fifteen years as a pastor of churches in Arkansas, Texas, and California he taught high school and middle school for twelve years. He has written an unpublished Civil War novel and is at work on a memoir, *The Minister and the Mafia*, which his writing coach calls a book of psychological essays. He was published in *The Guilded Pen* (2012, 2013, 2014, 2016). Harry is a member and past president of the SDWEG.

**JOHNSON-LABERTEW, S.**--Shelley Myrlane Johnson, writing as S. Johnson-Labertew, is a lifetime member of the San Diego Writers and Editors Guild, recipient of the Guild's Rhoda Riddell Lifetime Member award, member of Seattle's HUGO House, Seattle 7 attendee, Pacific NorthWest Writers Association, Romance Writers of America, National and Seattle Chapter, and a winner of NaNoWriMo 2014 and 2016. Shelley is now editing her first novel, *The Thirteenth Princess*, and working on short stories. She is also an ongoing member of the UW 2nd Draft Group and graduate of the University of Washington Popular Fiction Course. Born in Seattle and raised on a hill overlooking the beautiful Green River Valley (where she currently resides) in Kent, Washington, she attended Marylhurst College in Lake Oswego, Oregon, and lives with her husband and twenty-year-old Ragdoll Cat, Coco. Favorite things — reading, cooking, traveling, time with family and friends...WRITING.

**KLINOVA, DORA** — is an award-winning writer and poet. In 1992, Dora emigrated from the Ukraine and left behind everything, including her profession as an engineer-designer in the movie industry. Emigration pushed her to recreate herself. Dora's thoughts flooded out onto paper like a rushing stream. To her own surprise, the torrent of words was in English, not her native Russian. In March 2003, the International Society of Poets presented Dora a Merit Award for her poetry. Dora's works have been published in newspapers and magazines, performed at many theaters in San Diego, and were published in the anthology "Hot Chocolate for Seniors." Her first book, *A Melody from an Immigrant's Soul: A Collection of Memoirs, Essays, and Poetry,* a heartfelt story, has achieved worldwide success. Her second book, *The Queen of the Universe, The Vortex of Creation,* is a many-layered allegory for children and adults about power, courage, and the desire to achieve the highest peak of our life journey. Dora's third book, *Did You Ever Have the Chance to Marry an*

*American Multimillionaire?* is her personal story. <u>www.doraklinova.com.</u>

**LEECH, TOM** — is author of books covering a variety of topics. The most current *FUN ON THE JOB: Amusing and true tales from Rosie-the-Riveters to Rocket Scientists at a major (San Diego-based) aerospace company.* A topic getting much attention as 50 years since the wild year 1968 is described in Tom's book, *On the Road in '68: A year of turmoil, a journey of friendship*, about his own travel experiences that year. His years as Forum Editor for <u>San Diego Magazine Online</u> led to *Outdoors San Diego: Hiking, Biking & Camping.* Other current books include *Say It Like Shakespeare: The Bard's Timeless Tips for Successful Communication*, 2nd Ed. and *The Curious Adventures of Santa's Wayward Elves*, with co-author and wife Leslie. His AMACOM book, *How to Prepare, Stage & Deliver Winning Presentations*, is in its 3rd edition and has been acclaimed by many relevant publications. His poems have appeared in many anthologies and journals.

**LISZT, AUDREA IRELAND** — a legal US citizen, I was born in 1929 in Liverpool, England. Rain: I lived with it. One does when one abides in England, where the winters are cold and the summers are wet, and our family lived on the edge of debt. Fortunately, our family of five survived the Blitz, Liverpool being the second most bombed city after London. As the Liverpudlian Irish would say, "What Hitler did was wrong, wrong, wrong, worse than putting a holy-wafer on a non-Catholic tongue." Throughout it all, though, we kept a stiff upper-lip to save our king and the British nation, and in doing so we "Liverpudlian Scousers" won Winston Churchill's admiration. I left home at age 16, emigrated to Canada in 1951; in 1953, I drove a hot-off-the-line pink '54 Ford "Fordor" from Detroit, down Route 66, delivering it to a new car-dealer in Los Angeles. I later married, had two children, and, after the Sylmar earthquake destroyed our area, moved south to San Diego.

**MacILVAINE, MARY LOU, Ph.D.** — Mary Lou is a native San Diegan, born in Coronado and raised in Bird Rock. She says, "I write but rarely for publication. I have a youthful poem in an anthology, a medical article in a journal, and a number of blogs on my pretty website. I'm still growing, currently working on a mind/body memoir. Professionally, as Dr. MacIlvaine, Ph.D., I treat anxiety, depression, and psychosis in adults and children. Practicing since 1989, I've helped a number of people lead fuller lives with their emotions. In one's head is a crowded place to live. Between psyche and soma, I vote for soma for greatest satisfaction, fullest sensation, and most accurate perception. Renewed health is my passion. I'm also president of Gemcor, a small geothermal corporation that requires little tending. I live in Kensington with my polite dog. My website is: www.emotionalcontact.com. Enjoy."

**McMAHON, MICHAEL JUDE** — Michael was born in the East Wall area of Dublin, Ireland. He has been writing since he was ten years old. He has many poems and short stories in his portfolio, as well as two completed novels, *The Cloud Above The Platanos*, book one of a projected trilogy, and *The Sea Has No Dreams*. He is currently working on completing book two of the aforementioned trilogy. He has countless musical performance credits to his name and has received many awards for acting performances in plays ranging from Chekhov to Shakespeare. Since retiring from his job as a structural steel and masonry inspector, he has embarked on a full time writing career. He has made San Diego home for the past 31 years.

**NAIMAN, JOE** — Joe is a freelance writer and the co-author of the baseball history book, *The San Diego Padres Encyclopedia* (2002), and is the author of *The School with All the Catchers* (2012), a history of the Crawford High School baseball program. He is also the author of a novel, *Another Chance* (2006). Joe has been published in *The Guilded Pen* since 2012. He has been a member of the Society for American Baseball Research since 1980 and was the coordinator of SABR's 1993 national convention in San Diego.

**NEWTON, FRANK (FRANCISCO)** — was, for most of his working life, a national leader of Hispanic-American issues in journalism and public policy. He was founding director of the National Association of Hispanic Journalists and also founding director of the National Hispanic Leadership Agenda. He found time as well to work as a writer, editor, and publisher in a variety of capacities — including editing the Smithsonian's "New World" publication about the Columbus quincentenary; publishing "The Silver Wave" newspaper about older adult issues; and editing numerous newsletters for a variety of nonprofit organizations. Recently, he published a historical fiction novel about an Aztec youth, titled, *The Trials of Tizoc*. Frank edits and publishes the SDWEG newsletter, "A Writer's Life." He is a member of the SDWEG board of directors.

**PERRY, YVONNE NELSON** — Born, raised, and educated in the Hawaiian Islands, and of Polynesian descent, Yvonne's first book, *The Other Side of the Island*, is a collection of short stories set in a timeless Hawai`i. Although she didn't start writing fiction until her 60s...she had always been a columnist...forty-nine short stories have also been published in literary journals, magazines, and anthologies. An editor for years, she held creative writing classes in her home. A unique writers conference Yvonne staged in Balboa Park to prove conferences don't need to be so expensive, had well-known writer volunteers sitting under trees, teaching the craft of writing, "like Aristotle and his disciples." For nine years, she participated in Long Beach's "A Living Author in Every Classroom" program and continues to be invited to read her work in San Diego schools. She still teaches at the world-class Santa Barbara Writers Conference, now twenty-five years and ongoing. Her work-in-progress is another collection of short fiction set in the Pacific Rim. Her stories are about conditions of the human heart and evoke strong emotions. Yvonne is the recipient of SDWEG's Odin Award, for her many contributions to San Diego's writing community.

**PETERSON, RICHARD** — Rick has written magazine articles and was a former staff writer for <u>Wholistic Living News</u>. He authored the article "Stained Glass Television" in the *Journal of Popular Culture* (Vol. 19. No. 4); a chapter called "Electric Sisters" in *The God Pumpers: Religion in the Electronic Age* (Bowling Green State University Popular Press); and has been published in *The Guilded Pen* since 2012. He is working on a sci-fi suspense thriller. Rick serves on the Guild board of directors as Membership Chairman, and has been a judge for the San Diego Book Awards since 2008.

**PIZ, TY** — Ty raced Motocross and Flatrack from 1972 through 1979. In 1980 he switched to road racing until retiring in 2004. He has won three regional championships and twice finished Top Ten overall in the AMA Superbike Series onboard a Yamaha TZ-250 Grand Prix motorcycle. Ty is a Para-educator, working in the public-school system with high school students that have a wide range of special needs. He feels great to share his passion for life with these loving, caring young people. He has been published in *The Guilded Pen* since 2012.

**PRIMIANO, FRANK** — During academic and industrial careers, Frank published strictly nonfiction in scientific, engineering, and medical journals and textbooks. In retirement, he has let his imagination run wild, writing fiction with only an occasional short, autobiographical piece thrown in. He has been a finalist in the San Diego Book Awards' Unpublished Novel and Unpublished Short Story categories. His work has appeared in *The Guilded Pen* since 2015, and in anthologies published by San Diego Writers Ink and the Writers' Workshop of the San Diego

Community College Continuing Education Program, for which he is also an editor. Frank lived in Philadelphia and Cleveland before moving with his wife, Elaine, to San Diego.

**RAYBOLD, ARTHUR** — Arthur has penned the *Home from the Banks* (poetry collection). In process: a short story collection.

**SCHMIDT, DAVID J.** — David is an author, multilingual translator, and professional storyteller who splits his time between Mexico City and San Diego. He has published a variety of books, short stories, and articles in English and Spanish. His English-language titles include the "non-fiction horror" book, *Three Nights in the Clown Motel,* and *Holy Ghosts: True Tales from a Haunted Christian College,* a study of haunted places. His Spanish-language books *Más frío que la nieve: cuentos sobrenaturales de Rusia* and *Tunguska: luces en el cielo sobre Siberia* were published nationwide in Mexico last year. His ongoing series of ebooks, *The Tiny Staircase series,* covers a wide range of topics related to the mysterious, paranormal, and unexplained. In addition to his publications, he is the cohost of the podcast *To Russia with Love.* David speaks eleven languages and has been to 33 countries. He received his BA in psychology from Point Loma Nazarene University. HolyGhostStories@gmail.com; Twitter: @SchmidtTales; www.holyghoststories.com; Facebook:@HolyGhostStories; Amazon: https://www.amazon.com/David-J.-Schmidt/e/B00BXTBY7K; YouTube: Holy Ghosts www.youtube.com/channel/UCQkezKP2QocFTAKa_2GuRjQ/featured .

**SCHROEDER, MARDIE** — Mardie has been a member of the SDWEG for five years. She published her first novel, *Go West for Luck Go West for Love* in 2015 and republished it in 2018. She has contributed many pieces to *The Guilded Pen* since 2014. She is serving her second term as president of the Guild. Visit: www.mardieschroeder.com.

**SHAFER, PHILIP ROGER** — Philip has been a Guild member since 2000, and a long-time resident of the beach community of San Diego. He attended La Jolla High School and has degrees from San Diego State, The University of Idaho, and The University of Southern California. His eclectic career includes teacher, naval aviator, and community planner. Philip's first published pieces were *Permitting Geothermal Projects, Seismic Safety in Imperial County,* and a history, *Emmette and Emma.* In 1999, Philip started writing his nine-volume saga of the 20th Century, an historical romance-thriller series. The novels were published between 2009 and 2014: *Empire and Resistance, Tonkin Gold, The Scars of War, Merchants of Flesh, Like a Moth to the Flame, Worth Their Weight in Gold, Shepherd's*

*Secrets, The Good Shepherd,* and *Legacy.* Four of the saga's novels were San Diego Book Awards Finalists. *Shepherd's Secrets* won their award for Best Romance in 2011.

**SIRIGNANO, BARBARA** — In 1977, Barbara received a Bachelor of Science Degree in Nursing and a Public Health Credential from Mount St. Mary's College in Los Angeles. Her nursing career includes Air Force Flight Nursing, Critical Care, Home Health, School, and Oncology Nursing. Barbara has written several (unpublished) books through the years and now hopes to become a published author. Her genre is non-fiction and believes her best writing comes from her own personal experiences. Following the example of Laura Ingalls Wilder, Barbara writes about her life experiences in the latter part of the 20th Century, so that young people can understand what life was like back then. She is the mother of two Marines and one daughter serving in the Coast Guard. Barbara is currently a nanny/grannie and cares for her two young grandsons. She is very grateful for the opportunity to publish her story in the 2018 anthology, and for the lovely people she has met through the San Diego Writers and Editors Guild.

**TRAINOR, TERRI** — has enjoyed writing from the moment she wrapped her left hand around a pencil. The pleasure of creating new worlds was only trumped by the joy of making this one more pleasant and efficient for those around her. This led her into a career in computer programming, which got her wondering: can we re-program our own internal software? Our thoughts? Our feelings? Create better, happier outcomes for ourselves? This exploration led directly to writing, *Blessed-n-Lucky: How to Become a King or Queen of Manifestation.* Her one-act play "Three Little Words" was produced as part of New York's Theatre Studio, Inc (TSI) Playtime Series. She is currently refining an abduction screenplay featuring Santa Claus and his lead elf, Hans. A fiction novel involving saints and angels is currently collecting characters and plot points — hoping to grow into a series one day.

**WALLACE, RUTH L., Ph.D.** — Ruth has published two books on the relationships between nutrition and mental health, and is now retired from clinical practice in dietetics. She is a frequent contributor to the newsletter of the Behavioral Health Nutrition practice group, has presented at national conferences and provided educational webinars for clinical practitioners. She has been published in *The Guilded Pen* since 2012 and has served as Assistant Editor since 2015. Ruth is past president of SDWEG, has served on the board of directors from 2009 to 2016, and served five years as editor of *The Writer's Life*, the monthly newsletter of SDWEG. She initiated the SDWEG Marketing Support Group and Open Mic Night which enhance member-to-member communication. Ruth enjoys traveling, and especially likes to read books on consciousness and spirituality. She was recently awarded the Albert Nelson Marquis Lifetime Achievement Award by the Marquis Who's Who Publications Board.

**WINTERS, GARY** — Gary authored *The Deer Dancer*, a novel about a Yaqui boy in Mexico. *The Deer Dancer* won the silver medal from UC Irvine for the Chicano/Latino Literary Prize; runner-up in the San Diego Book Awards; Best Novel 2010 Mensa Creative Awards; bronze 2011 Book of the Year award for Multicultural Fiction in *ForeWord Reviews Magazine*. The book has been in the curriculum at Southwestern College, where *Poets & Writers Magazine* awarded Gary an honorarium to speak. *The Deer Dancer* is currently used at Juvenile Hall, and is in local Indian and county libraries. He has won awards for short story and photojournalism and his poetry has won international and national awards including winner of a Mensa global contest that was published in a hundred countries. His fiction and poetry have appeared in numerous anthologies and in such diverse publications as *Whisperings, A Literary and Visual Culture Magazine; The Caribbean Writer*, a literary journal of the University of the Virgin Islands; the San Francisco-based experimental/alternative multimedia journal *Free the Marque*; and *BEAT-itude*, the magazine's National Beat Poetry Festival 10-Year Anthology. The magazine, established in 1959 in San Francisco, is dedicated to the preservation and promotion of Beat poetry.

**YAROS, KEN, D.D.S.** — Ken, an alumnus of Albright College, received his DDS degree from Temple University. He spent six years serving with the Air Force and seven years serving with the Connecticut Air National Guard, attaining the rank of Major. Now semi-retired after 45 years of practice and teaching Dental Hygiene, he has turned his hand to writing short stories both non-fiction and fiction. He has been a contributor to *The Guilded Pen* since 2013 and was published in the national OASIS Journal 2014. Ken often writes under his pen name: KAY Allen, and is putting together an anthology of short stories for Kindle publication. Ken serves as a director at large on the SDWEG board.

**YEAMAN, SANDRA** — Sandra has lived and worked in 12 countries, most of them so small you probably haven't heard of them. She is working on a novel based on her experiences in Iran in the 1970s. She currently serves as SDWEG webmaster and social media manager and has been published in *The Guilded Pen* since 2013. The Guild recognized the positive impact of her contributions by presenting her with a Rhoda Riddell Builders Award in 2018. She blogs at sandrayeaman.com.

**ZAJAC, AMY E.** — Amy lives in San Marcos, California. Her first book, *It Started With Patton, Teresa Leska's Story, A Memoir* (2012), is her mother's compelling story as a Nazi political hostage. Amy has many stories published in anthologies since 2009, such as, *Chicken Soup for the Soul — From Lemons to Lemonade*, released in 2013. She has been a yearly contributor to *The Guilded Pen* since 2012. Amy's first novel, *Foredestined*, a story of enlightenment after global destruction, was published in December 2013. Currently, Amy is working on her dad's memoir. E-mail: azajac10@yahoo.com.

**ZOLFAGHARI, VAL** — Val has lived in the USA, Canada, Spain, England, Turkey, and his native land Iran (Persia). His educational background is in Engineering and Education. He graduated from the University of California at Irvine with Masters and Bachelor degrees in Engineering and pursued a technical career. In the 1990s, he earned a Master's degree in Education and Mathematics, and Administrative credentials. He taught secondary mathematics and was president of a teachers' union for two terms. He retired in 2013 and after a year of vacation started writing short stories based on his political and teaching experiences. Val has been a board member and has also been published in *The Guilded Pen* anthologies since 2015. Email: valzolfaghari@yahoo.ca.

Made in the USA
Columbia, SC
29 October 2018